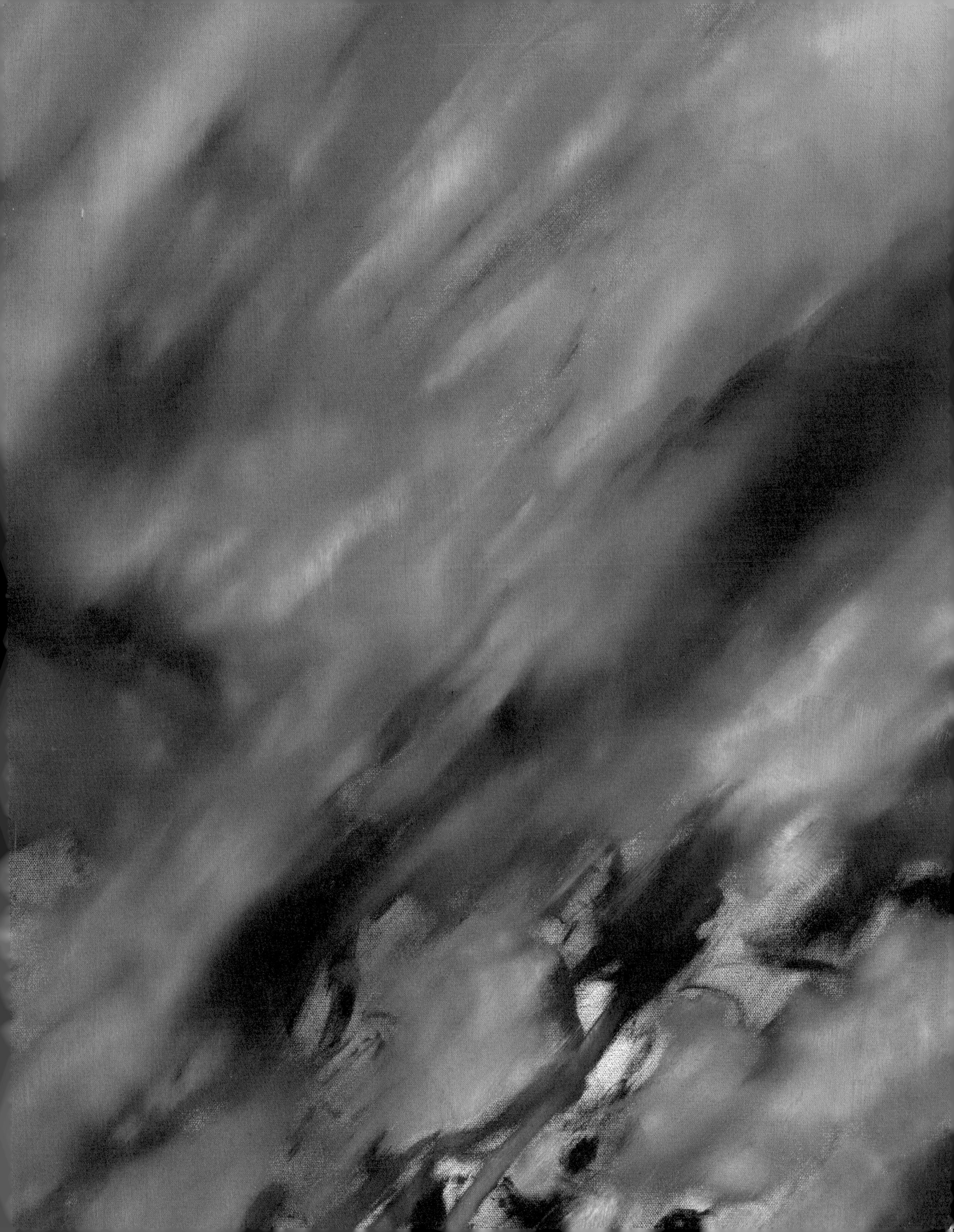

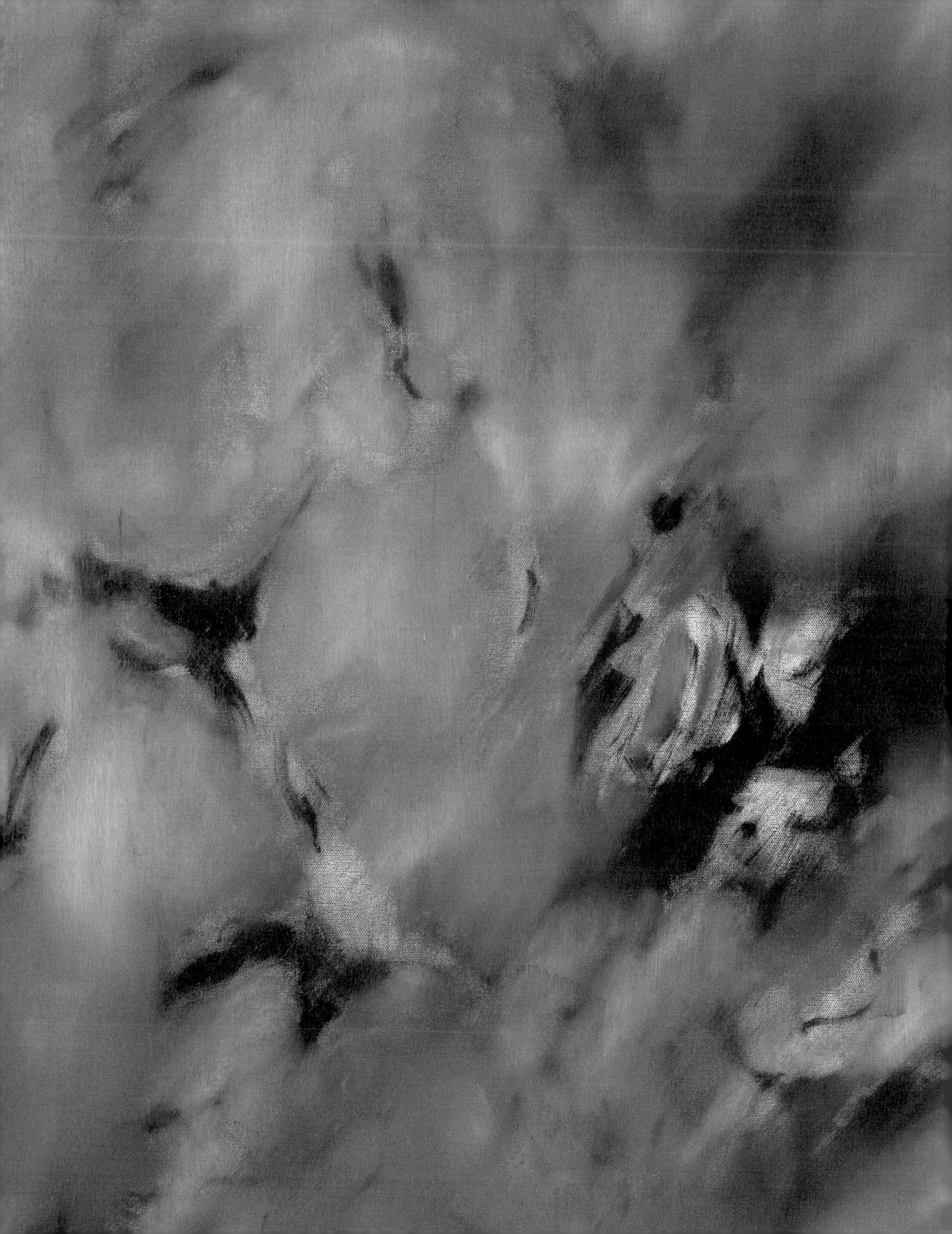

Janiva Ellis

Rats

Institute of Contemporary Art, Miami
DelMonico Books • D.A.P. New York

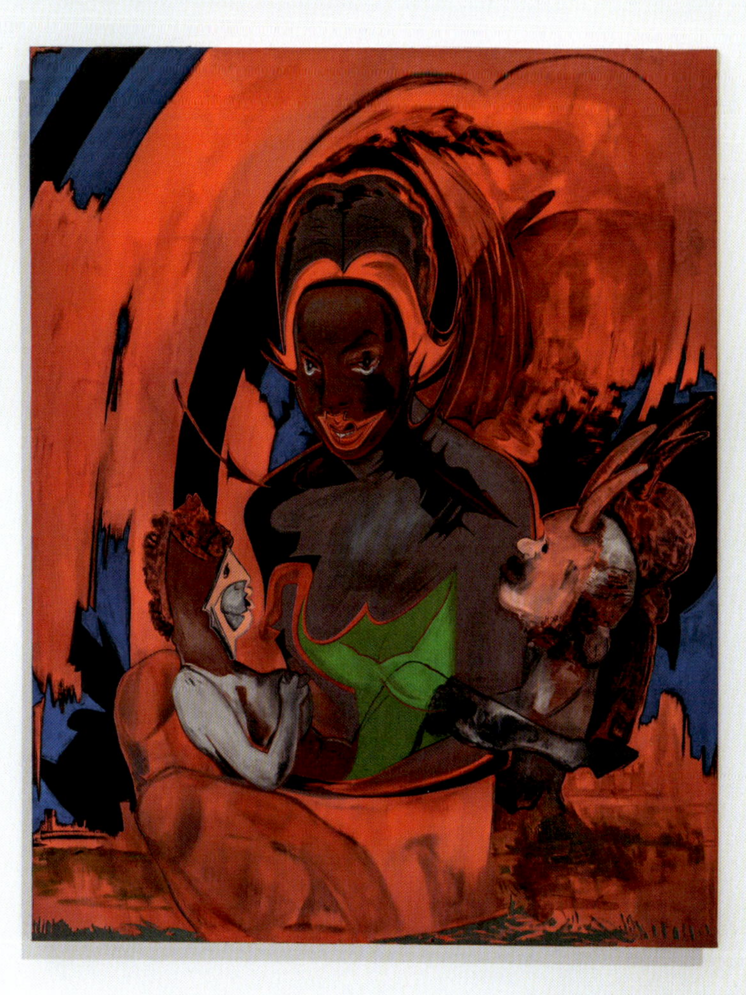

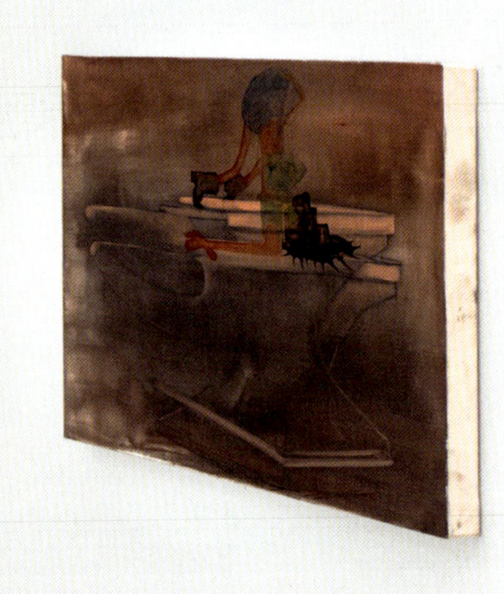

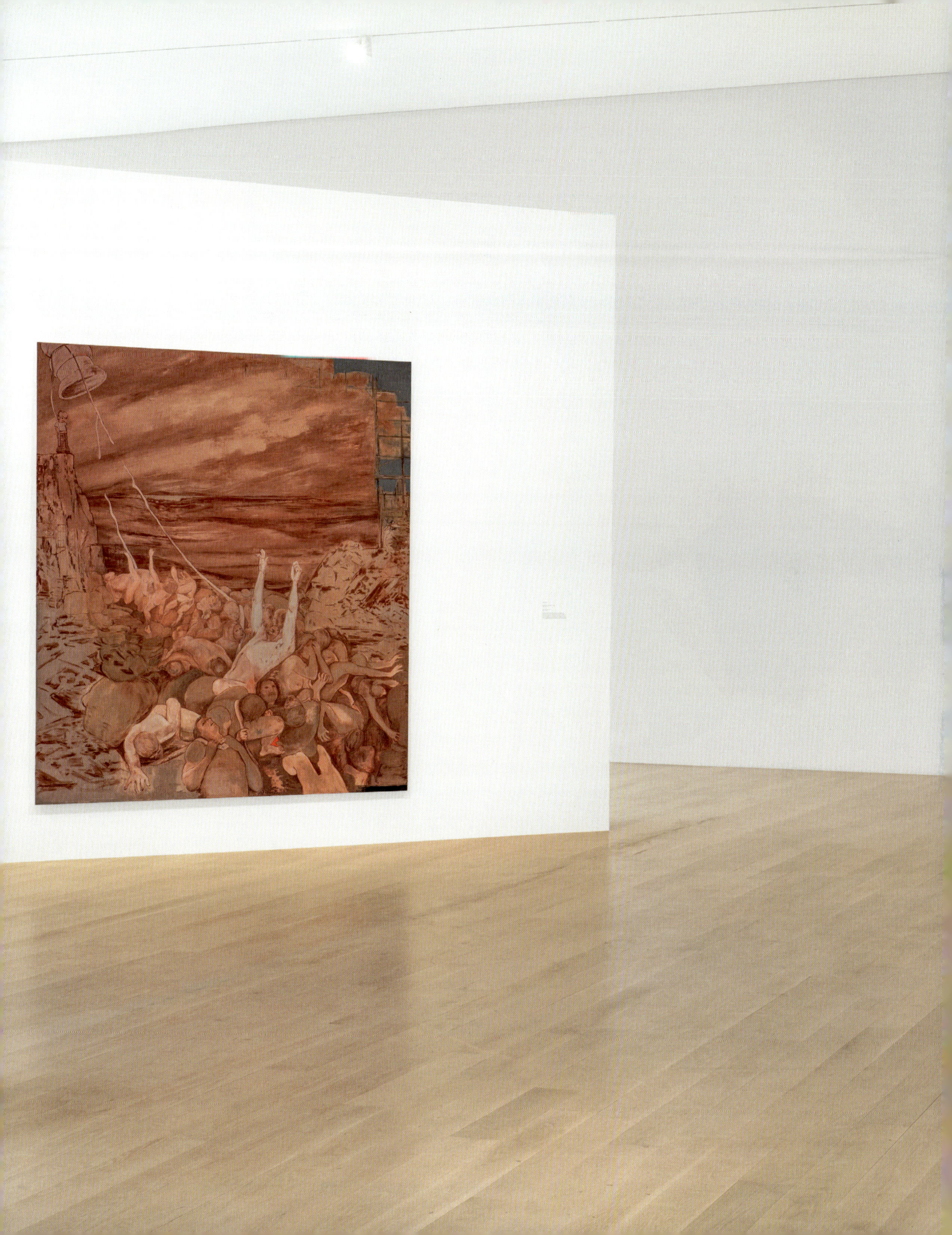

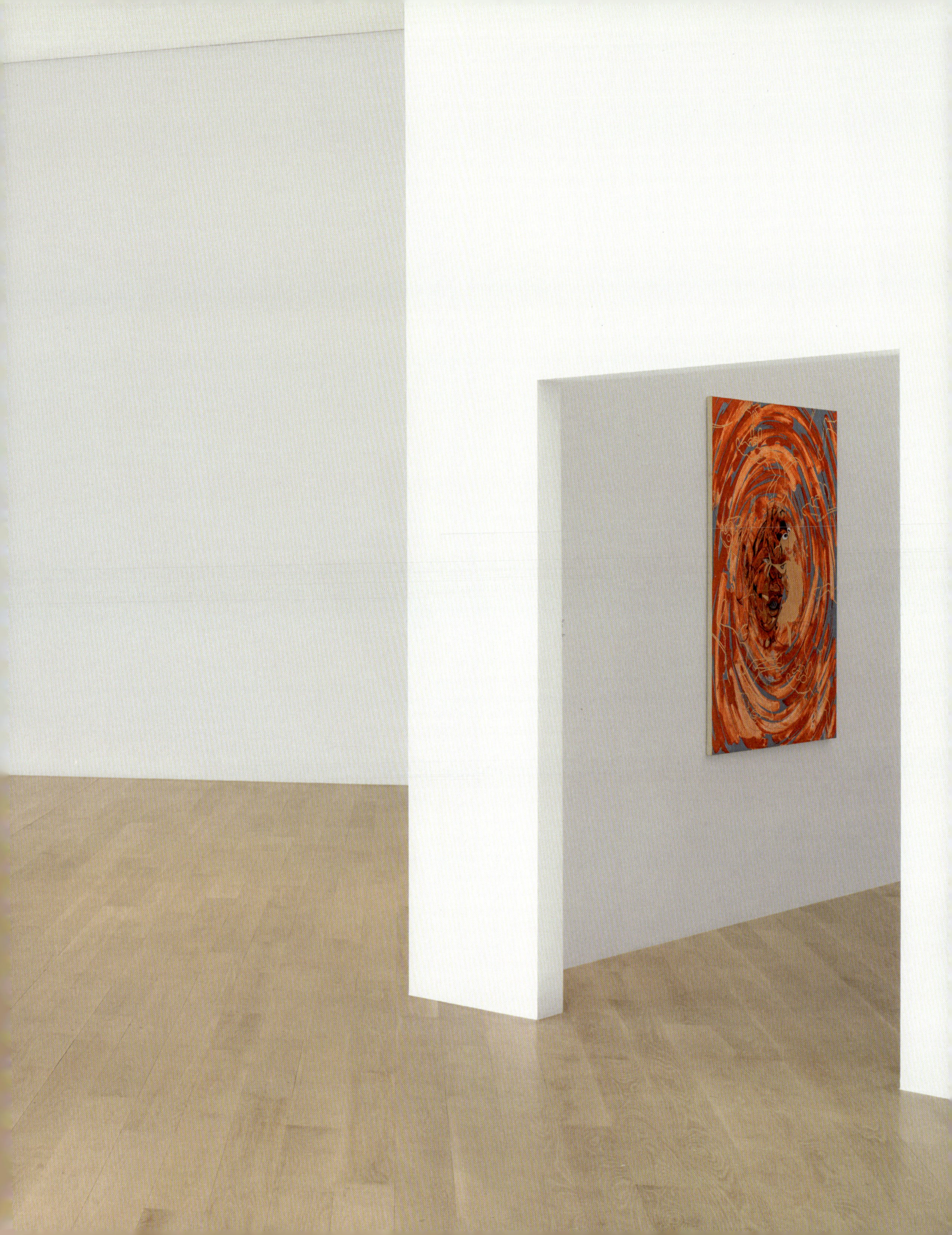

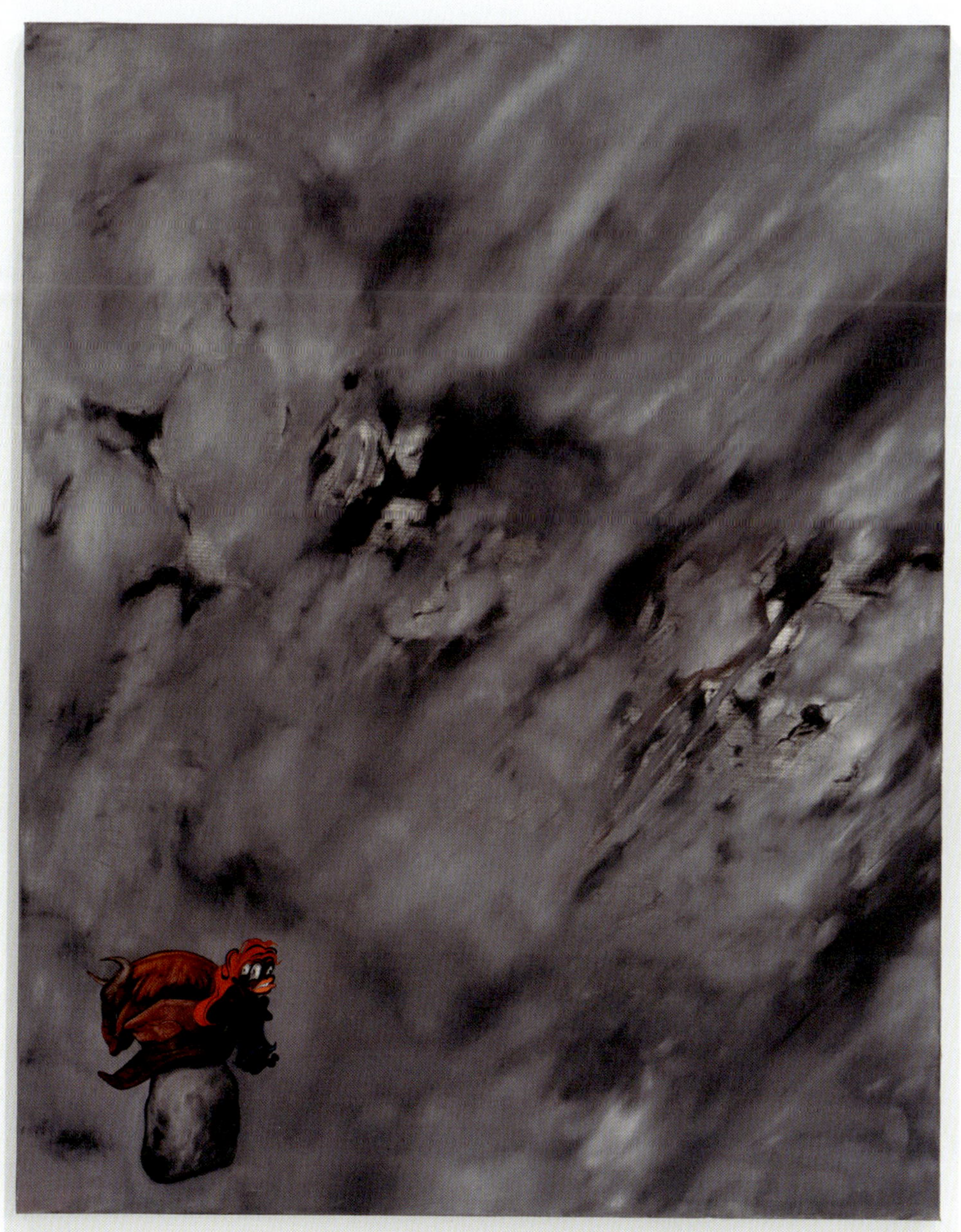

Contents

Foreword — p. 09

Alex Gartenfeld
Stephanie Seidel

Works (2017–2018) — p. 11

Red-Hot Cannonballs and Bloody Knives: Janiva Ellis's White Scourge — p. 79

Jessica Bell Brown

Works (2019–2020) — p. 85

Of Entrapment and Other White Supremacist Things: An Interview — p. 127

Olivia K. Young, Ph.D.
Janiva Ellis

Rats (2021) — p. 135

List of Works — p. 174

Alex Gartenfeld   Artistic Director

Stephanie Seidel   Curator
Institute of Contemporary Art, Miami

The Institute of Contemporary Art, Miami, is honored to present "Janiva Ellis: Rats," and to have the opportunity to host the artist's first solo museum exhibition. Ellis is a critical voice in contemporary painting; her works provoke important conversations through her dexterous use of wide-ranging strategies including landscape, abstraction, and references to mainstream cartoons. Ellis's work interrogates the pervasiveness of certain images, examining their contexts and resonances and sardonically reframing their visual and emotional narratives.

Ellis produces abundant imagery, both invented and appropriated, that she draws from a broad array of materials, including art history and pop culture, to comment on the insidious nature of white existentialist mythology and its denial of itself as a brutal social and structural force. Ellis's critical approach to figuration paints Blackness expansively, communicating the complexity of navigating such a lopsided and violent landscape. "Rats" comprises twelve extraordinary paintings created in the transformative years since 2019. This important body of work demonstrates Ellis's bold experimentation, as she thinks through ideas related to entrapment, infestation, and mistakes.

The inventive design of this publication is by Eric Hu. Ellis's profound works are matched by insightful contributions to the discourse on painting by Jessica Bell Brown and Olivia K. Young. We acknowledge the catalogue contributors for their generous and groundbreaking considerations of Ellis's work.

ICA Miami presents field-advancing exhibitions thanks to our partnership with the Knight Foundation, specifically the Knight Contemporary Art Fund at The Miami Foundation. Additional support for "Janiva Ellis: Rats" is provided by Ray Ellen and Allan Yarkin; 47 Canal, New York; and the Miami Design District.

ICA Miami's permanent collection is an engine and record for our exhibitions. We were honored to be the first museum to acquire work by the artist when, in 2018, we accessioned Ellis's profound painting *Prescribed Ambush* (2018), thanks to funding from the Simkins family.

We thank Janiva Ellis for her brilliant efforts that resulted in "Rats," and congratulate the artist on creating work that significantly advances the critical potential for painting.

Works (2017–2018)

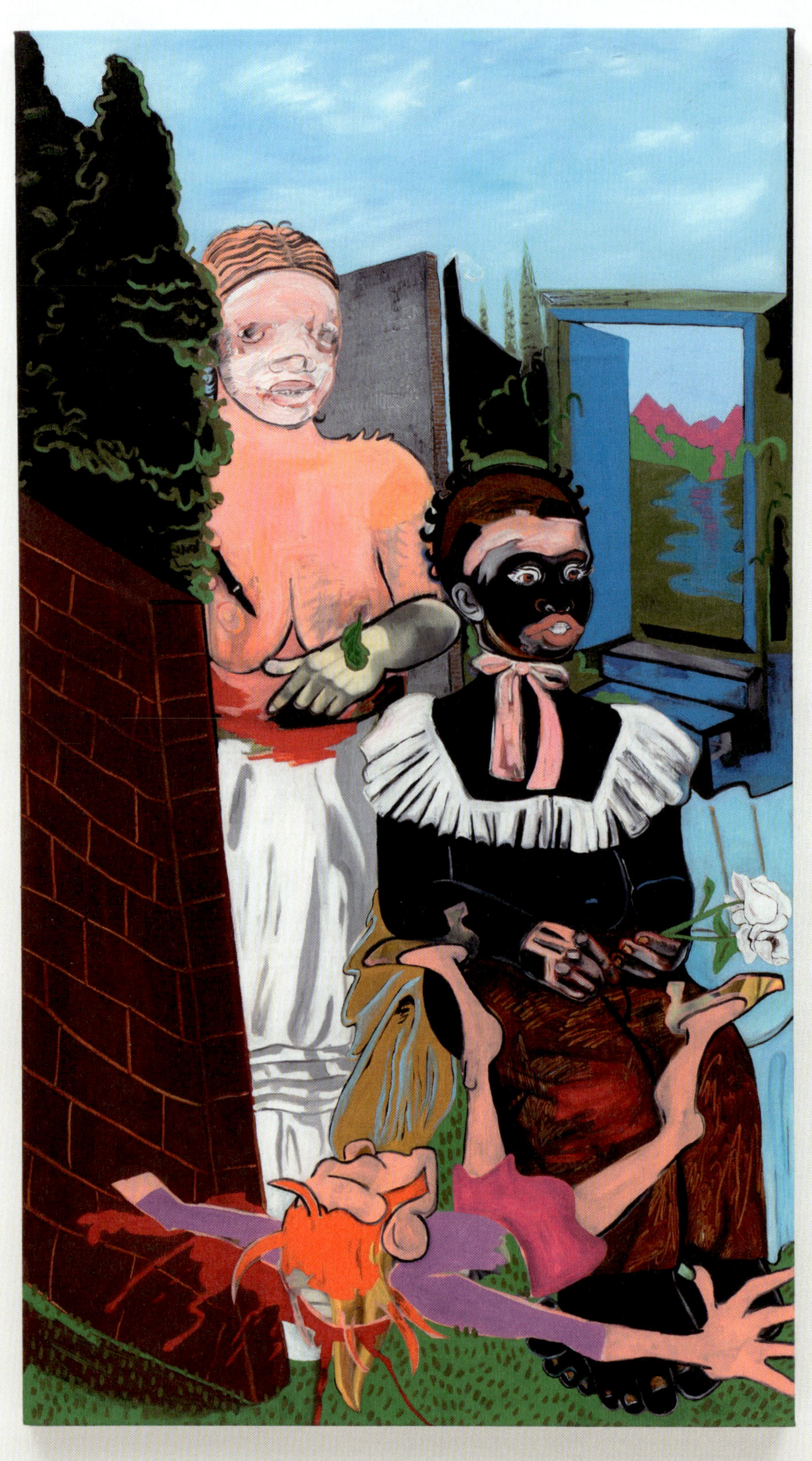

Something Anxiety 2017
Oil on panel
60 × 60 in. (152.4 × 152.4 cm)

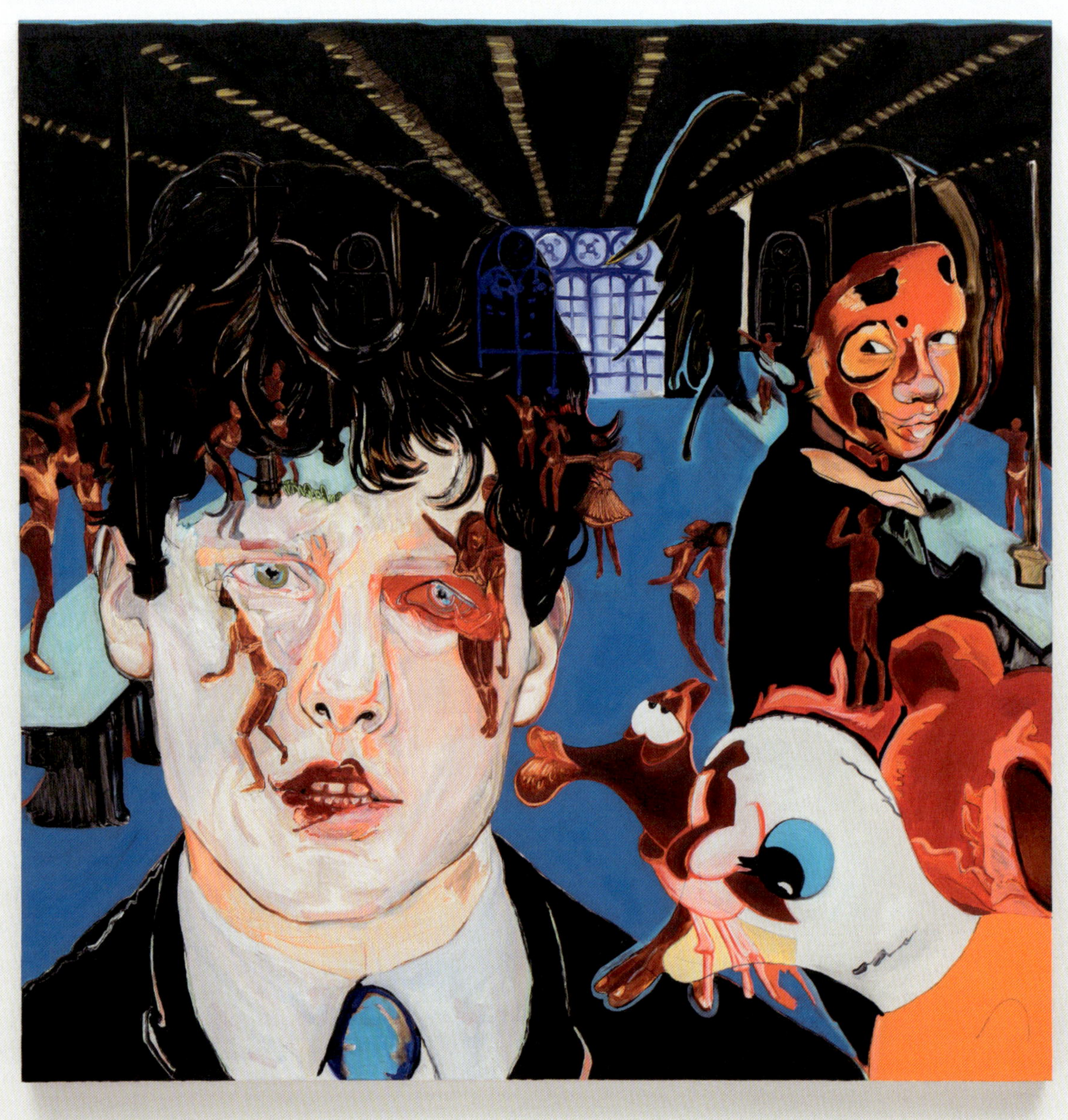

Open Pour Reality 2017
Oil on canvas
35 ½ × 35 ½ in. (90.2 × 90.2 cm)

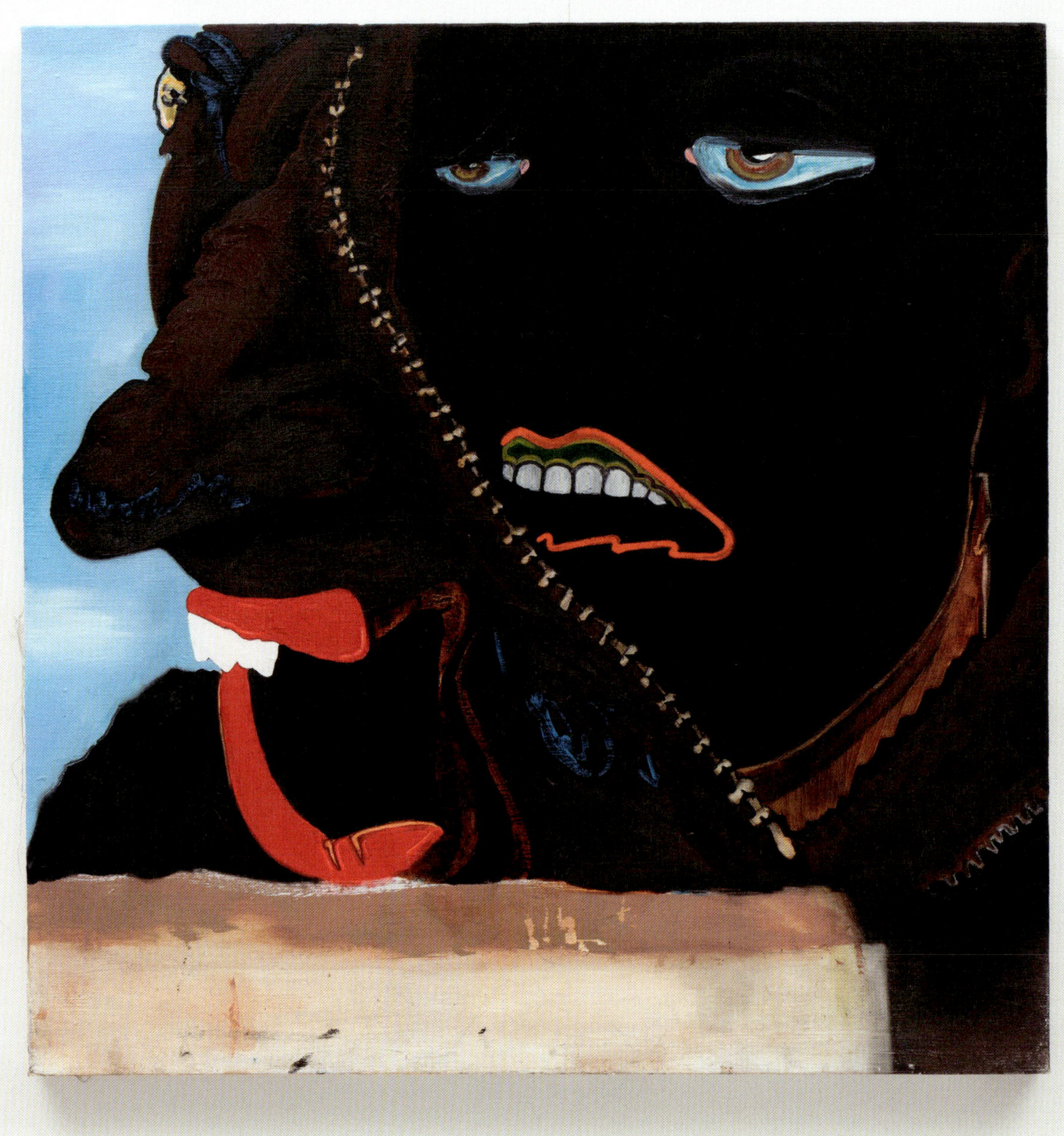

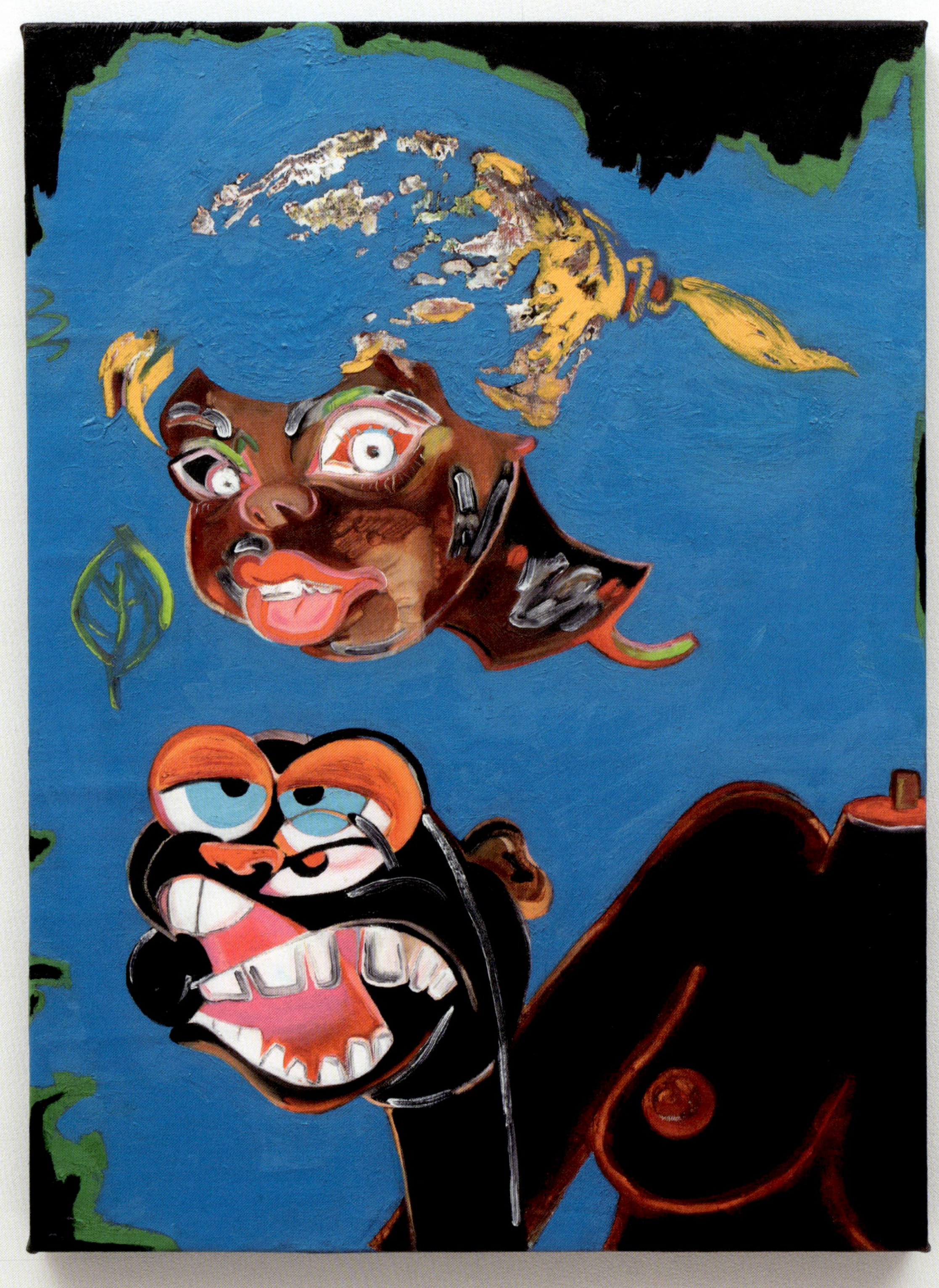

Memorializing My Industry   2017
In Sculpture
Oil on canvas
47 ½ × 34 ½ in. (120.7 × 87.6 cm)

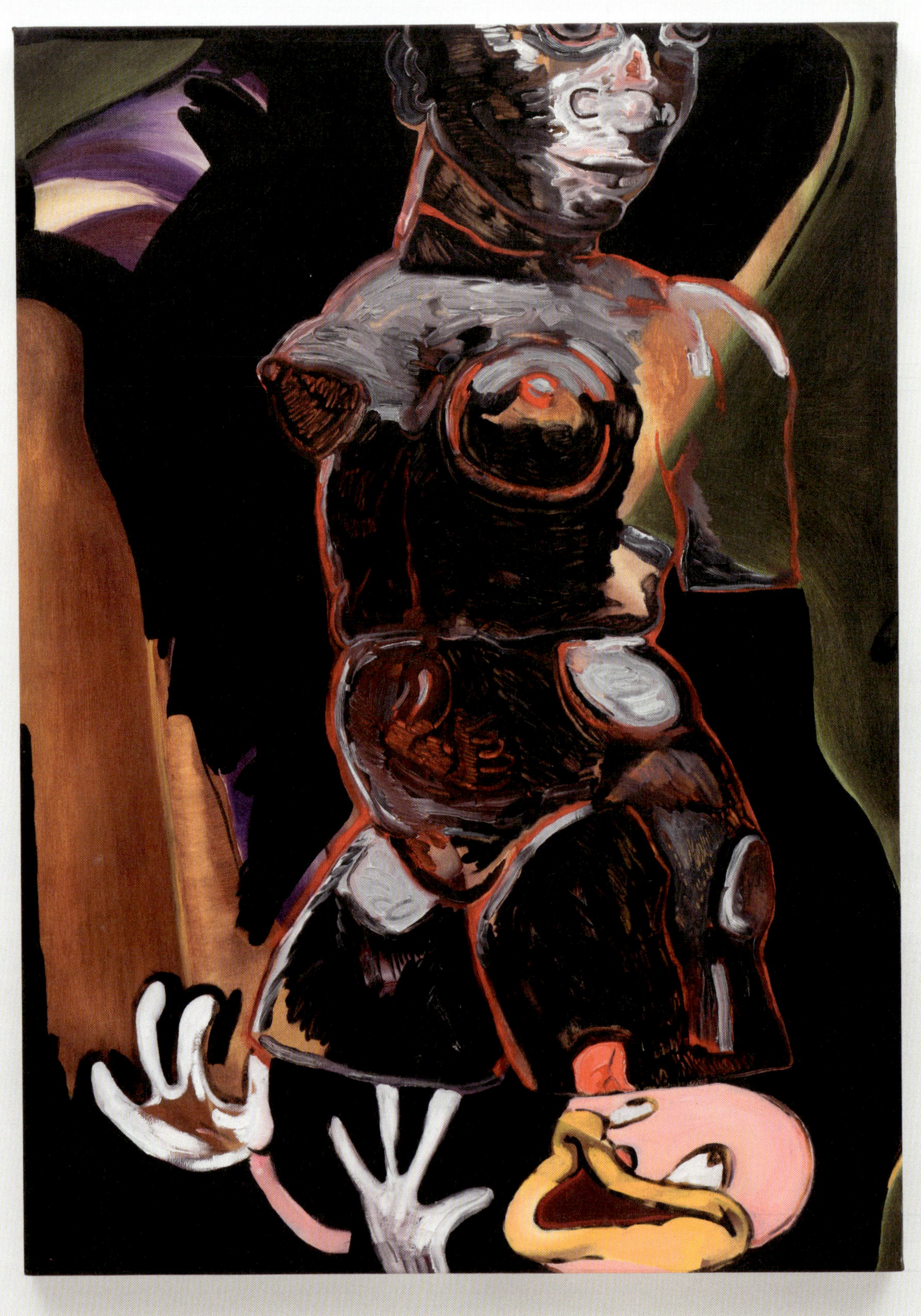

Hi-ho The Derry-o 2017
Oil on canvas
27 ½ × 24 in. (69.9 × 61 cm)

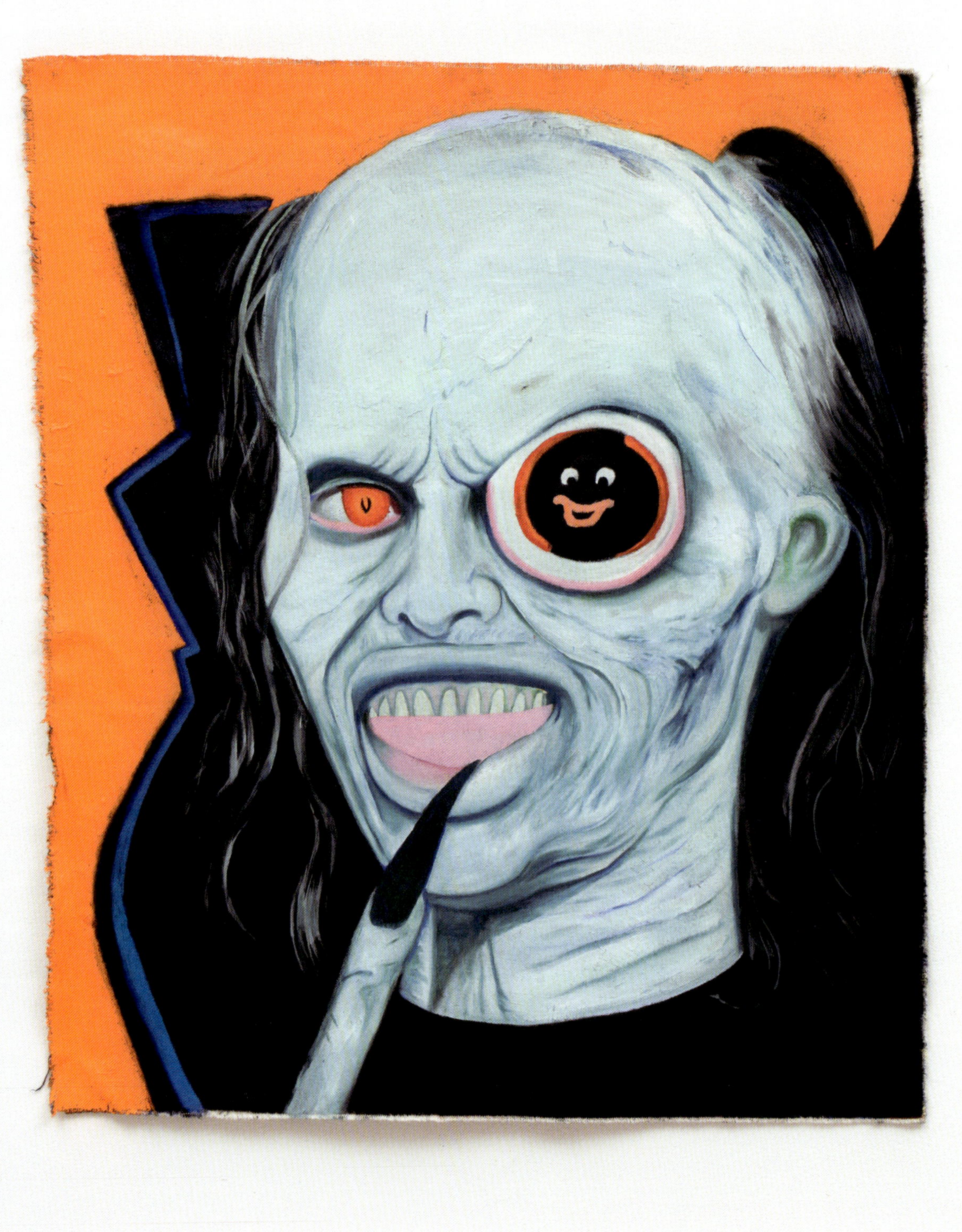

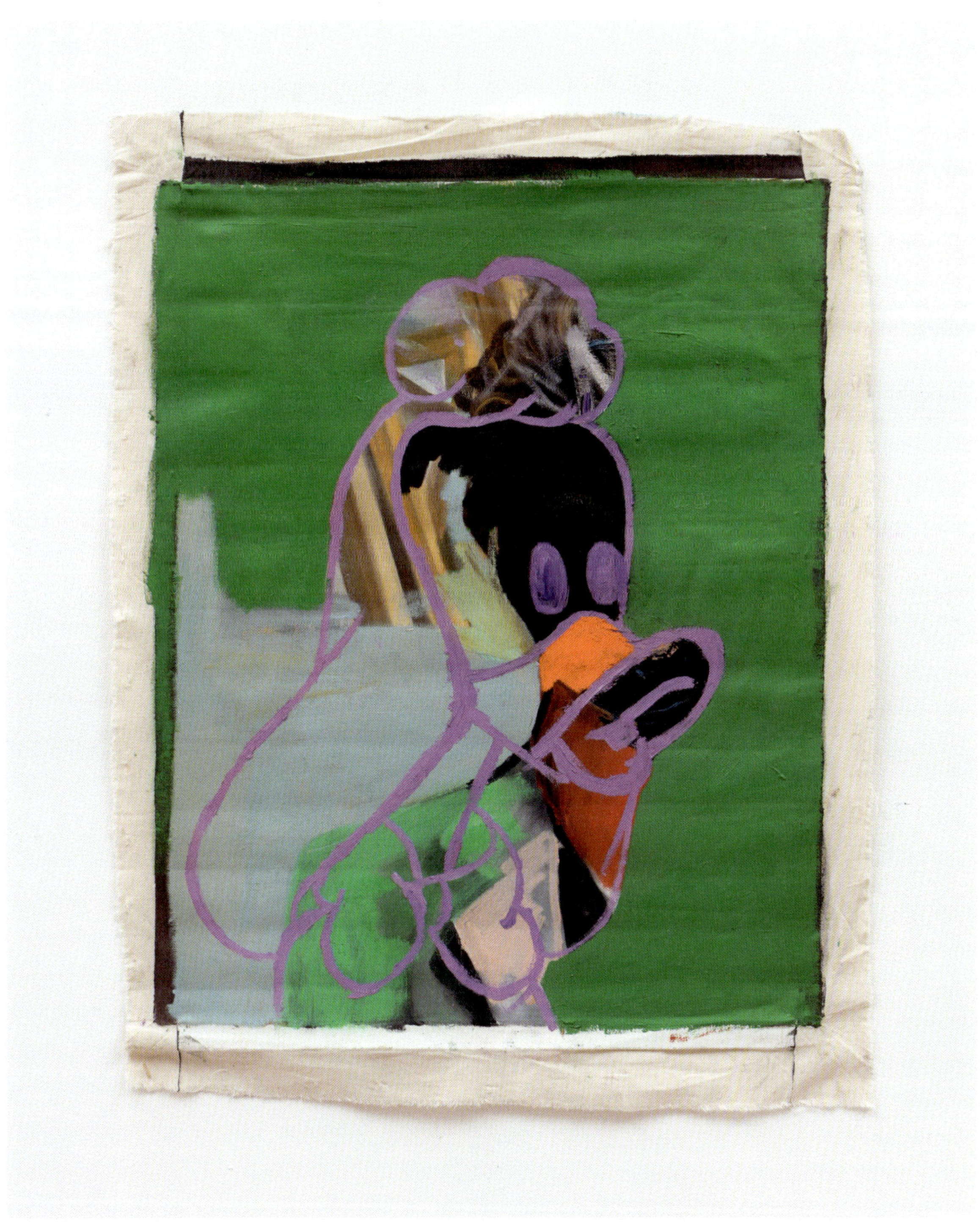

Duck Duck Deuce 2017
Oil on canvas
23 × 19 in. (58.4 × 48.3 cm)

Runk'd 2017
Oil on canvas
14 ½ × 10 in. (36.8 × 25.4 cm)

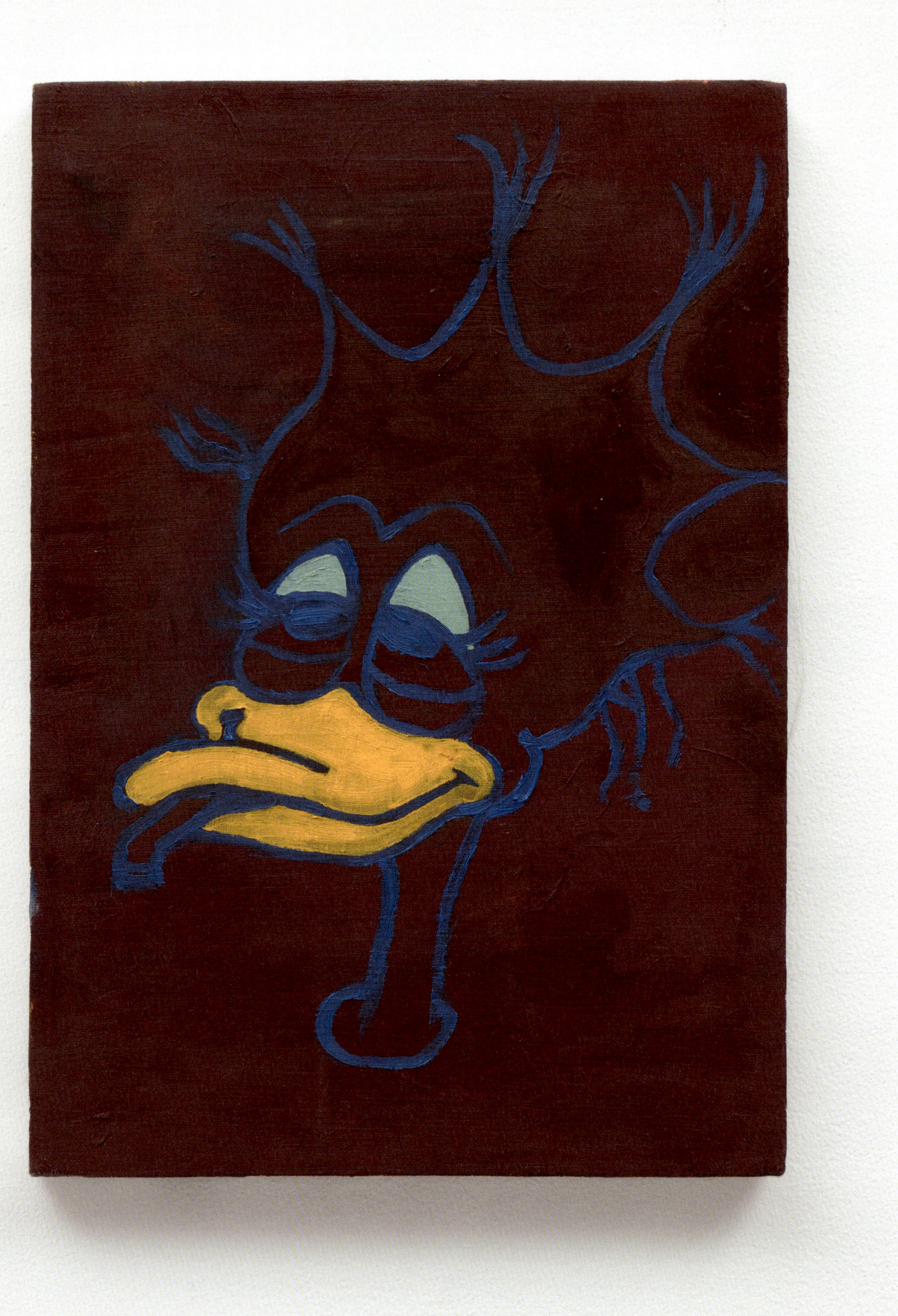

Fire Walk With Me 2   2017
Oil on canvas
12 × 9 in. (30.5 × 22.9 cm)

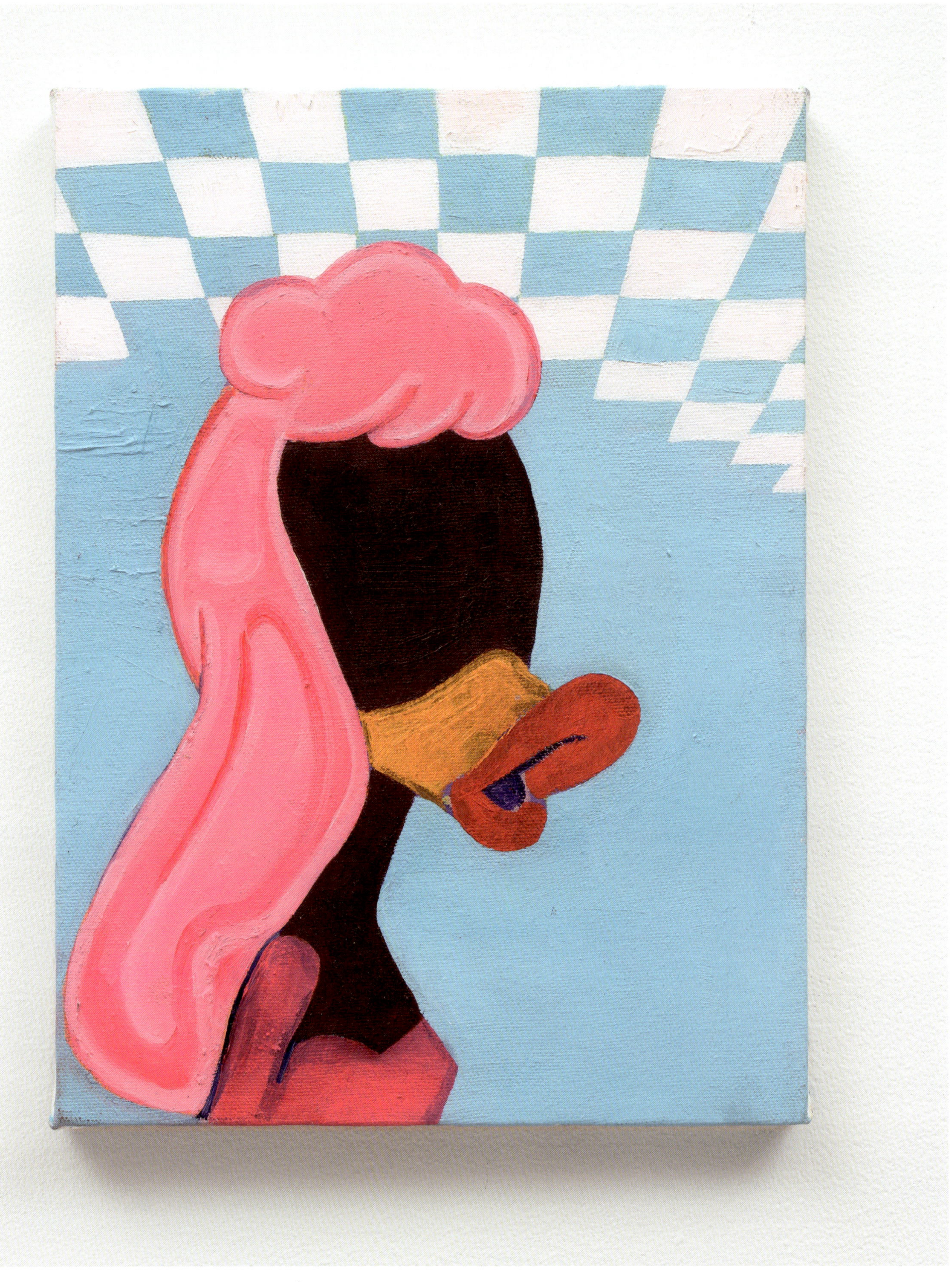

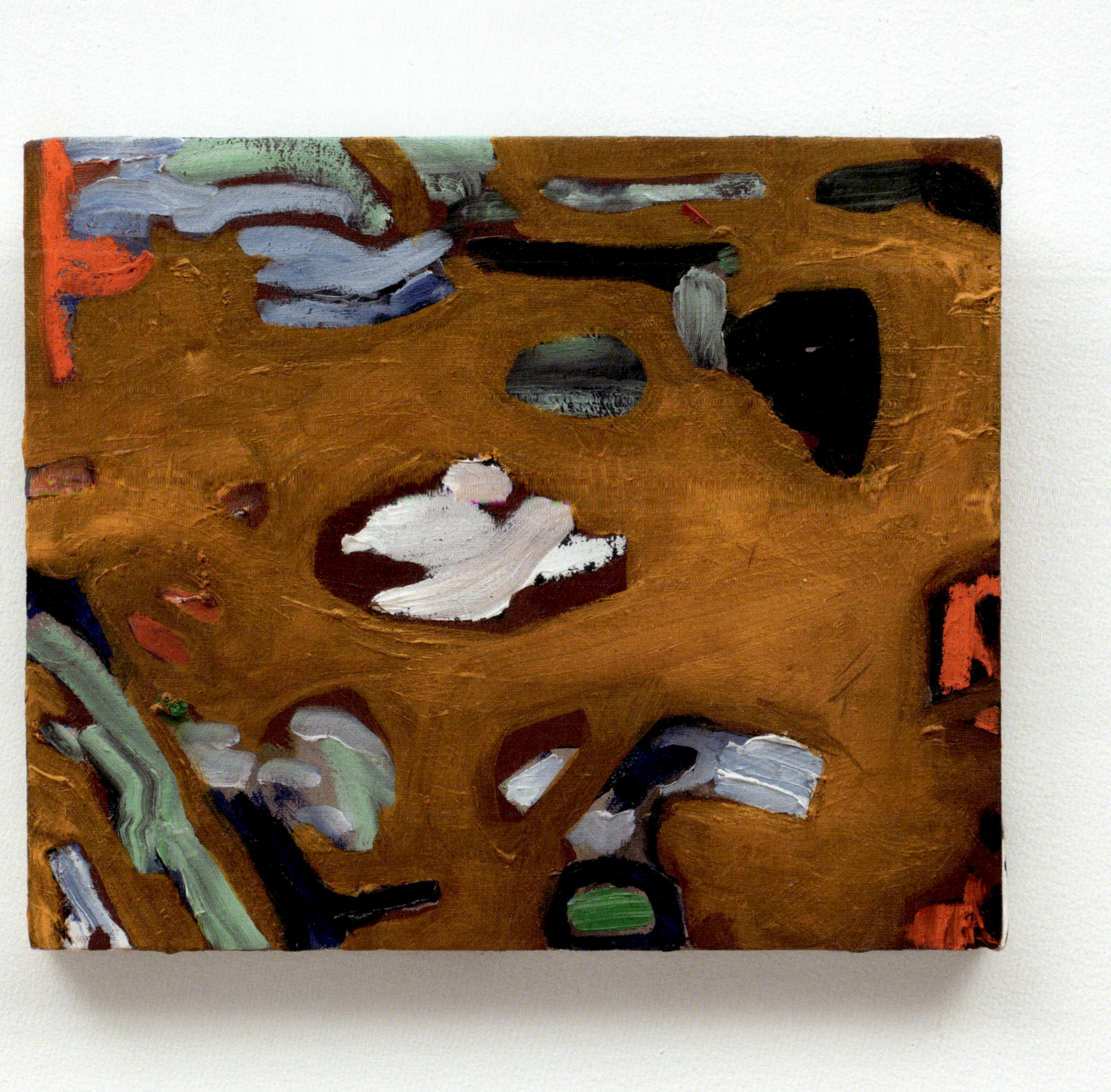

Abrandoment 2017
Oil on canvas
11 ½ × 8 in. (29.2 × 20.3 cm)

Bloodlust Halo 2017
Oil on canvas
40 × 30 in. (101.6 × 76.2 cm)

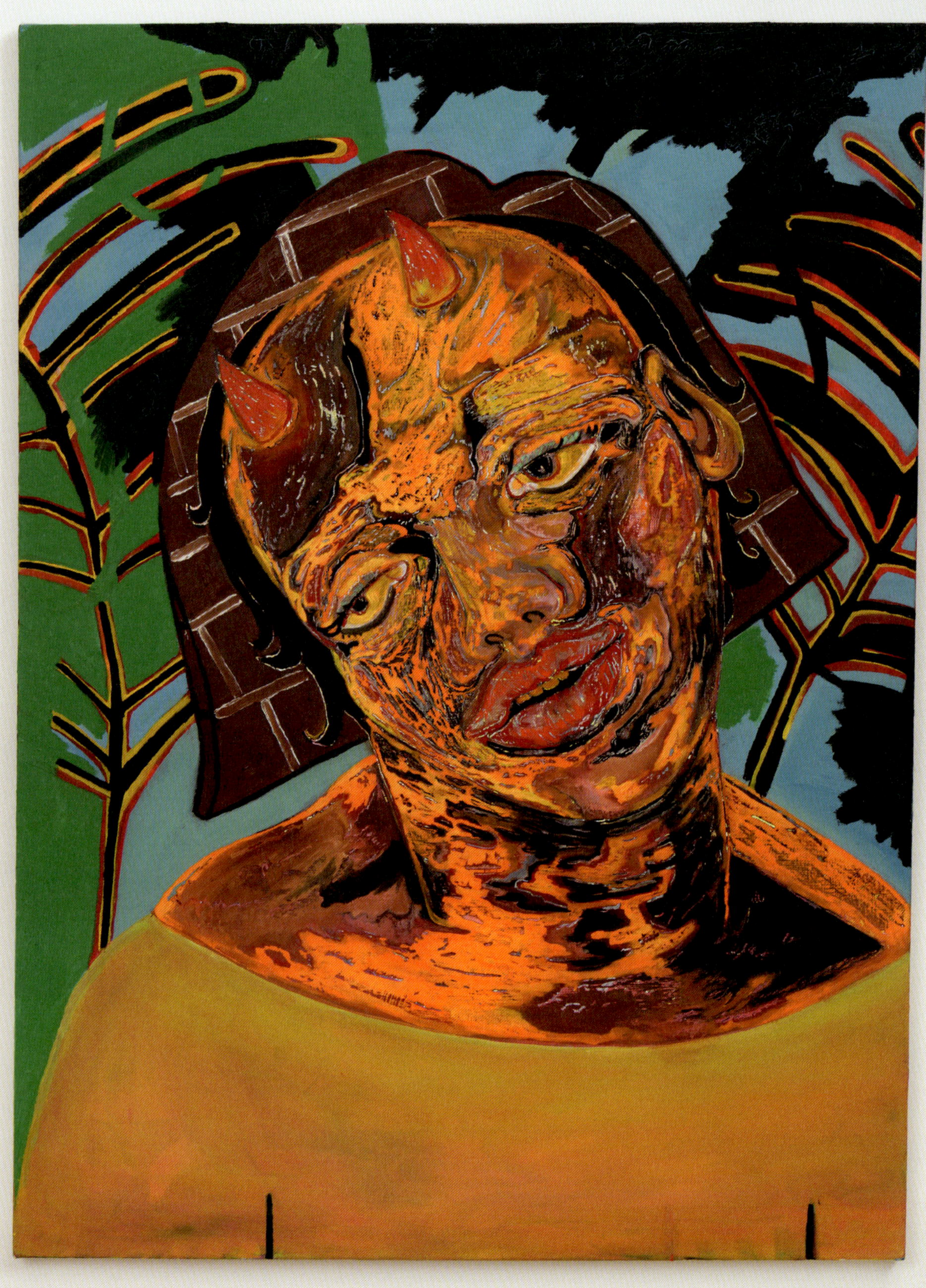

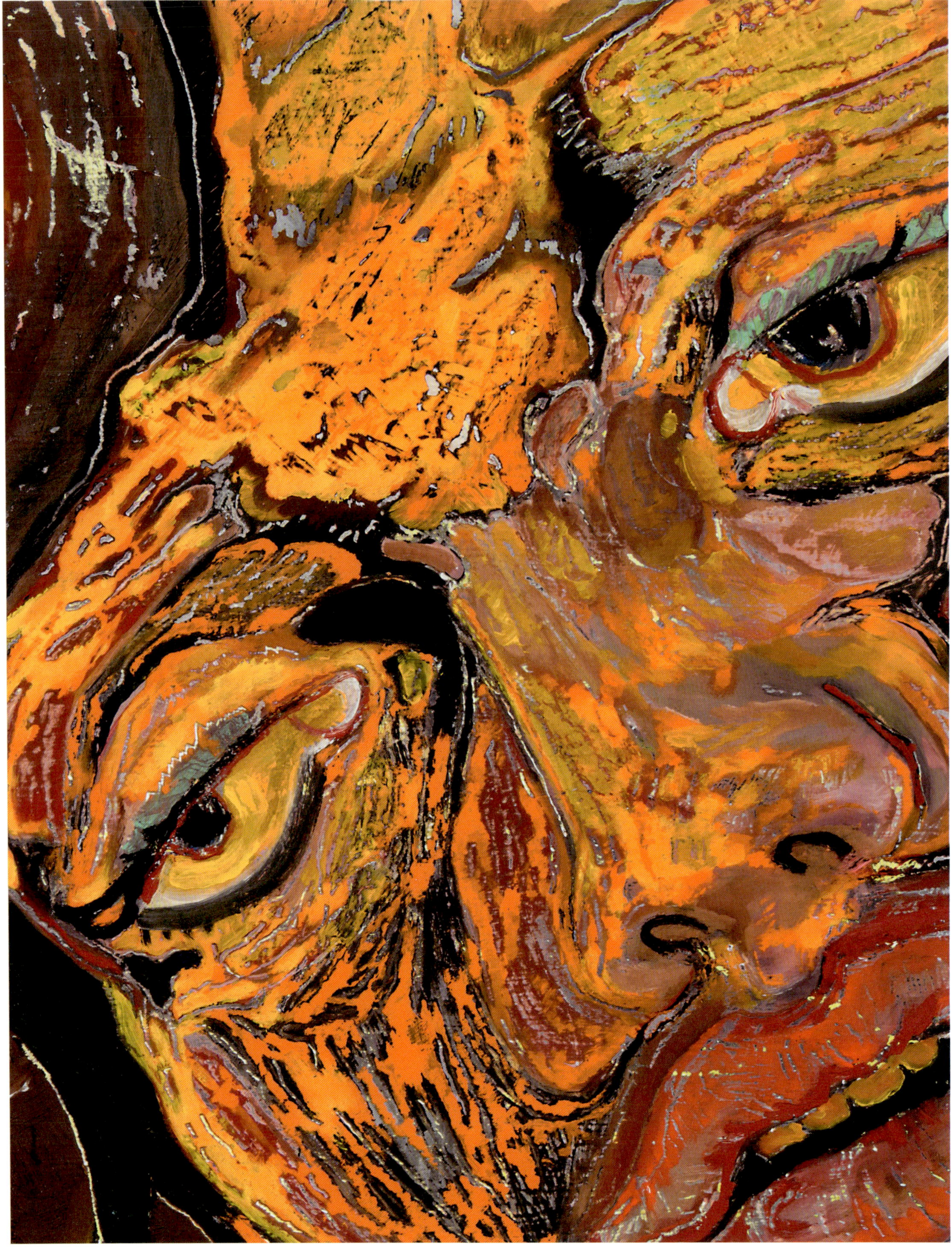

The Okiest Doke   2017
Oil on canvas
40 × 30 in. (101.6 × 76.2 cm)

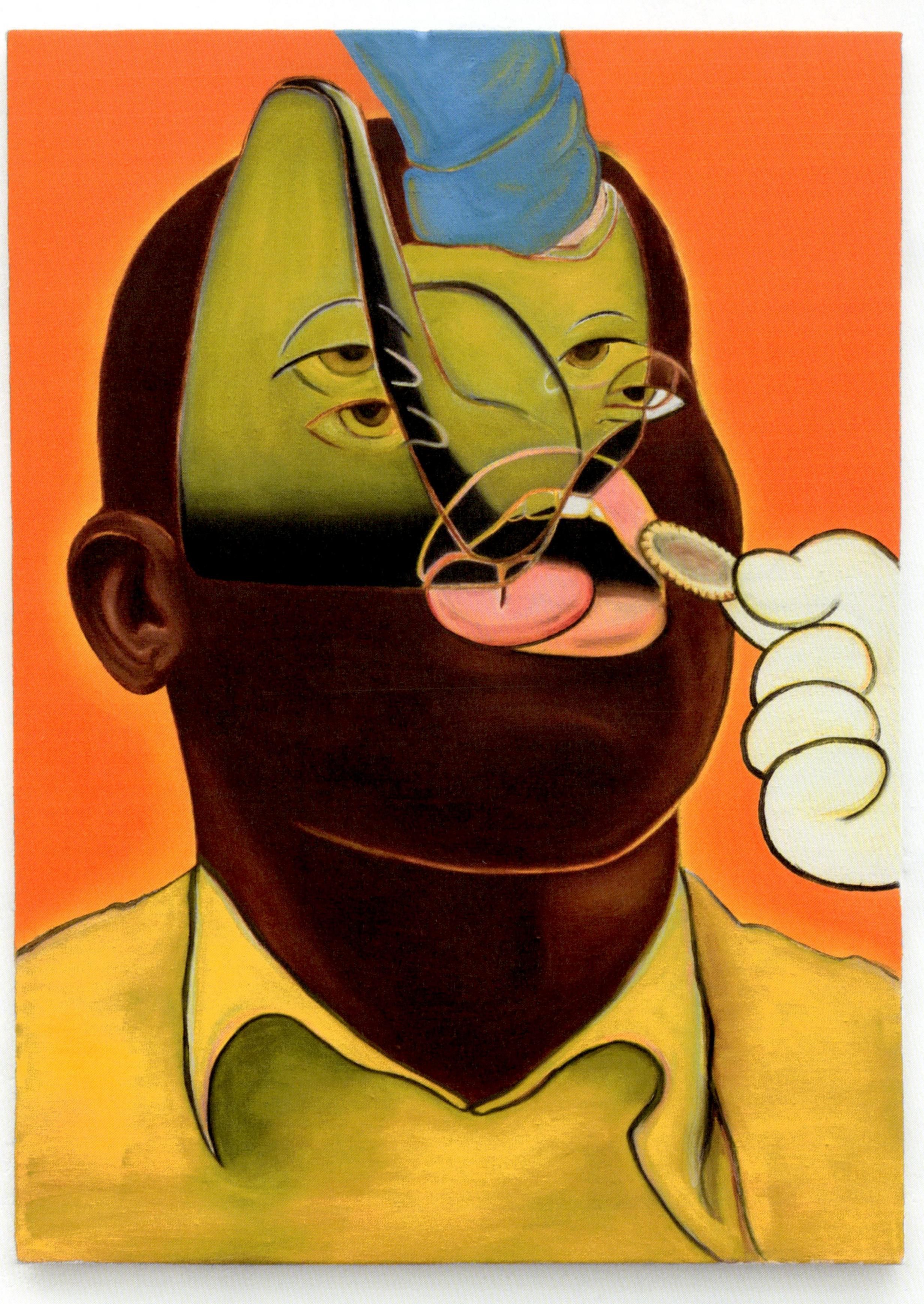

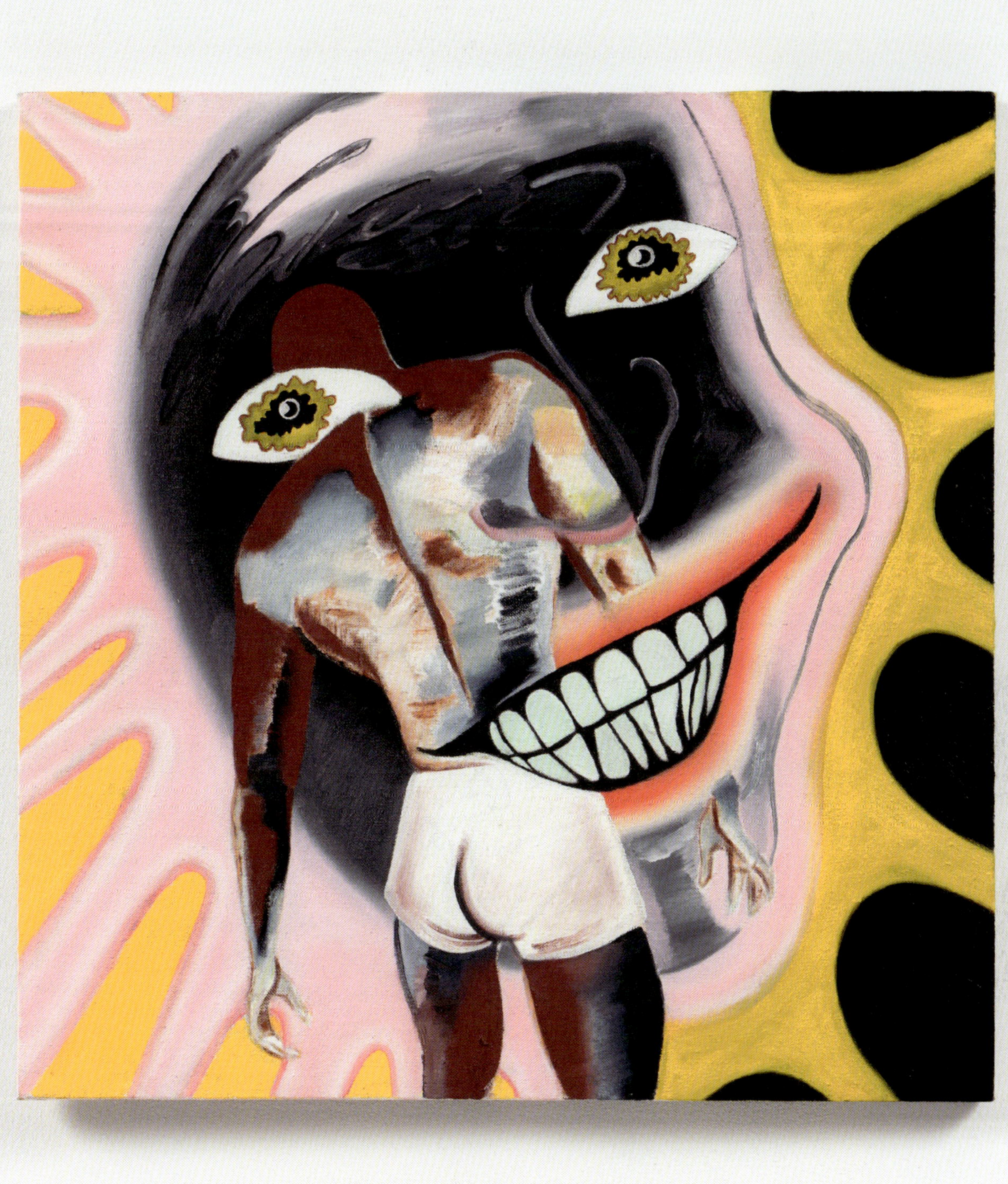

Gaze Cage 2017
Oil on canvas
24 × 24 in. (61 × 61 cm)

Cotton Eyed Misery Business 2017
Oil on canvas
36 × 24 in. (91.4 × 61 cm)

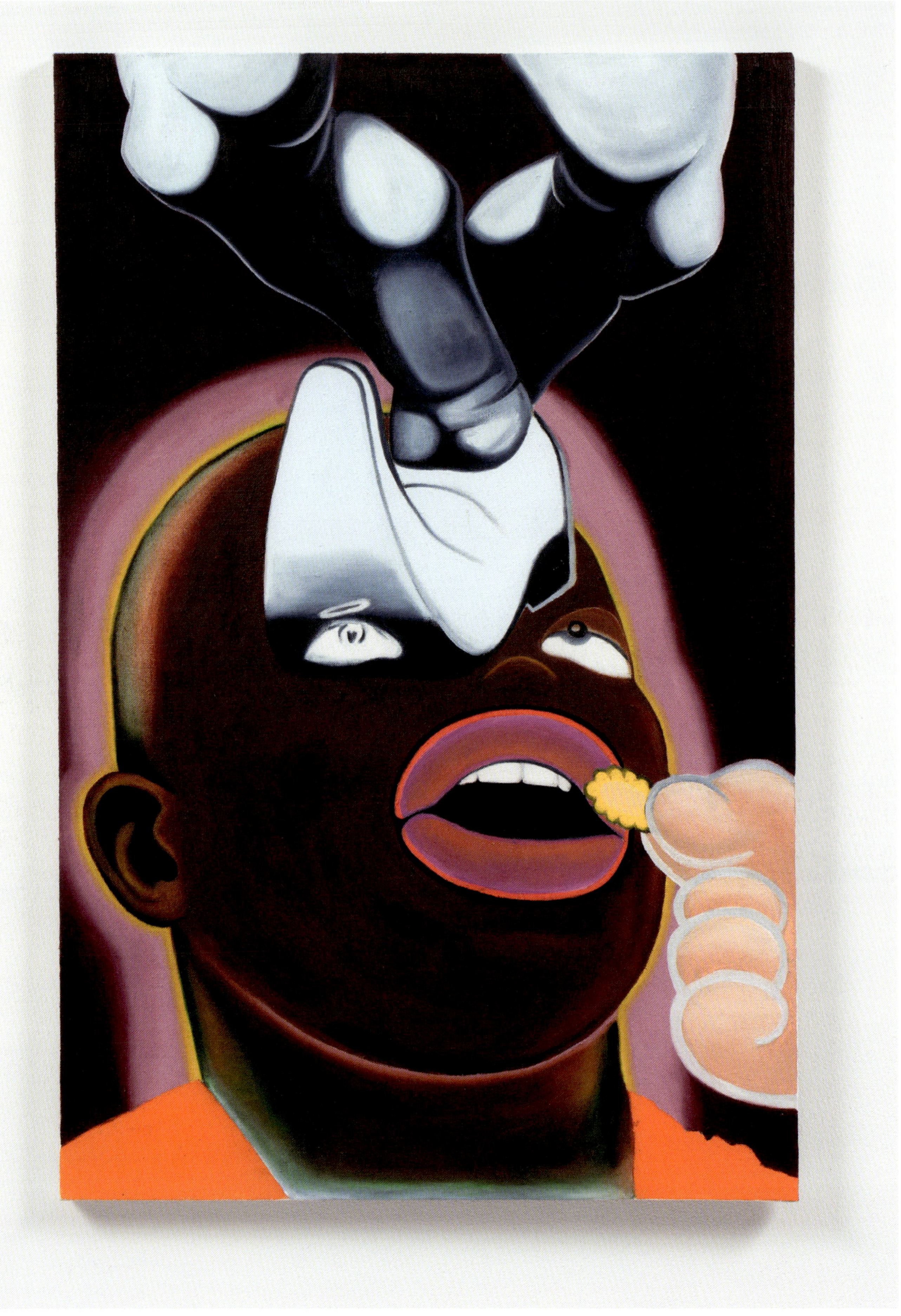

Doubt Guardian 2   2017
Oil on canvas
60 × 48 in. (152.4 × 121.9 cm)

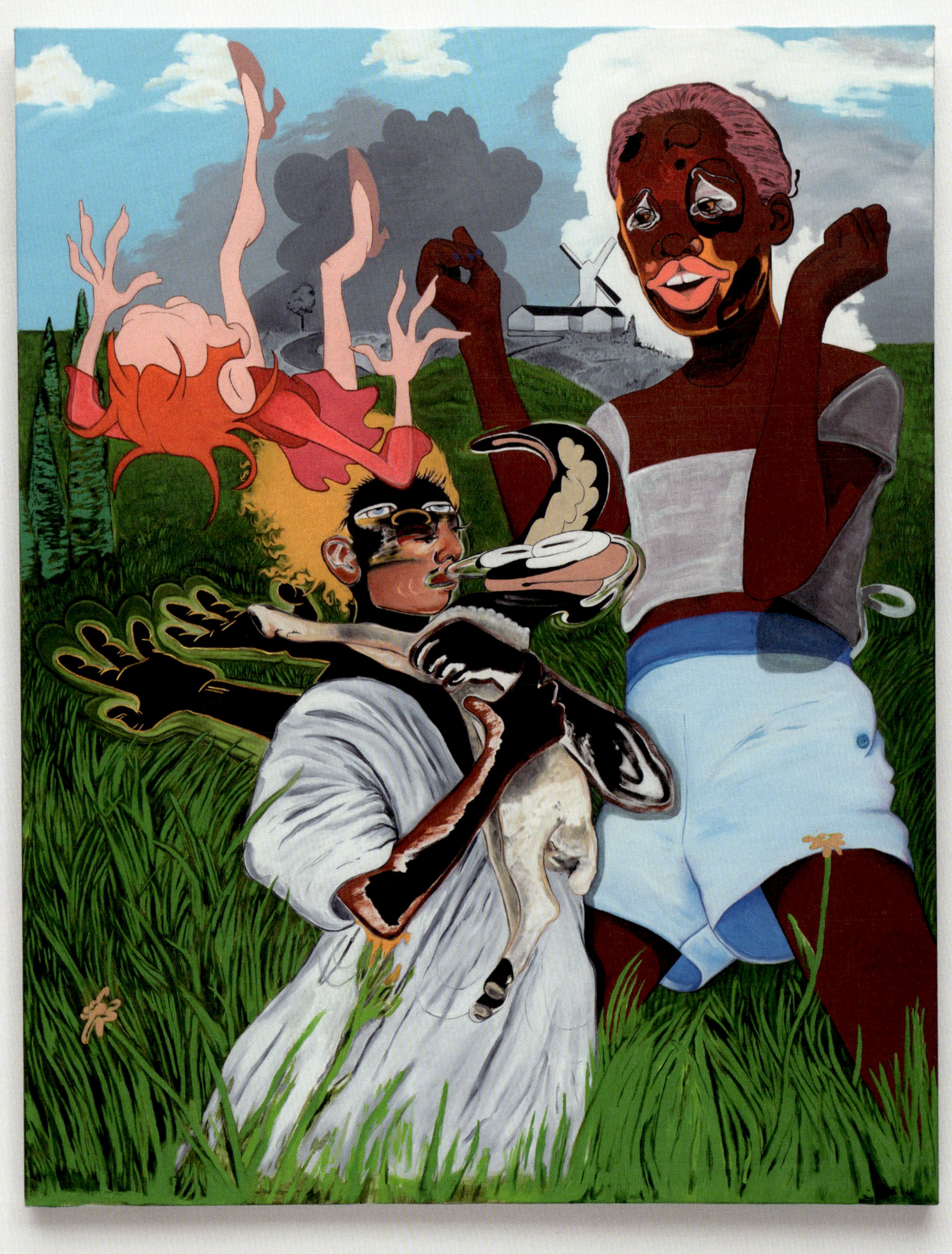

Thrill Issues   2017
Oil on canvas
95 × 77 in. (241.3 × 195.6 cm)

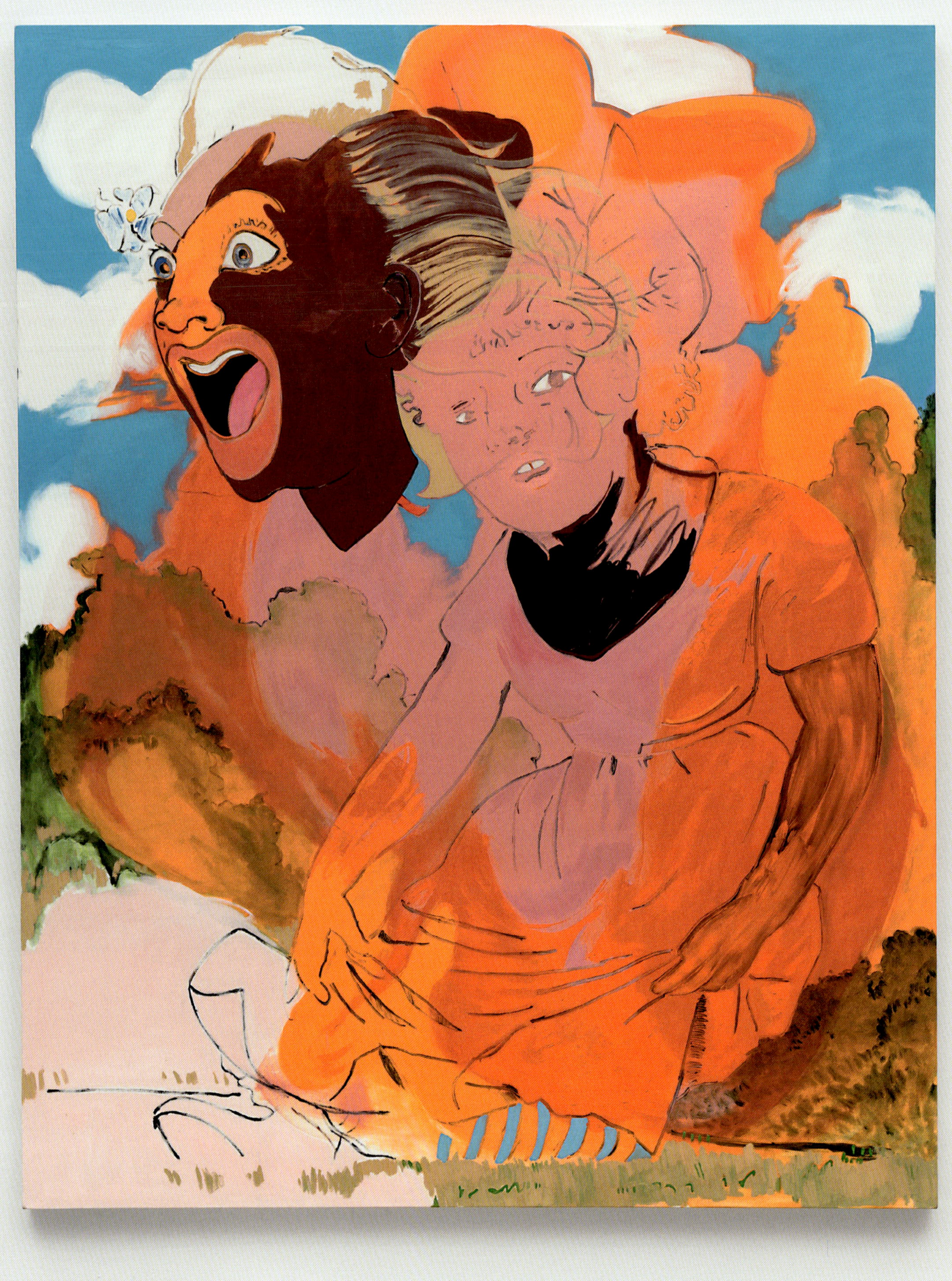

Curb Check Regular,   2018
Black Chick
Oil on canvas
70 × 76 in. (177.8 × 193 cm)

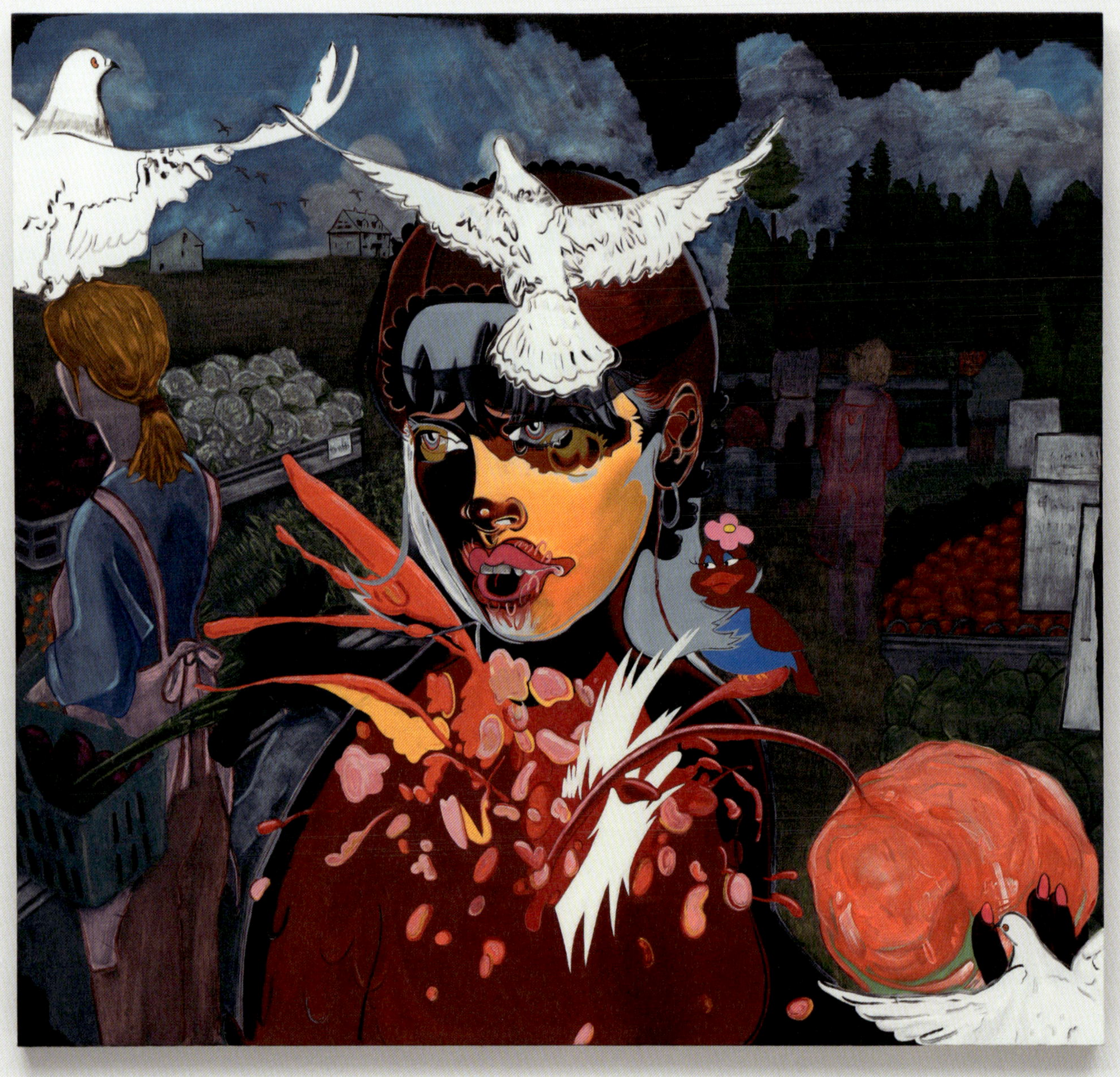

Keebler's Revenge   2018
Oil on canvas
40 × 48 in. (101.6 × 121.9 cm)

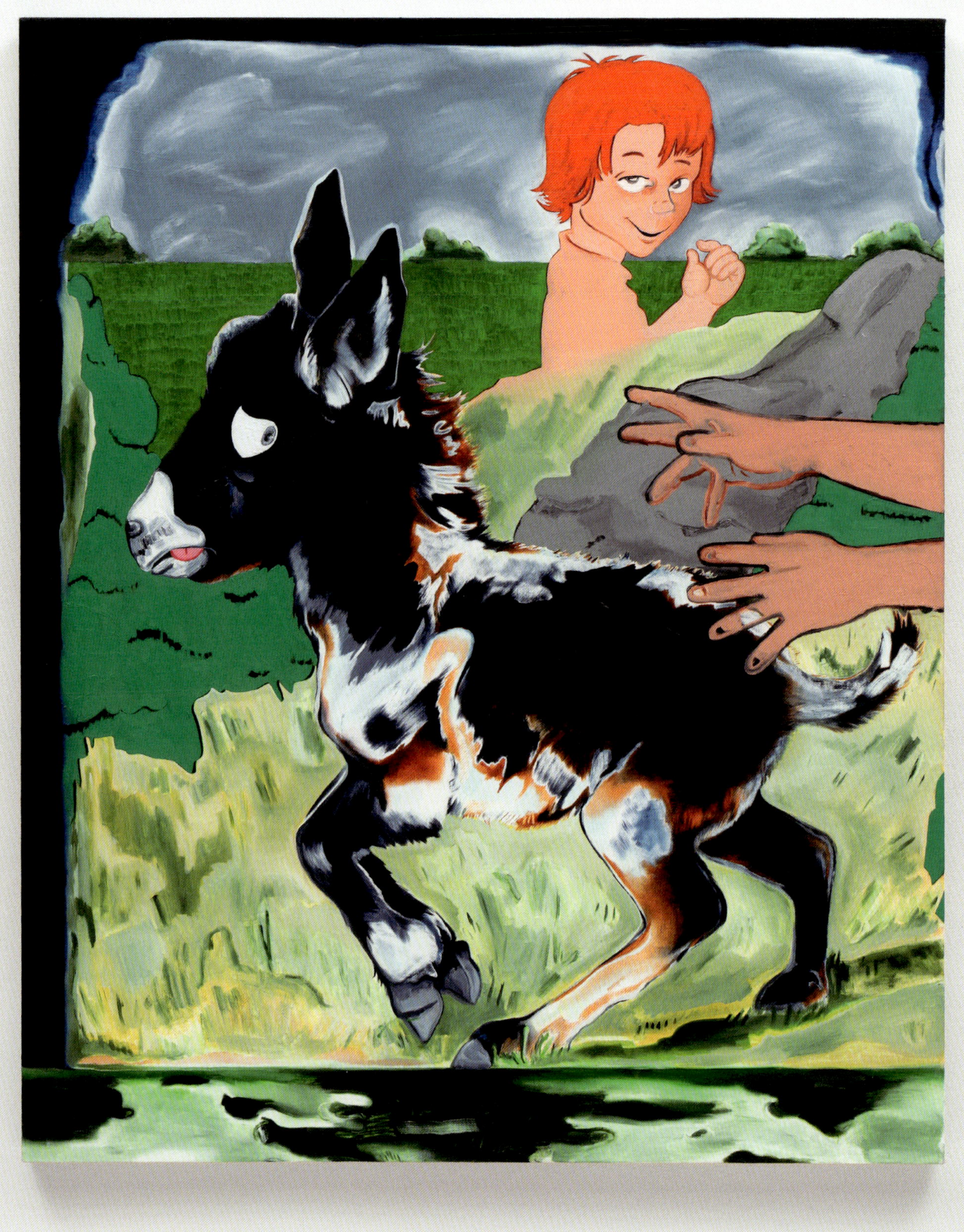

Doubt Guardian   2018
Oil on canvas
48 × 48 in. (121.9 × 121.9 cm)

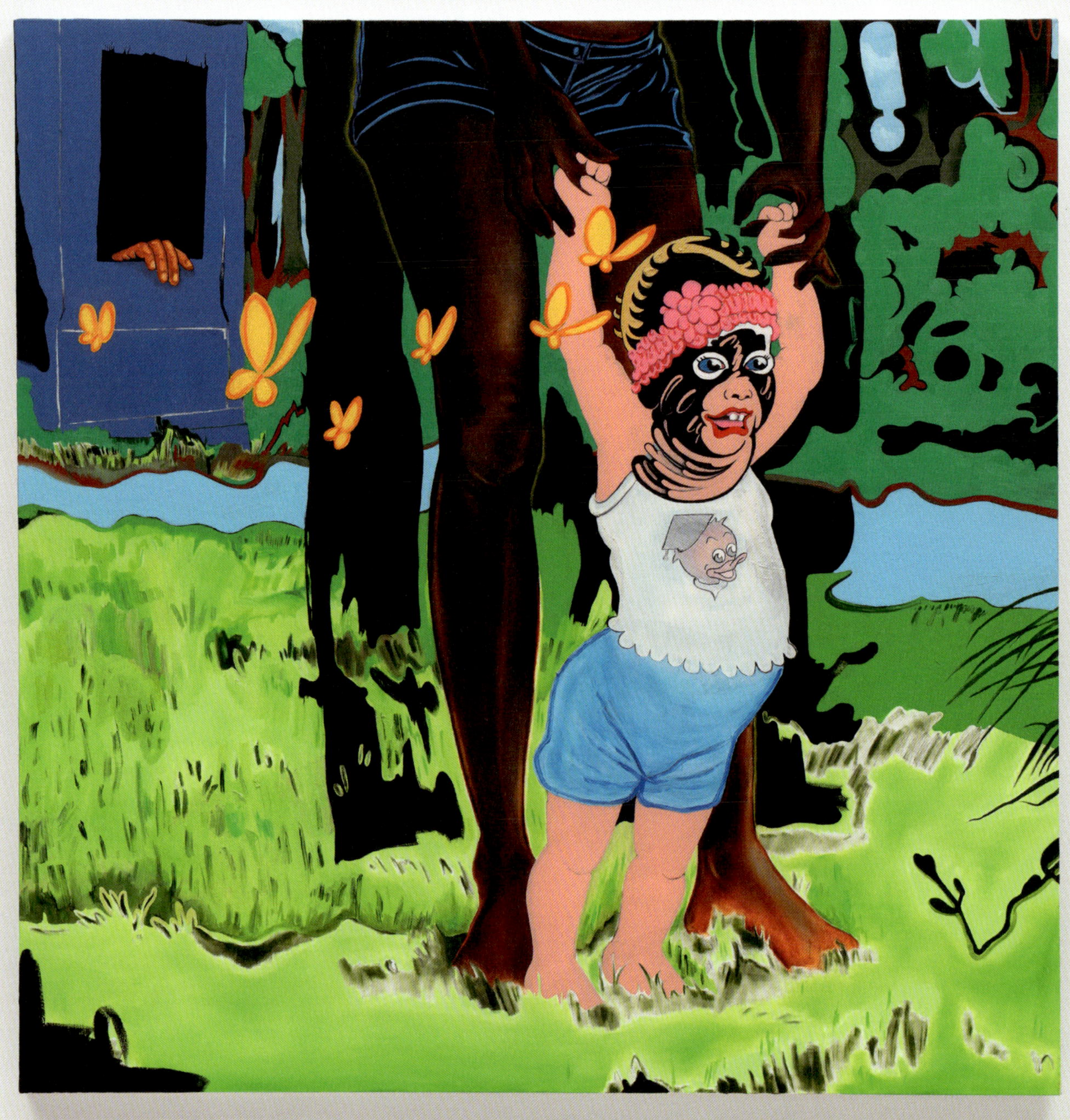

Thumper Tantrum   2018
Oil on canvas
20 × 16 in. (50.8 × 40.6 cm)

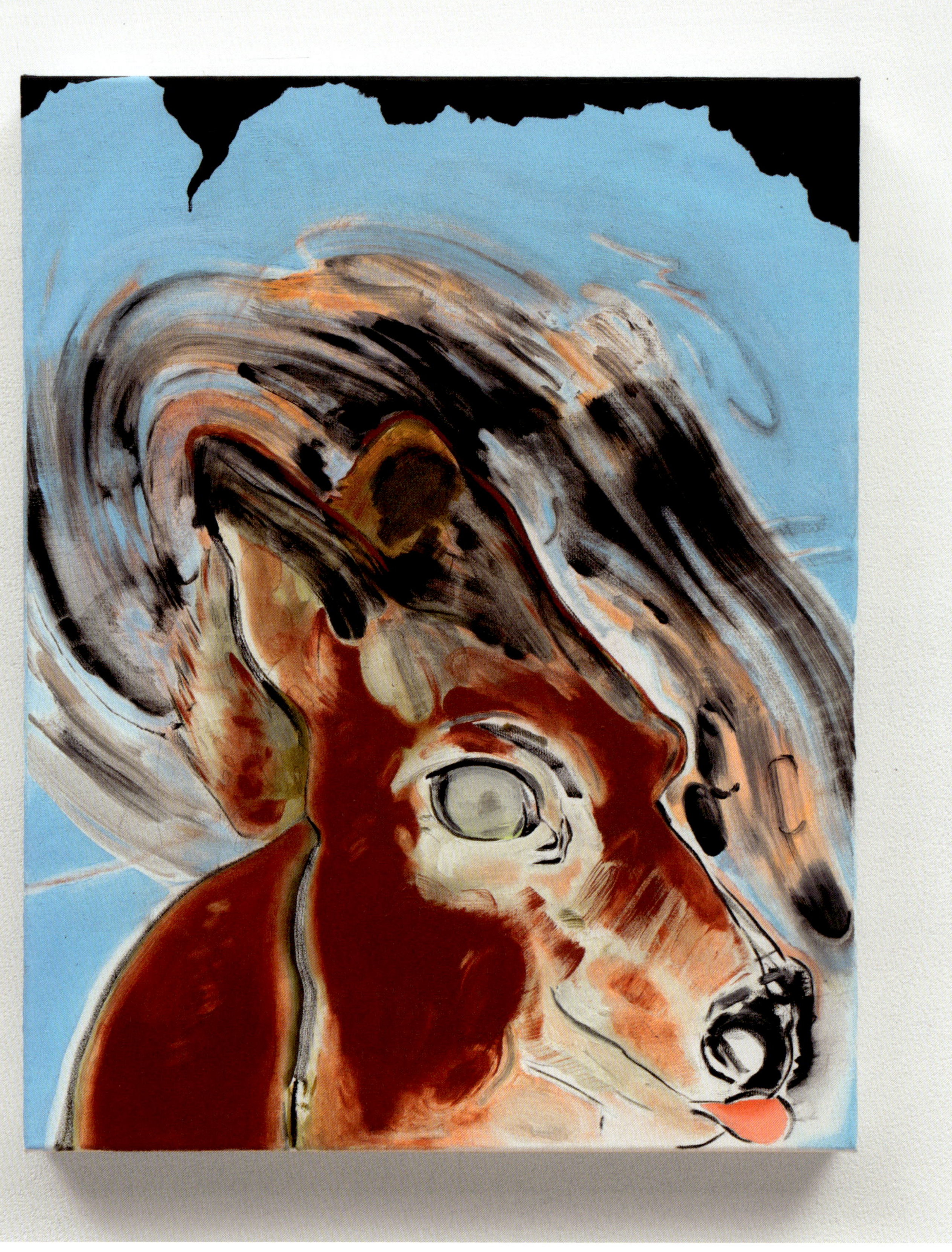

Bimini Boop Bullaby 2018
Oil on canvas
30 × 24 in. (76.2 × 61 cm)

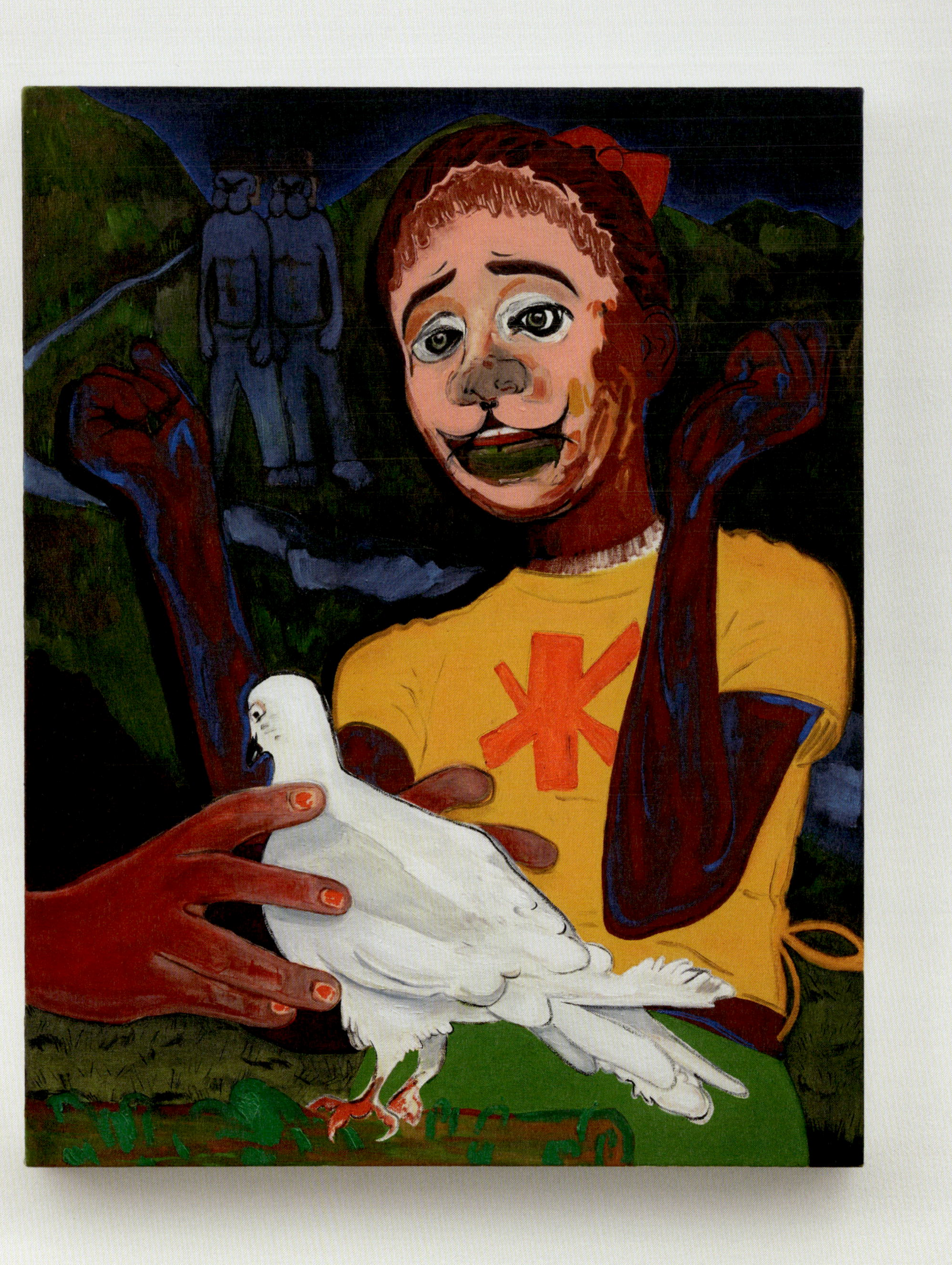

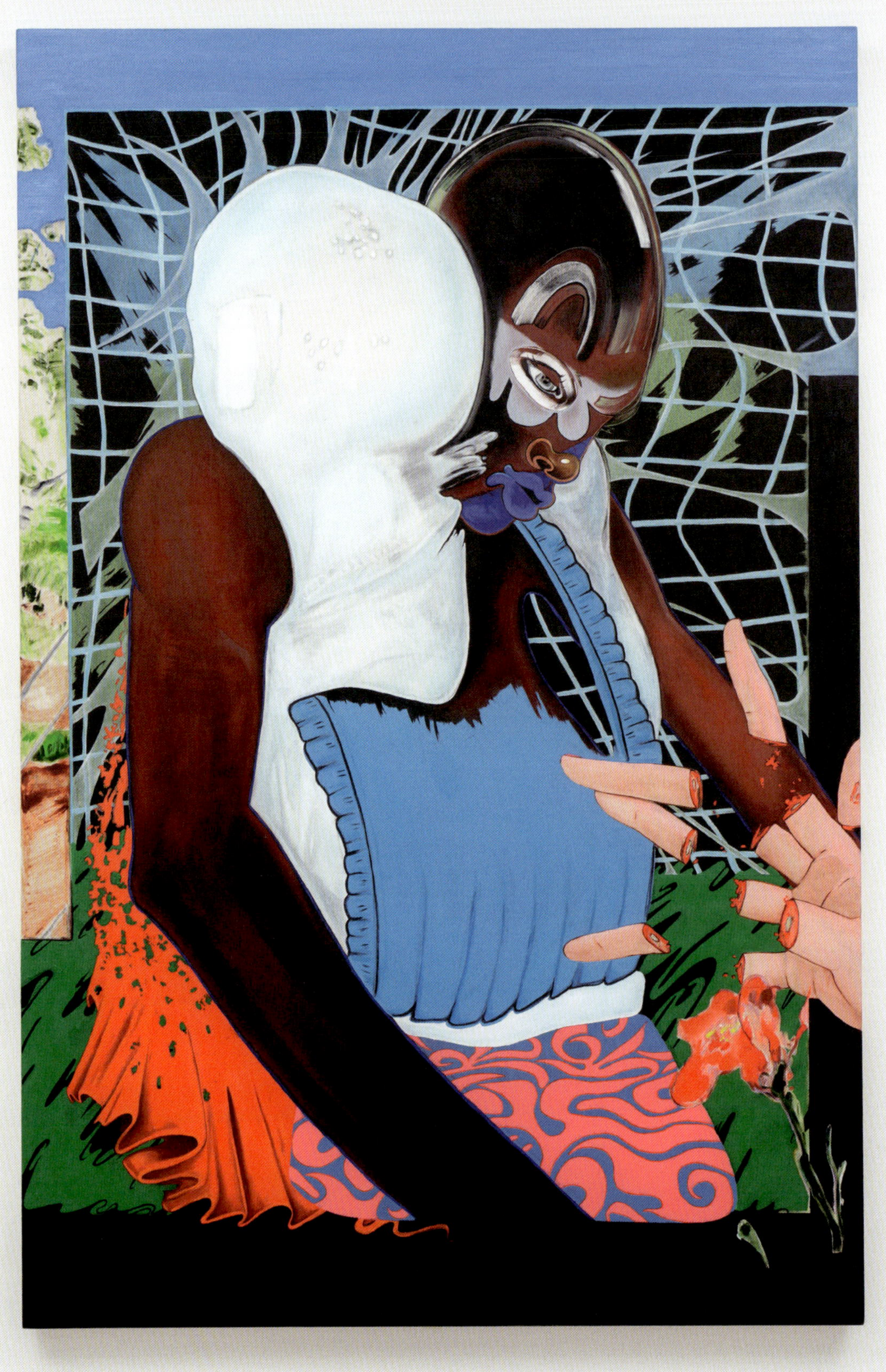

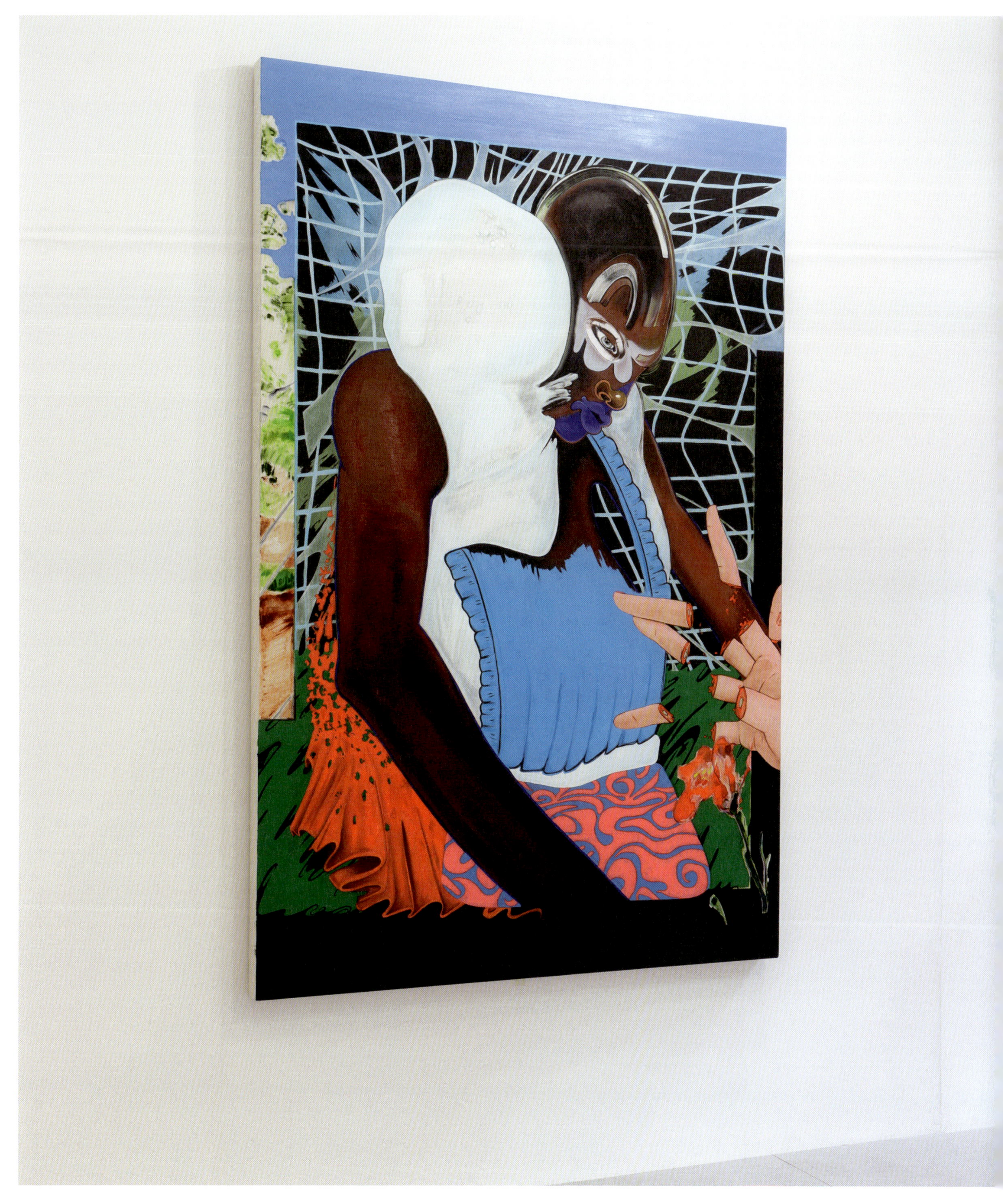

A Devotion Deficit   2018
Oil on canvas
72 × 48 in. (182.9 × 121.9 cm)

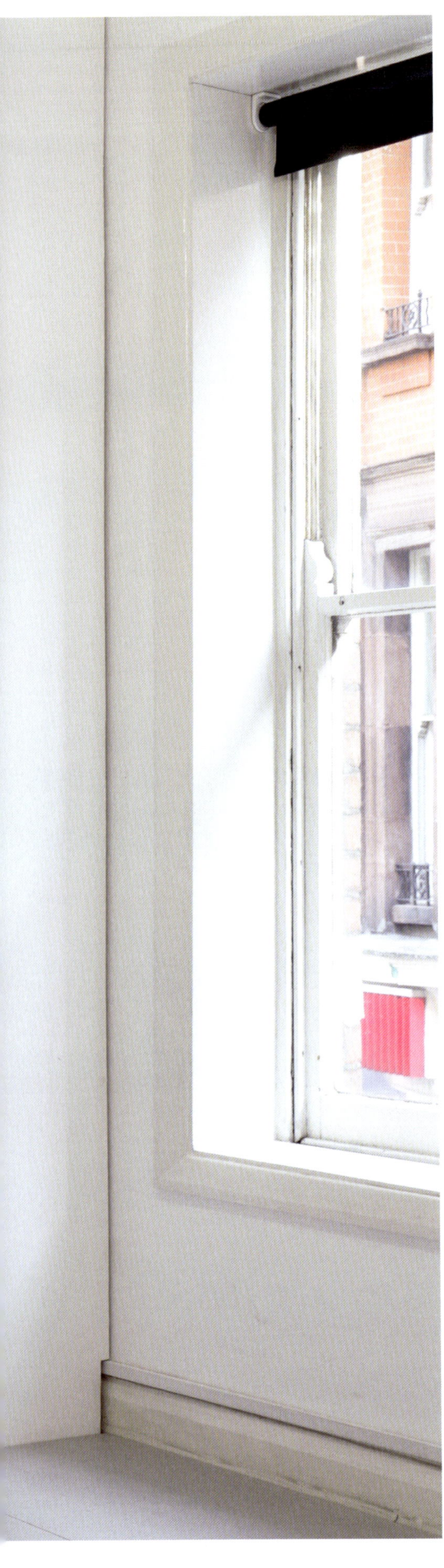

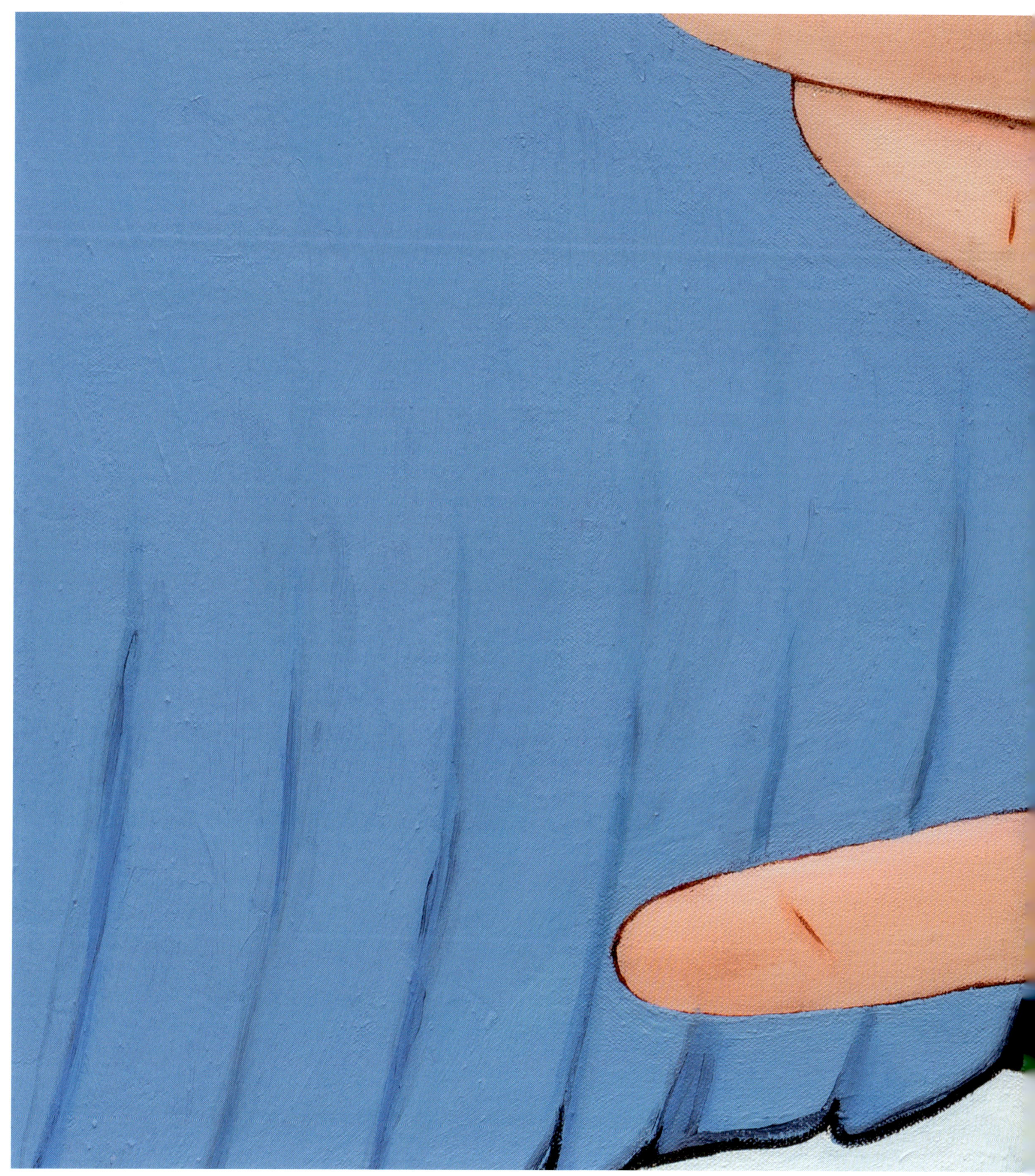

A Devotion Deficit   2018   detail
Oil on canvas
72 × 48 in. (182.9 × 121.9 cm)

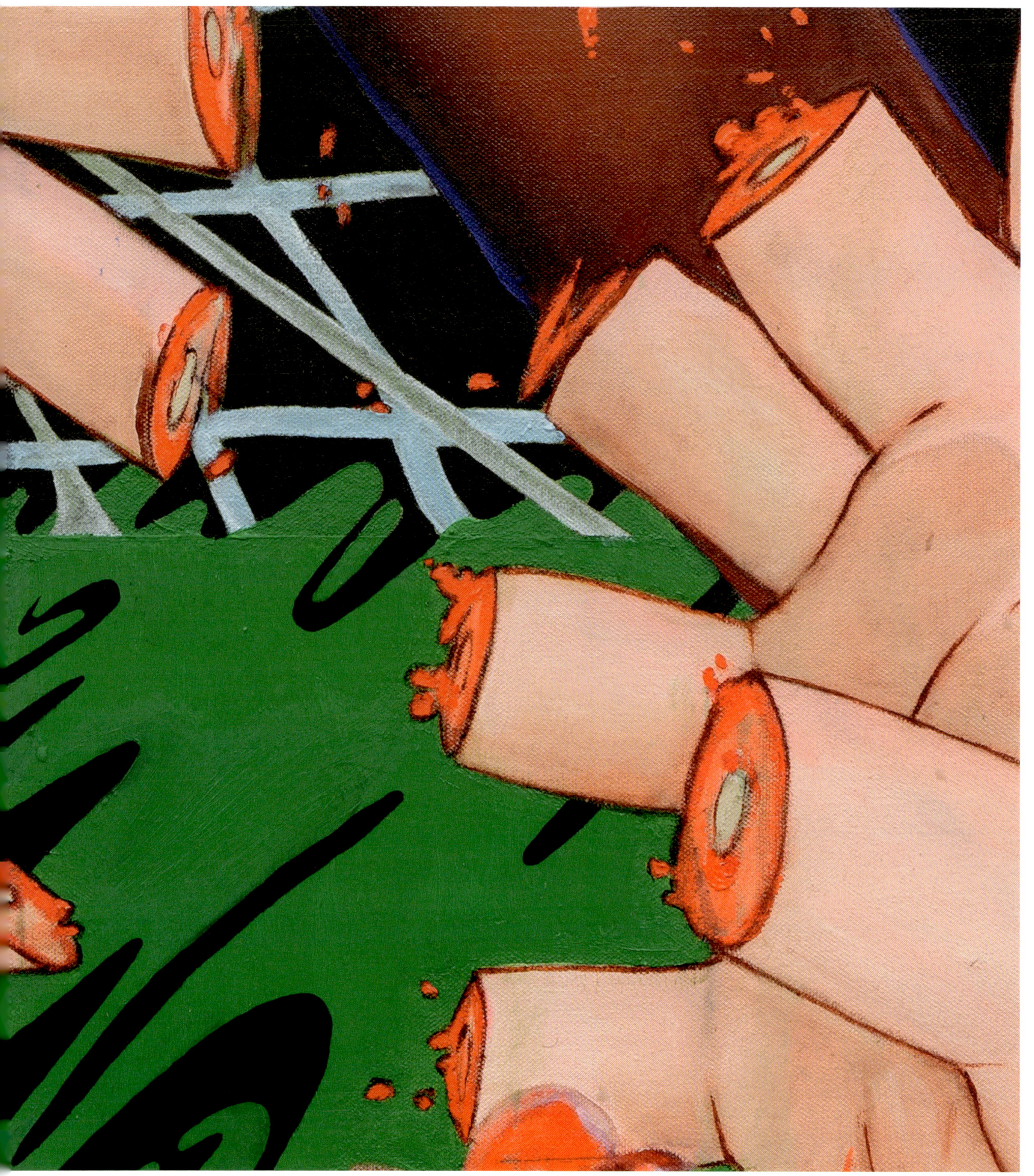

Bramble's Briar Patch   2018
Oil on canvas
40 × 30 in. (101.6 × 76.2 cm)

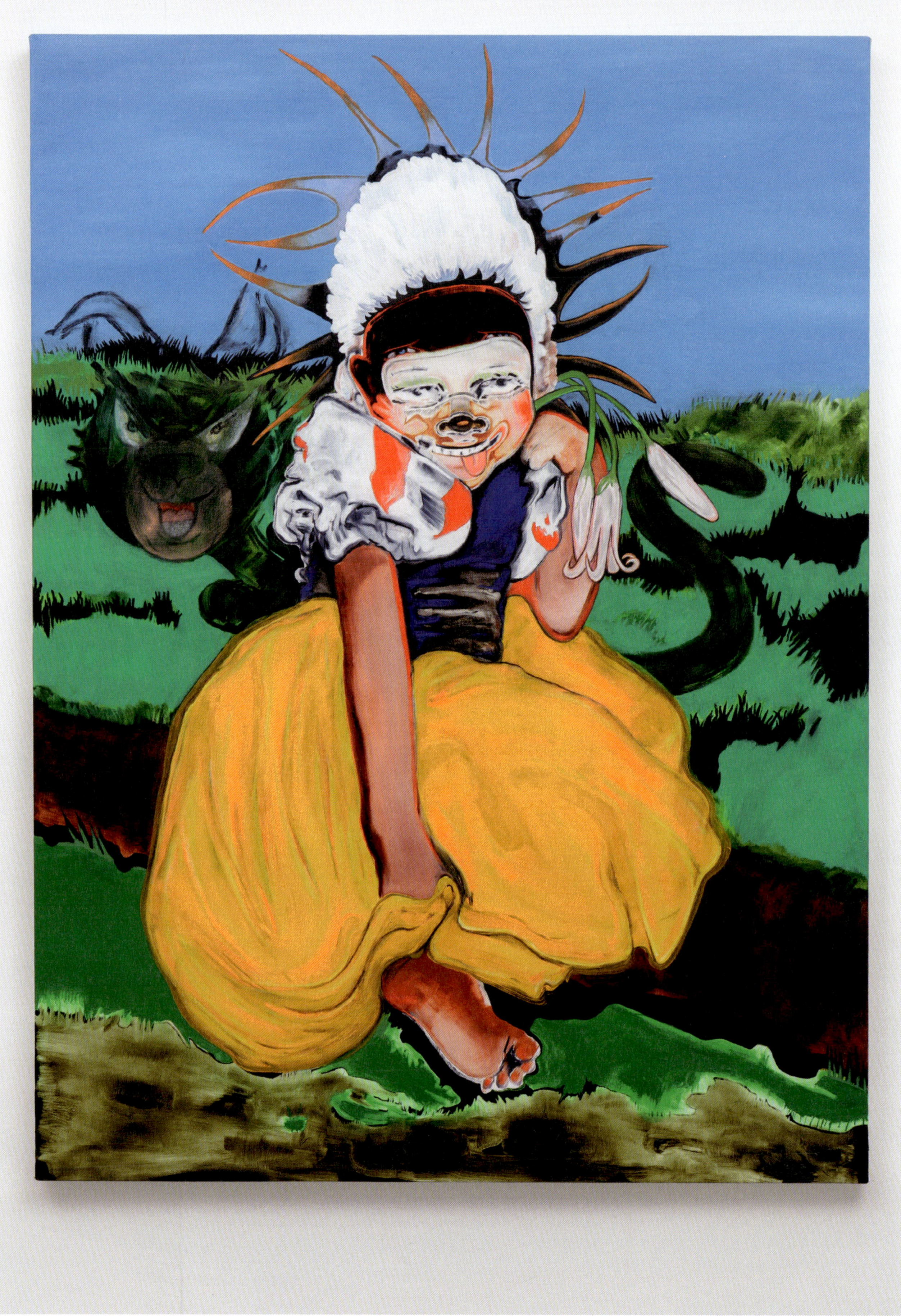

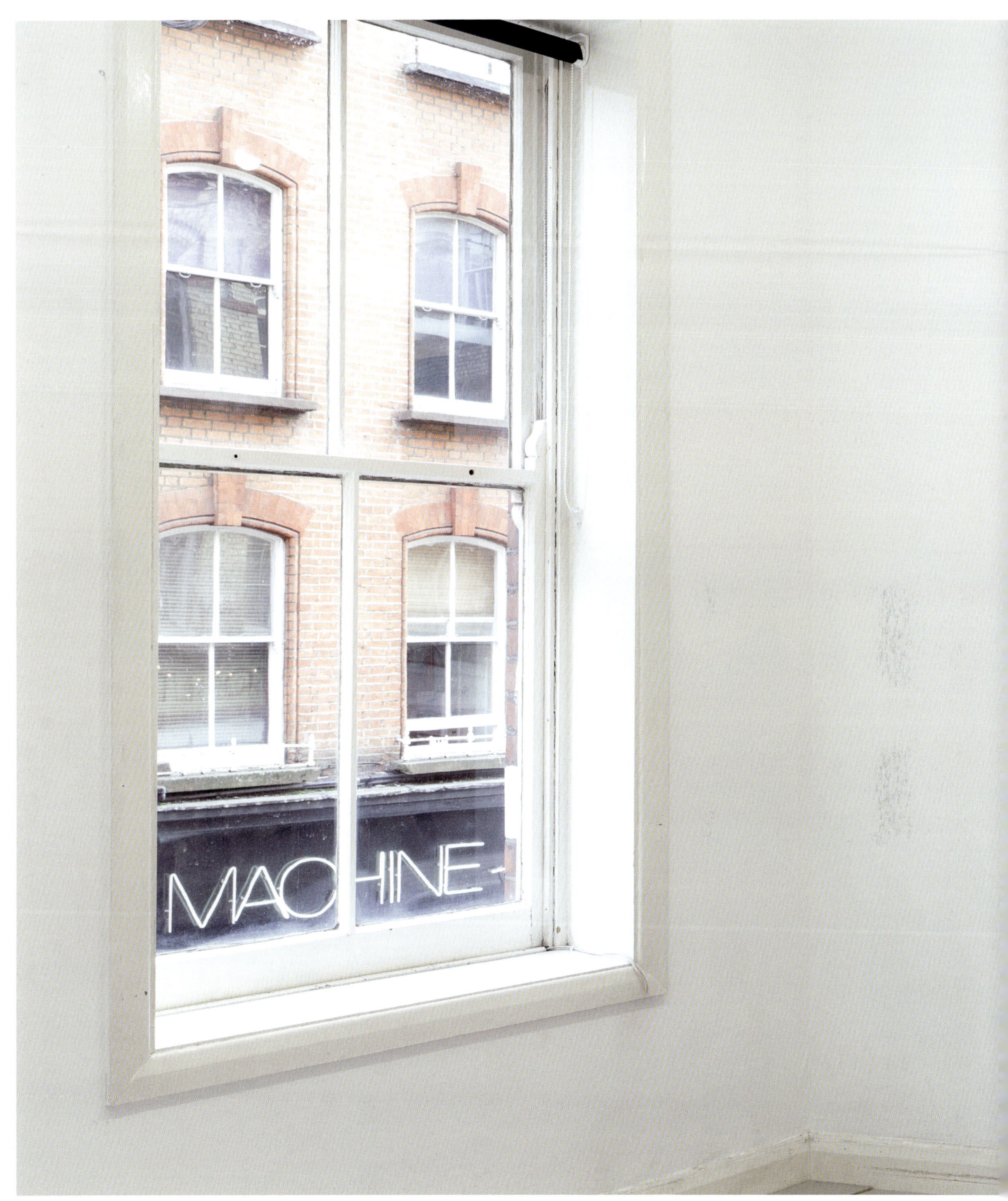

Full-Fledged Safari Syndrome   2018
Oil on canvas
48 × 59 ½ in. (121.9 × 151.1 cm)

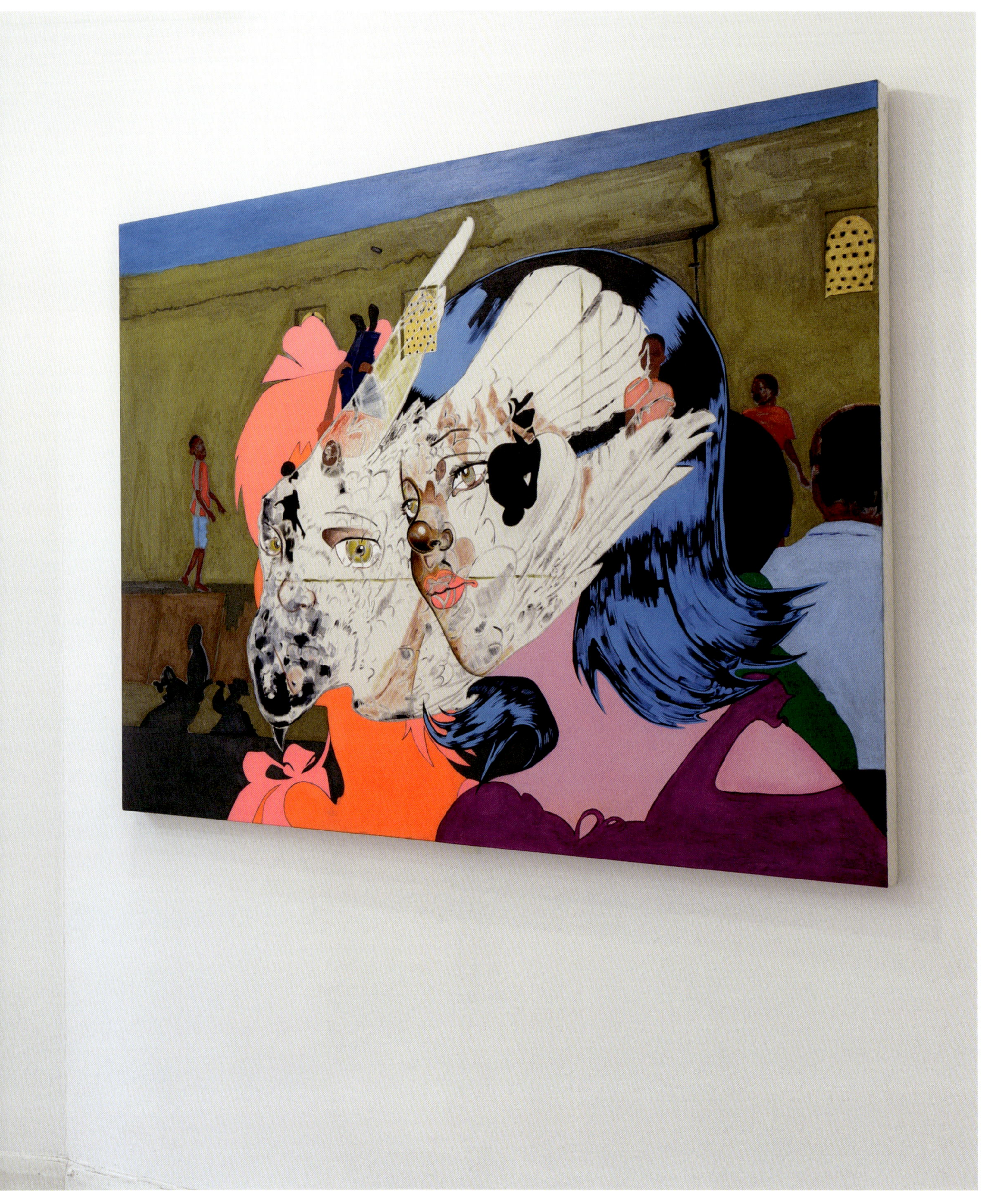

Full-Fledged Safari Syndrome   2018
Oil on canvas
48 × 59 ½ in. (121.9 × 151.1 cm)

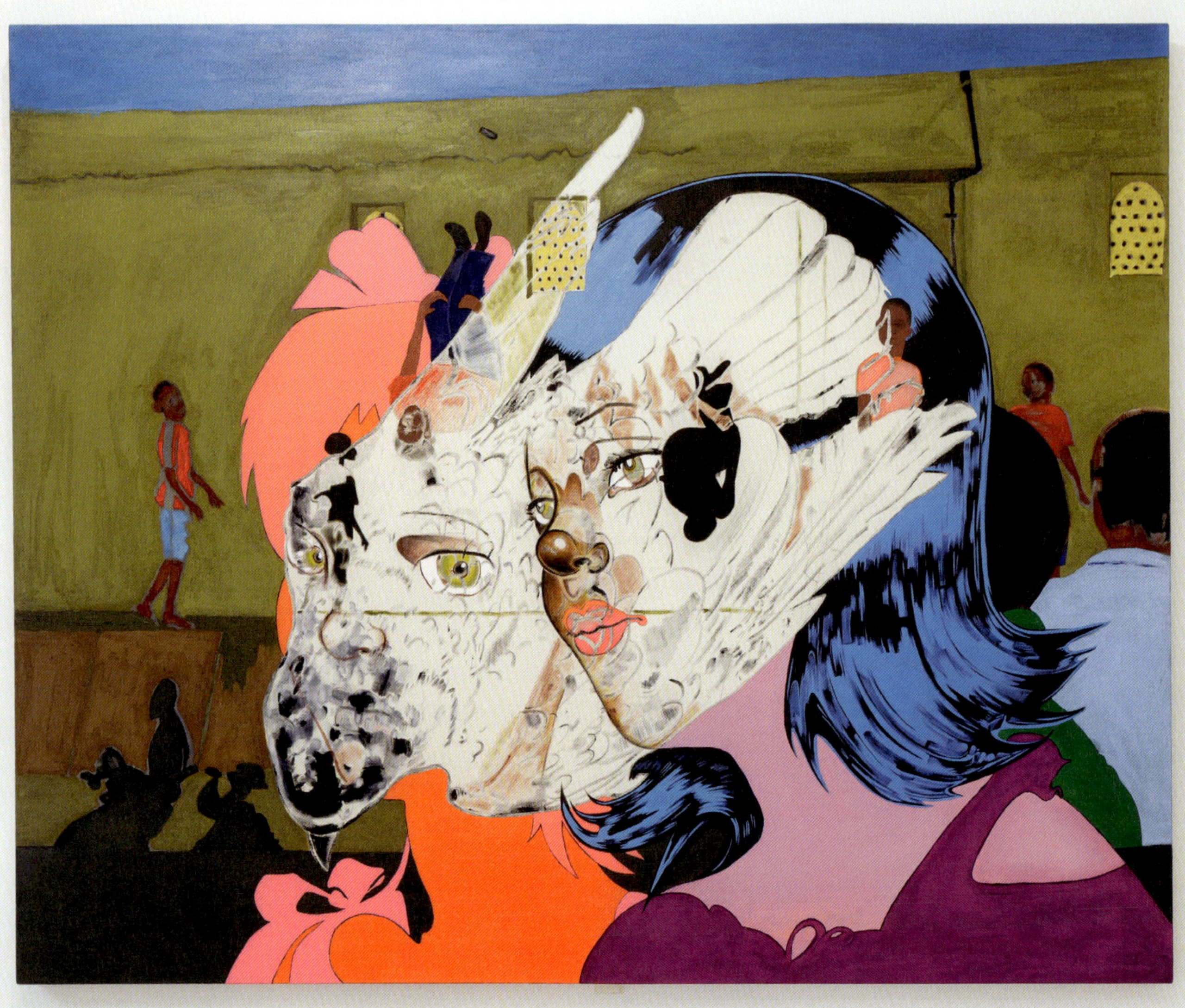

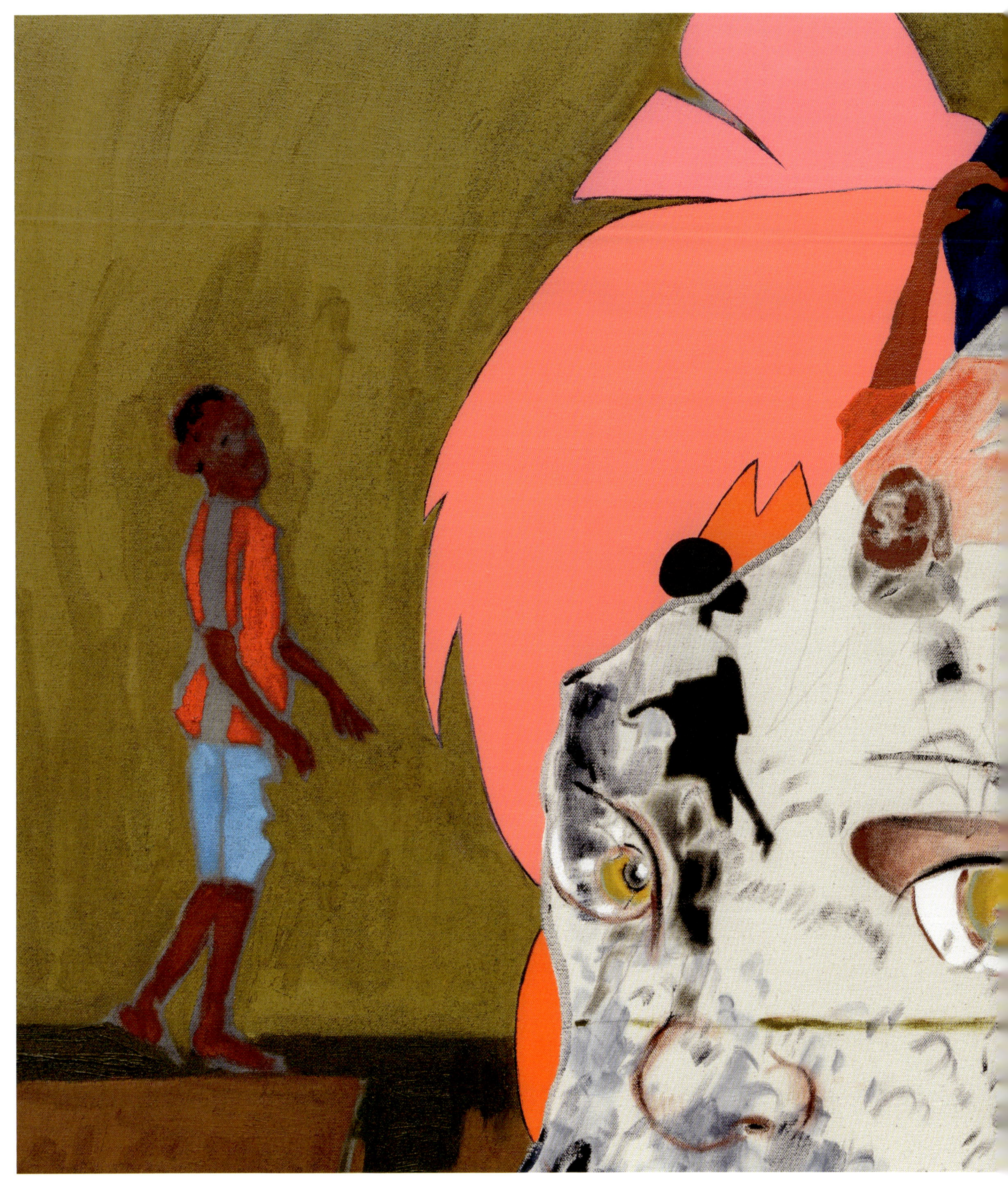

Full-Fledged Safari Syndrome   2018   detail
Oil on canvas
48 × 59 ½ in. (121.9 × 151.1 cm)

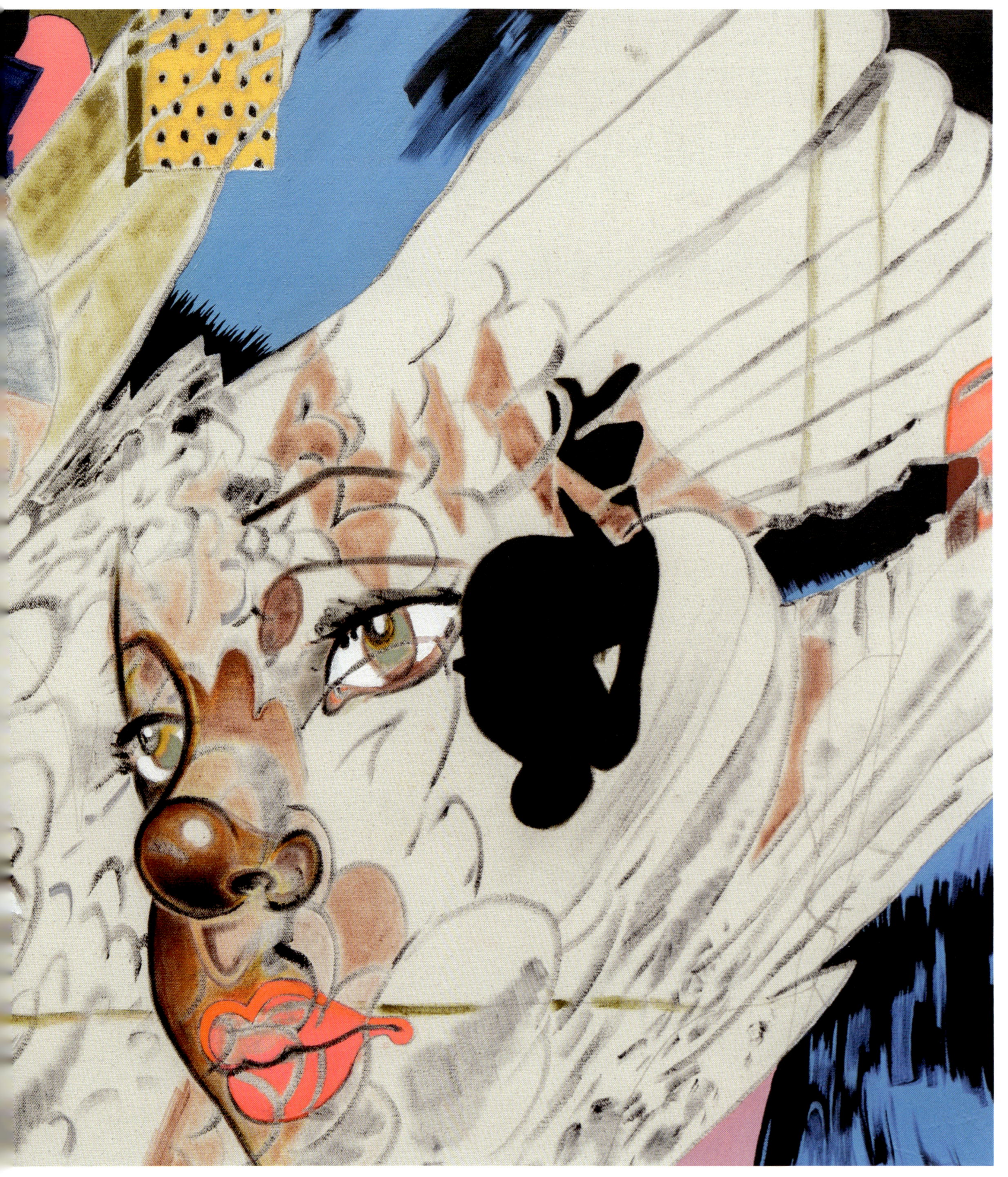

Playful But Bites 2018
Oil on canvas
20 × 16 in. (50.8 × 40.6 cm)

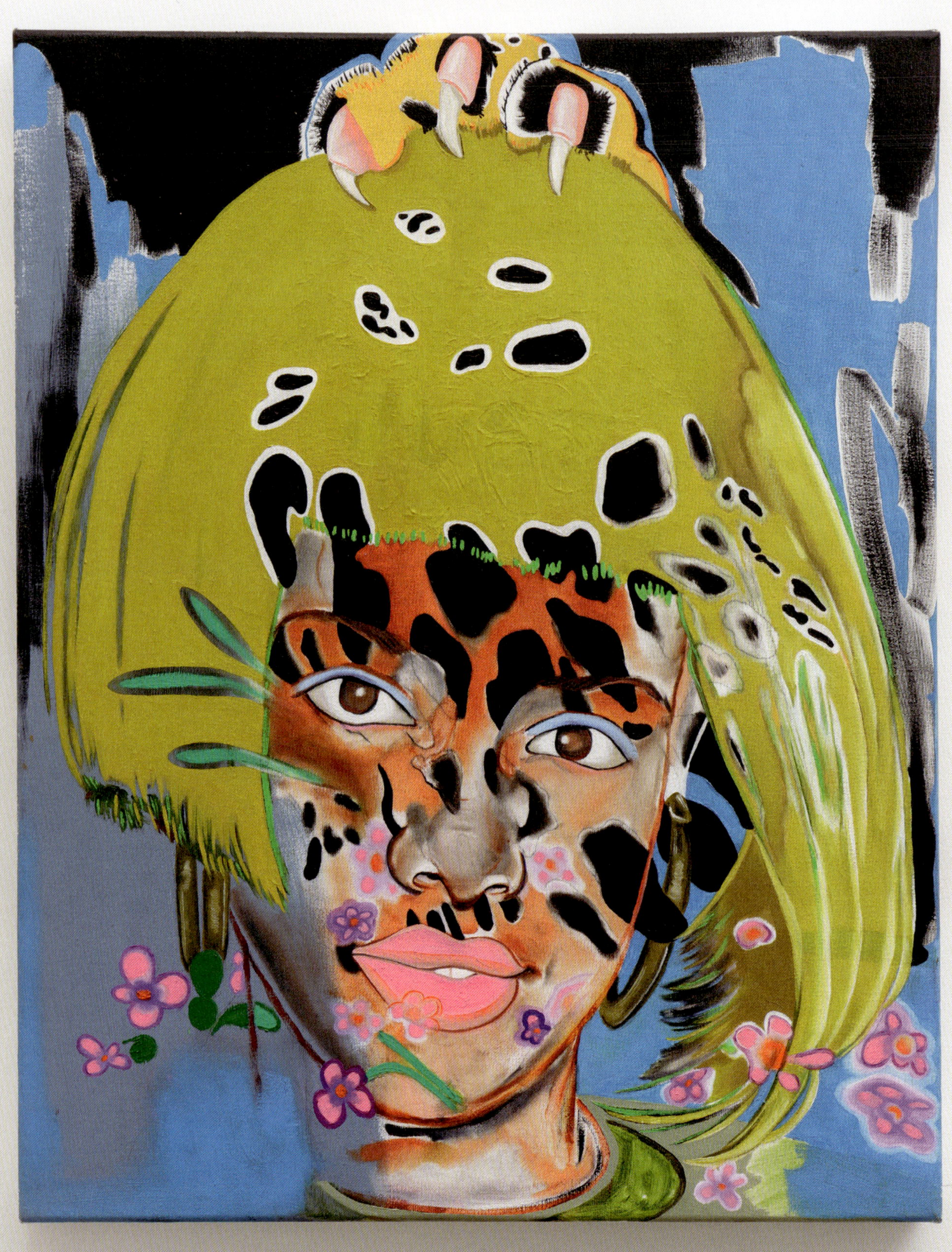

Scripture for the Enemy   2018
Oil on canvas
48 × 36 in. (121.9 × 91.4 cm)

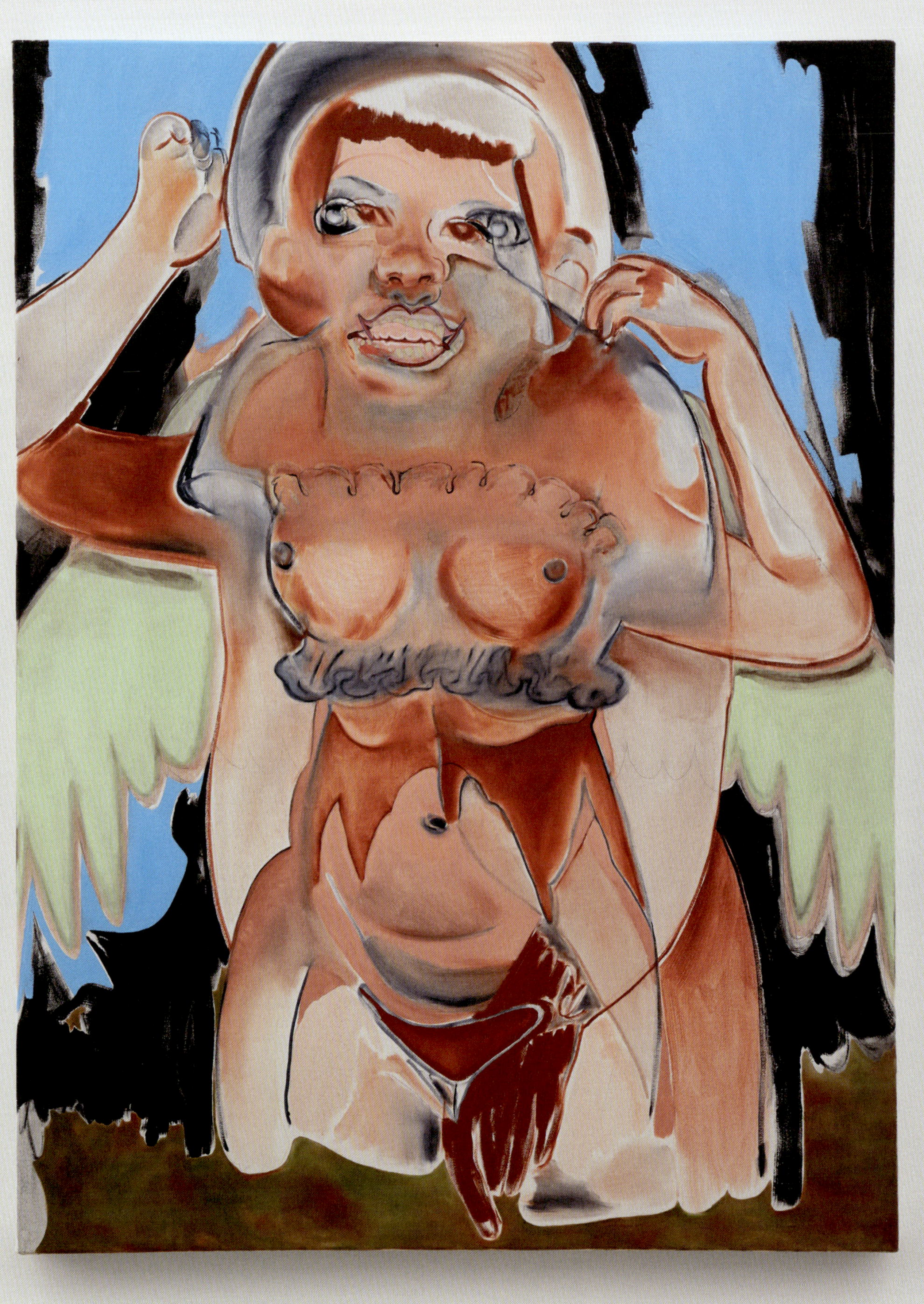

Rube Boy Leisure Obstacle   2018
Oil on canvas
36 × 42 in. (91.4 × 106.7 cm)

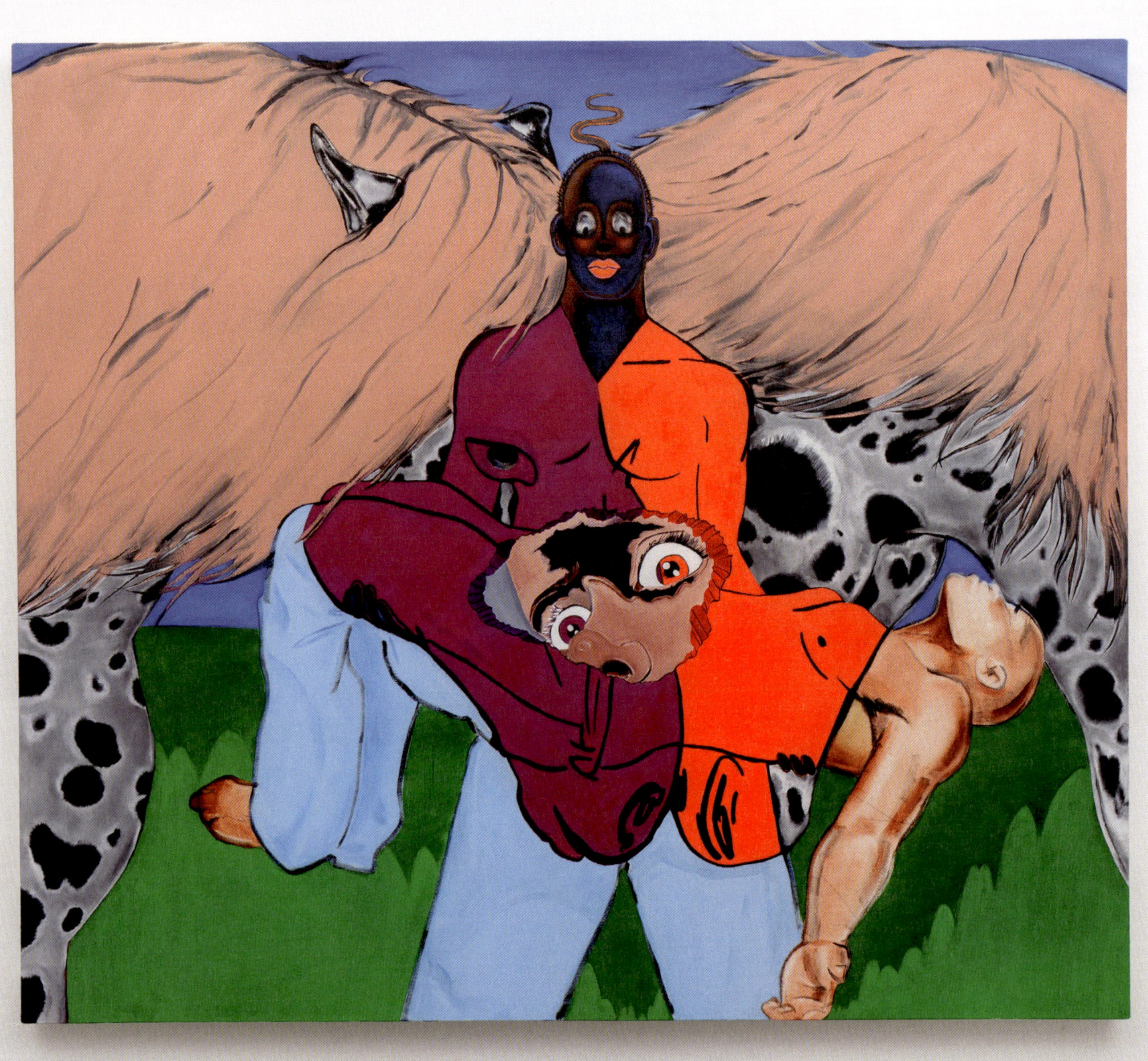

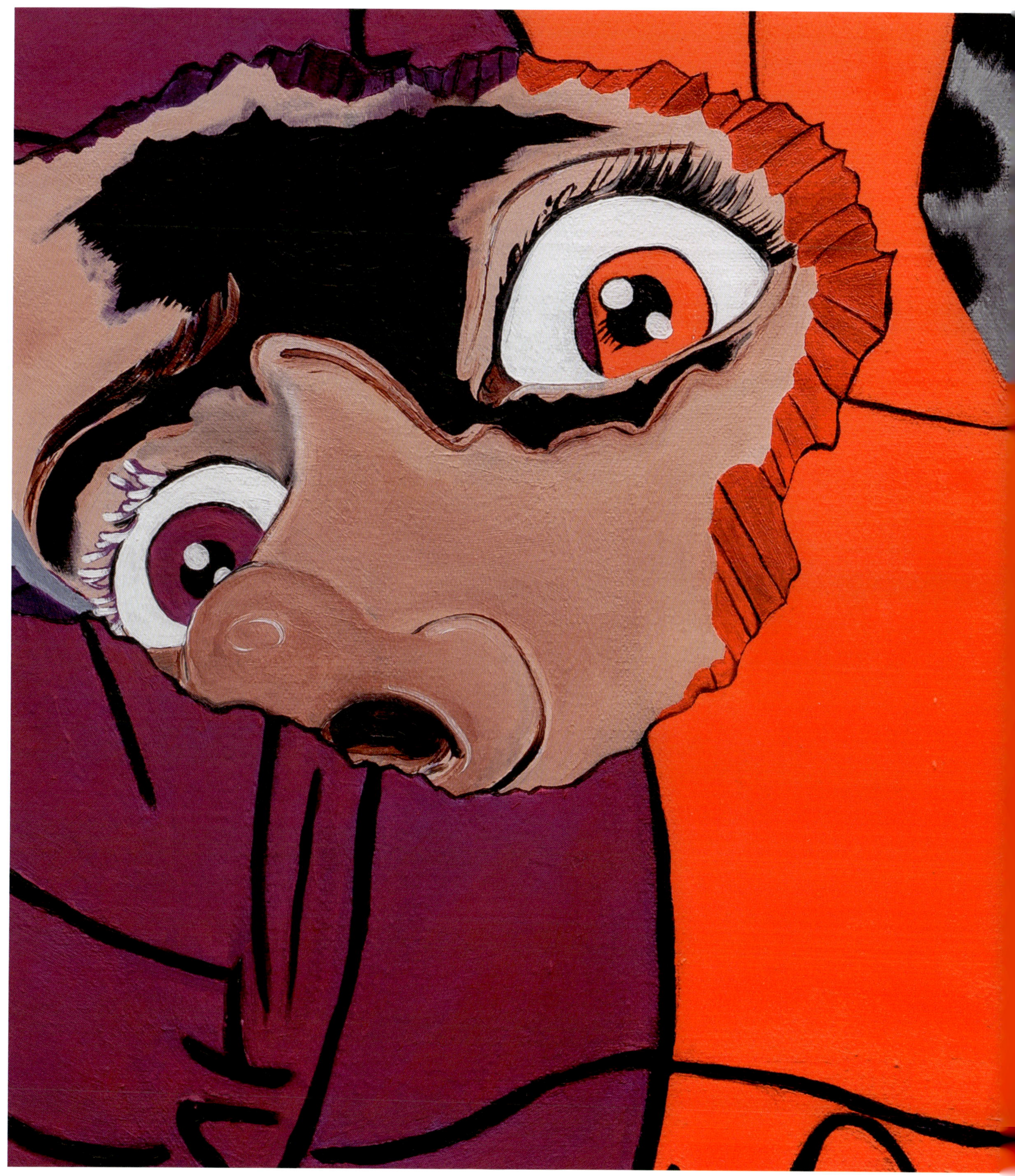

Rube Boy Leisure Obstacle   2018   detail
Oil on canvas
36 × 42 in. (91.4 × 106.7 cm)

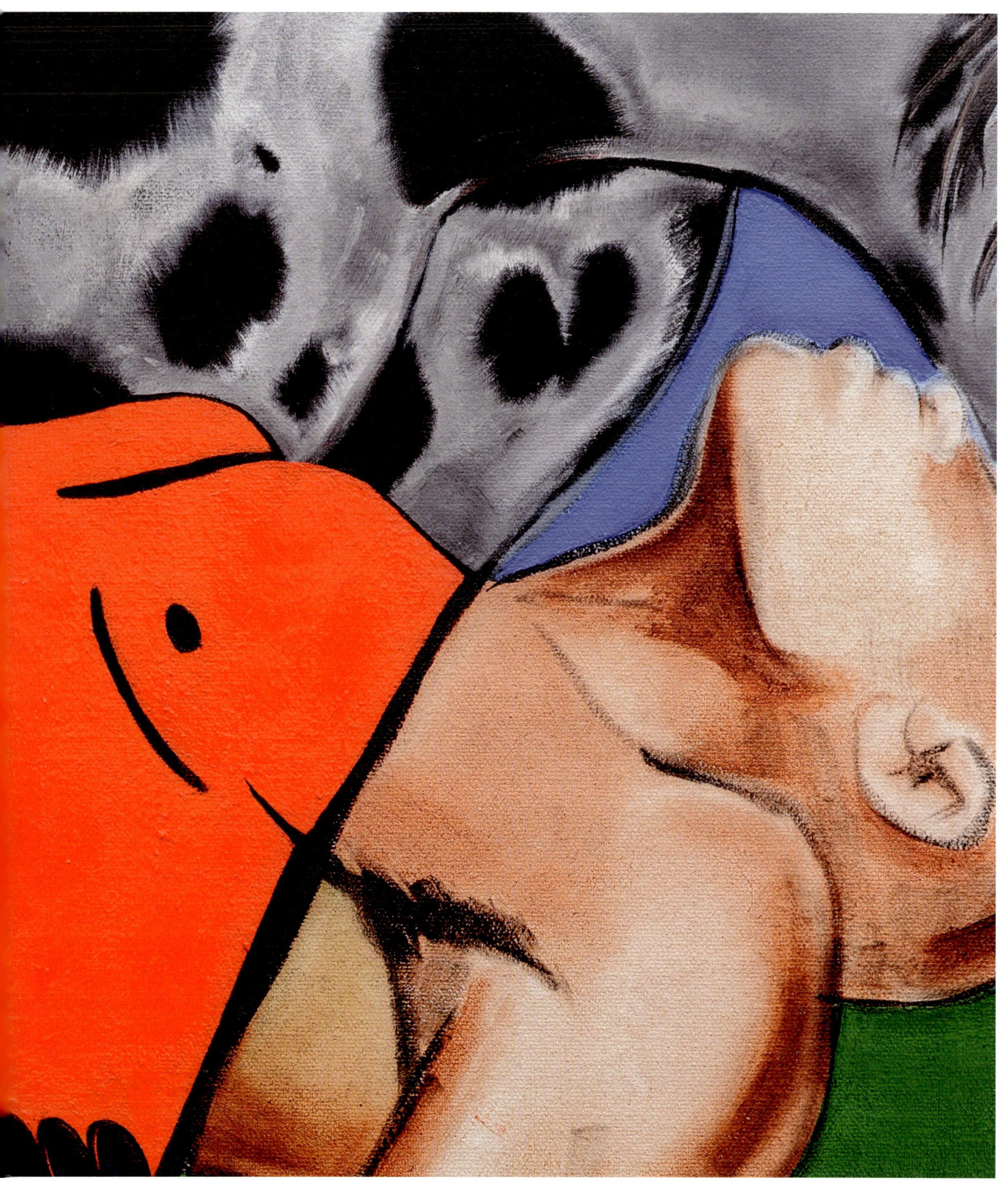

Prescribed Ambush 2018
Oil on canvas
42 × 36 in. (106.7 × 91.4 cm)

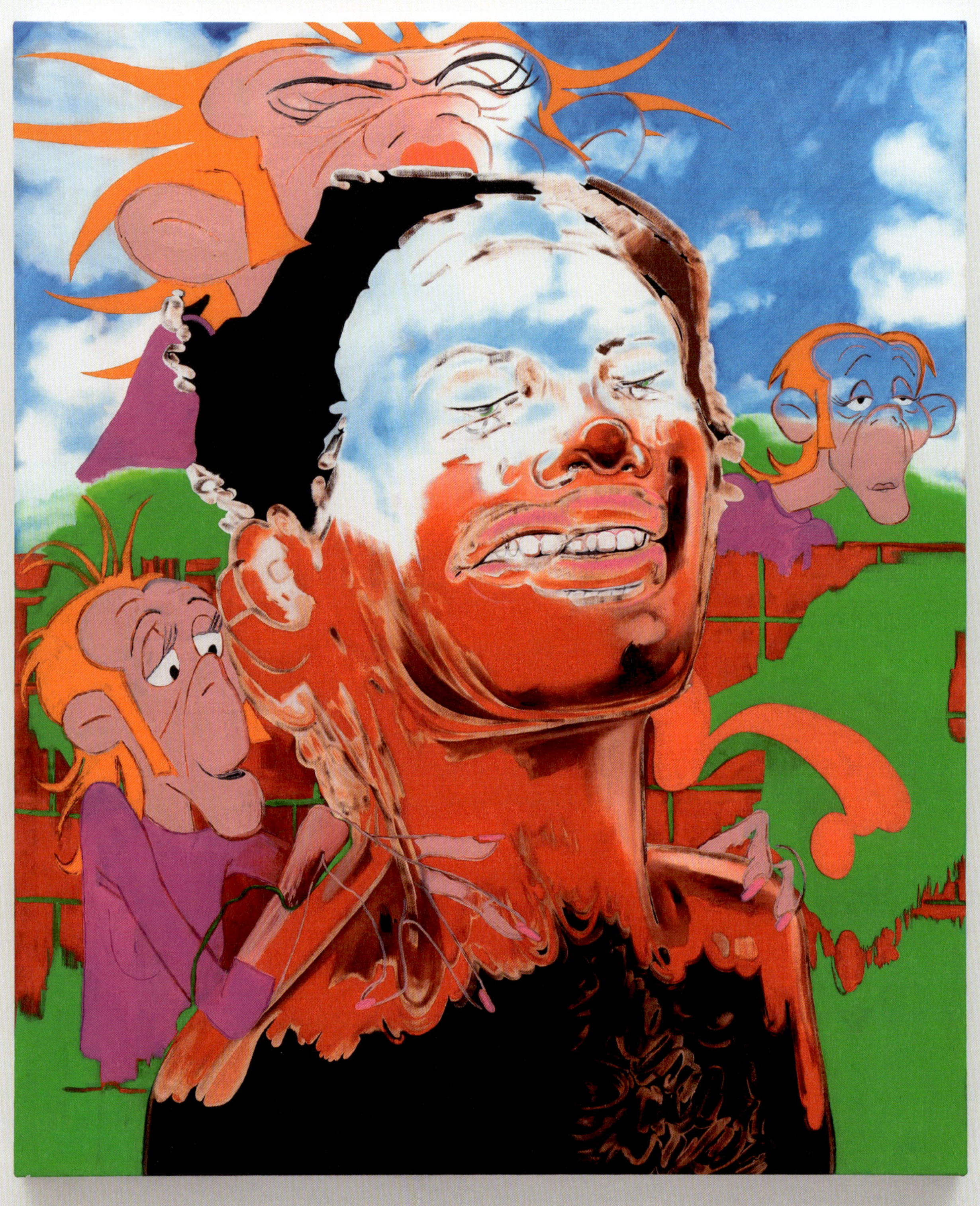

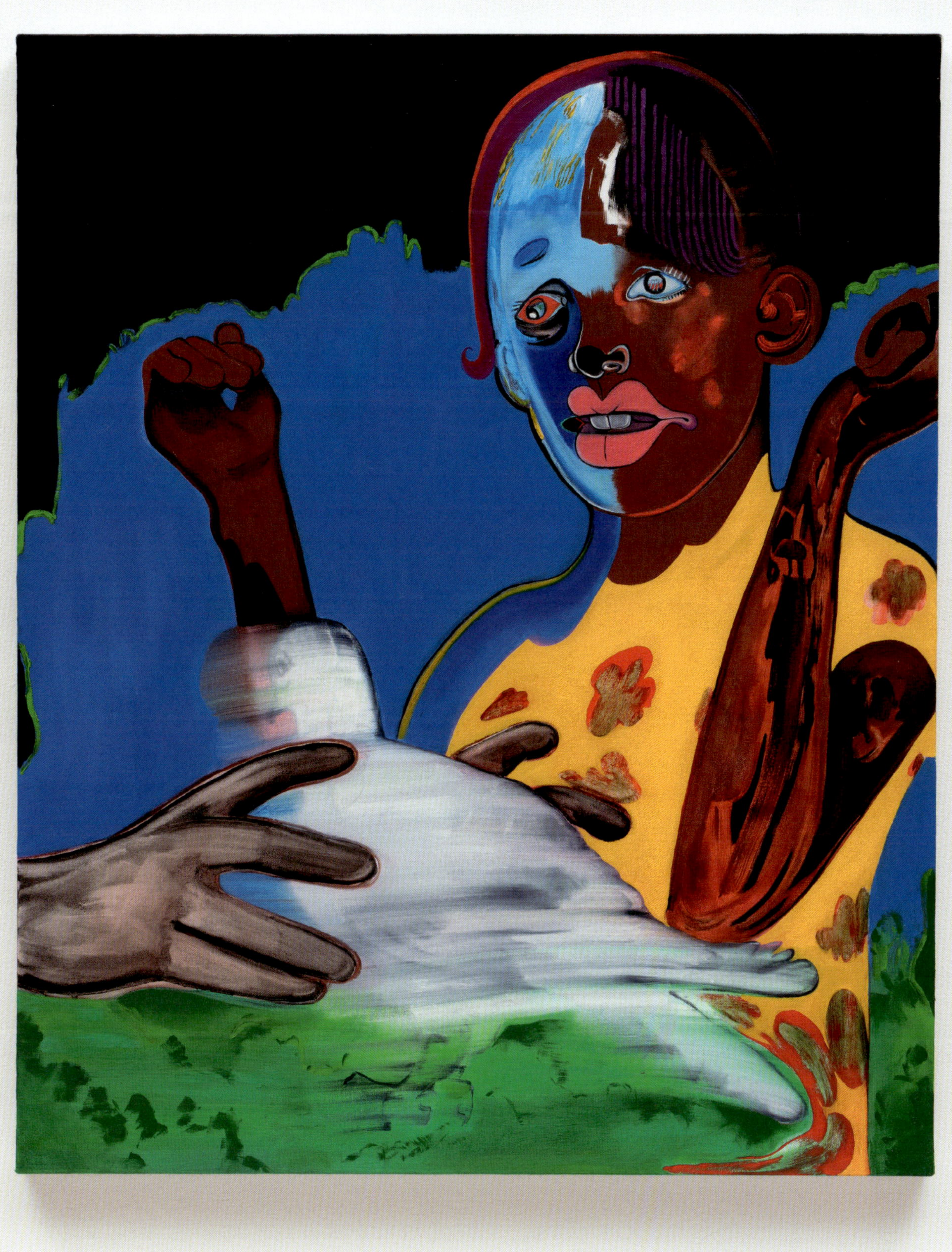

None of Our Dreams Are Pipe   2018
Oil on canvas
36 × 30 in. (91.4 × 76.2 cm)

Thought Iron Frontier   2018
Oil on canvas
46 × 40 in. (116.8 × 101.6 cm)

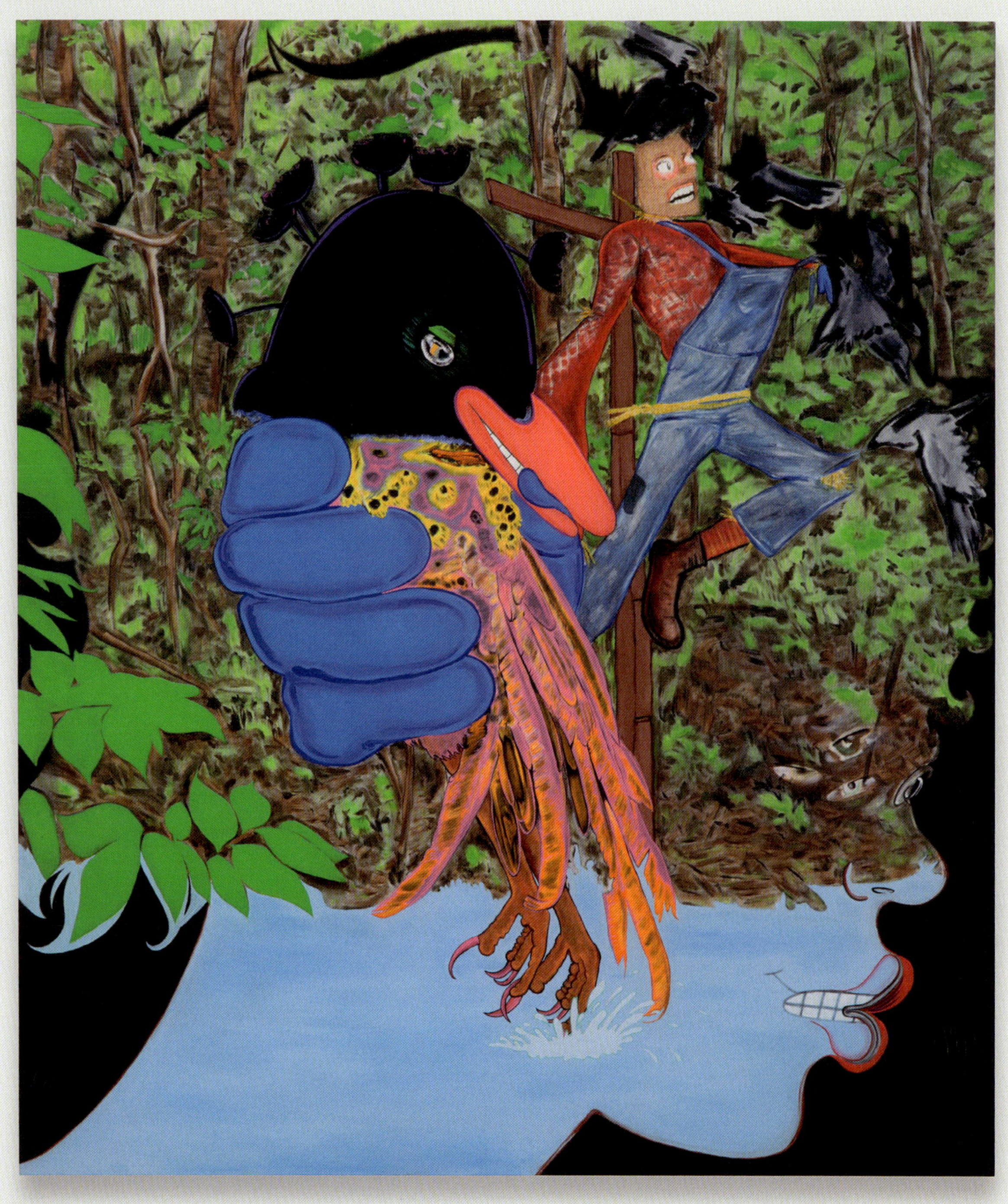

Fire Walk with Me 2018
Oil on canvas
23 × 35 in. (58.4 × 88.9 cm)

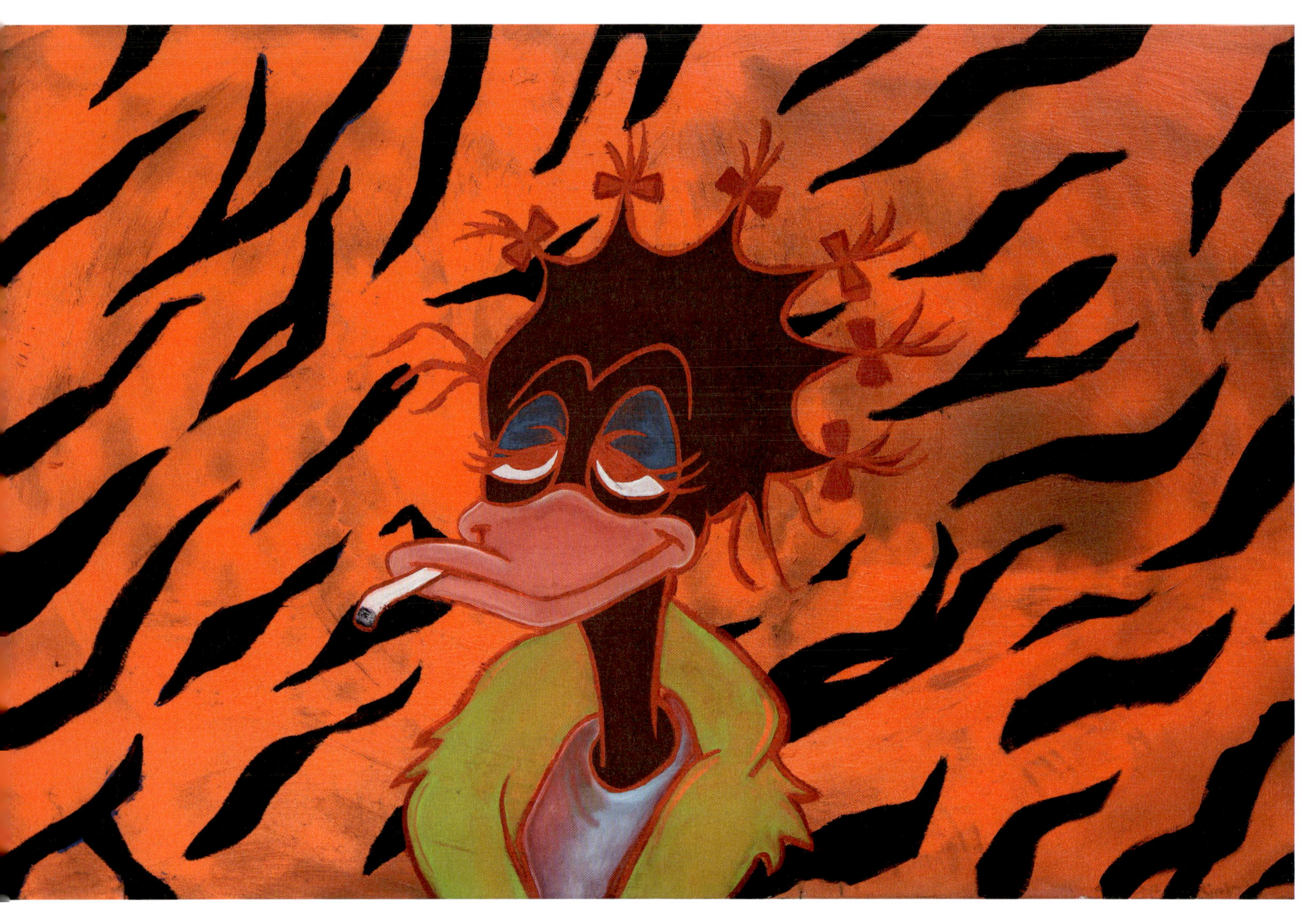

We are at some sort of borderline. A black blob tears through a gray wall. This nonhuman, nonanimal form receives in its mouth an encroaching white body. The figure is nude except for a pair of high leather boots that cushion its rear end. Scale is telling here. Not only this dark, amorphous form, but the very architecture of this odd scene towers over the white figure. Ellis reduces this key signifier down to a diminutive size. The white body, plugged somewhat comfortably into the blob, like a head in the sand, seems willfully unaware of its status as an unwanted guest. The sky may be blue, but the mood is bleak. Ellis stages a dynamic that is at once fraught and cheeky. The artist depicts a scene that by and large presents white obliviousness. The blow here is that Ellis points to the imposition as something that is structural, rather than operating on the affective dimensions of Black pain. *Nectar Troth* (2021) is part of a new body of architectural and figurative paintings Janiva Ellis has made on the occasion of the exhibition "Rats."

Adept in figurative, landscape, pastoral, and abstract modes of painting, Ellis interweaves art historical genres to find currency in the gaps between experience and structure, and in modes that are equally playful, precise, and punishing. Many past critics have honed in on racialized encapsulations of the work that skew toward the artist's identity as a Black woman and away from whiteness as a totalizing and brutal force. Arguably any insistence upon Black conditions cannot be untethered from Black being. Neat and uncomplicated synopses regarding Blackness and Black femme experiences fall short of the expanse her work as an intellectual project seeks to achieve. "Rats" conjures notions of pests, infestation, infection, impurity, and chaos, in other words, an unwanted presence not easily expelled.

Ellis's recent paintings throw into relief major questions around national identity, industry, and progress and their respective pictorial alignments. In this current era of increased political divisions and tensions, her work asks us to consider the historical consistency of consequences to whiteness. From white anxiety founded in blue-collar disenfranchisement in middle America to racism cloaked in liberalism, the continuity of such consequences has gone through eras of increased or decreased visibility and detection. Ellis is markedly concerned about the surreptitious forces of whiteness as aligned with liberal or "progressive" sentiment. In either case and along the spectrum, Black life can just as easily become the object of knowledge and a projection screen for desire and disdain. Walker Evans's photographs in *Let Us Now Praise Famous Men* (1941, with James Agee) were a direct reference for Ellis. Evans traveled across the American South documenting the harrowing devastation caused by the Great Depression, photographing three families of cotton farmers in rural Alabama. His subjects were poor, white laborers, though it is equally important to remember that just before mid-century more than half of the nation's population of Black Americans still resided in the South. The other half of the story—disenfranchised Black sharecroppers, Jim Crow segregation, white racial resentment, and extrajudicial lynchings—remains to be told. In the largely grayscale painting *Bloodlust Halo* (2021), Ellis calls attention to the manner in which notions of death loom over Evans's choice of subject, in this case a white child's grave with makeshift markers in Hale County, Alabama.

Considering narratives around American regionalism and labor, for early-twentieth-century painter Charles Demuth, Cubist-inspired abstraction gave way to a highly stylized mode of picturing the industrial landscape of his hometown of Lancaster, Pennsylvania. In the 1927 painting *My Egypt*, Demuth depicts a concrete grain silo painted in a precisionist style. Demuth, along with peers Charles Sheeler and Paul Strand, searched for a way to imagine American industry through a machine-like aesthetic. Precisionism, influenced by Cubism, was a celebration of industrialization and technological advancement, but through the cultivation of a distinct American style and subject matter. Demuth took an almost photorealistic approach to painting, erasing the mark of his hand with minimal brush strokes. Like the erasure of the artist's hand, *My Egypt* merely suggests evidence of human life through the rooftops of tenement houses that flank each side of the silo. In 1927, Lancaster coal miners were embroiled in one of the largest state-wide labor strikes at the time, but rather than picturing any workers as drivers of the engine of industrial change, Demuth commemorates the silo and places it on par with the pyramids of the ancient Egyptians. Even the pollution and smoke billowing out of the chimney seems to be foreclosed to the gloriousness and promise of this massive building. The sky is still a pristine blue; two prisms of light cut across the picture and beam down like halos onto its form. Ellis's contemporary take on girders, anvils, bridges, and scaffolds are doubly encoded, calling into question the presumed neutrality of architectural and industrial symbols of progress and evolution, and recapitulating their terrorizing way of making invisible the asymmetrical structures of power. They are no longer mundane or benign, but become vehicles for the infestation that Ellis releases onto art history.

Recalling Charles C. Ebbets's classic photograph *Lunch atop a Skyscraper* (1932), in *From Whom the Bell Tolls* (2021) Ellis presents a gray monochrome and an obliteration exposing a metal support or girder. It's an image of construction and destruction, where edges and boundaries converge. At the same time, Ellis's opening, torn through the canvas with a trompe l'oeil effect, signals a distrust of the perceived stability of imagery. Not unlike her past figurative paintings that indulge in uncertainty, with superimposed treatments of skin and bodies in pleasure and angst, such as *Bramble's Briar Patch* (2018), this work peddles in foul play, suspicion, and empty provocation. If the aim is to pull back the many complicated layers that form some semblance of subjectivity, then Ellis's fabulations are meant to be unstable, and parasitic even. The artist evokes a poetics of dissonance, which she conjures through selective pin pricks at images of pivotal, iconographic moments in art history. Precious Okoyomon's astute analysis of Ellis's 2019 show at 47 Canal rings true here: "These are haunting images and their capacity to stump us is I think a dislocation of the painter's own feeling of being stumped by the deracinating interdiction of anti-blackness and its gratuitous violence being reverted onto her viewers. This kind of transgression is critical. It doesn't reinscribe violence or rehearse it in painting, dangerously forcing us to see it again, but instead reproduces the feeling of that violence going unseen as it almost always does, remaining invisible or incommunicable entirely." [1]

Ellis deals in the affective register of violence as it is enacted upon Black people, in this case by referencing forms that emerge from the built environment. One can see Ellis's paintings and hurriedly assess that the works deal in Black experience

of hysteria brought about by racism. This is a grave misinterpretation. Okoyomon rightly put their finger on one of the myriad ways in which Ellis's work operates, which is to say that her paintings make visible the invisible pervasiveness of whiteness and its violent infliction on Black people. Ellis's oeuvre finds as its kindred a Fanonian conception of a "decolonization" of whiteness that "reeks of red-hot cannonballs and bloody knives." [2]

Furthermore, Ellis's project is tied to what poet and literary scholar Denise Ferreira da Silva frames as a Poethics of Blackness, an analytical framework in excess of historical, capitalist, scientific facticity: "From without the World as we know it, where the Category of Blackness exists in/as thought—always already a referent of commodity, an object, and the other, as fact beyond evidence—a Poethics of Blackness would announce a whole range of possibilities for knowing, doing, and existing. For releasing Blackness from the registers of the object, the commodity, or the other would halt the trial of Trayvon Martin's killer before it is added to the already huge library of racial facts and precedents that authorize racial violence." [3]

Thus the artist has deployed a reversal of Black signifiers. Paramount of note is that the prominence of Black skin, unreliable as it was in her earlier machinations, has all but disappeared. By exorcising topical depictions of Blackness, she has pulled the rug out from underneath us, and we have fallen through a kind of trap door of her making. But how can symbols like anvils, scaffolds, girders, and grain silos signify white violence? Ellis draws parallels to the poetics of these types of representations that can no longer remain alienated from the social and political histories they evince. How can we celebrate art of industry, progress, and Americanness, and look away from the violence that such representations predicate?

In an interview from June 25, 2020, Sonya Renee Taylor spoke about antiracist work in the wake of George Floyd's death at the hands of Minneapolis police officers. The poet and activist emphasized racism as a part of the primordial makeup of our nation: "Our society speaks racism. It has spoken racism since the day we were born. Of course you are racist. The idea that somehow, this blanket of idea has fallen on everyone's head except for yours, is magical thinking. And it's useless." [4] Drawing directly from Taylor, Ellis has referred to "white delusion" in the critical responses to her paintings, and in the totalizing commentary on Blackness devoid of any nuanced understanding of white domination and violence. Delusion has long been a theme in Ellis's work, as an affliction of mental derangement or deception. With "Rats," Ellis makes explicit her interest in white delusion as a mode of currency. [5]

The project of contemporary representation is bankrupt without an incisive analysis of whiteness. After all, race is but a concept, not a biological fact, as scholar Nell Irvin Painter asserts in her magnanimous historical account of whiteness from antiquity to the present. "The meanings of white race reach into concepts of labor, gender, and class and images of personal beauty that seldom appear in analysis of race," she asserts. [6] Whiteness has an unshakeable grasp on how we understand concepts of value and worth in art history, from distinguishing which artists we designate as "masters" to which artworks we venerate as historically and socially significant. It is only when we are able to recognize the interpolation of Blackness, or otherness, that we can get a peek into the "soft" architecture of the grip of whiteness on culture.

One of the first exhibitions to attempt to reckon with the implications of whiteness in art was Maurice Berger's landmark show "White: Whiteness and Race in Contemporary Art" at the International Center of Photography, New York, in 2003–04. In its catalogue, legal scholar Patricia J. Williams argues that "whiteness is a kind of cultural canvas upon which American existence is depicted in a myriad of artful visions of the possible. Whiteness is the site of privileged imagining, the invisible standard. It is whatever it wants to be. And Blackness has been for too many generations whatever was left over." She continues, explaining that race has always maintained a "lack of unifying theme or crisp clear edges" because "its history has been just that: mercurial and contingent. Race is a careless, deeply unconscious and highly aesthetic phenomenon, even if that aesthetic deprives us of greater vision."[7] Williams points to the very nature of the problem that Ellis attempts to chart in "Rats." Objects and symbols are not benign, but are instead powerful reminders of whiteness as a dangerous floating signifier, akin to a beautifully ripened red tomato that, unbeknownst to its gardener, is rotting from the inside out.

Ellis's paintings inadvertently point to art historical tropes and phenomena that have peddled in seizing the conditions of racial difference in the beholder's share. Take Thomas Eakins's 1876 painting *Will Schuster and Blackman Going Shooting for Rail*. Eakins renders a hunting scene along the Delaware River in which two men occupy a boat, one well-to-do, white, and named, the other a raced and nameless hired aide. Michael Fried argues that the "most remarkable feature" of the painting is the "incandescent red of Schuster's long-sleeved shirt, which by virtue of its coloristic explosiveness repels the viewer from the painting as with the force of a blast."[8] Fried focuses on the viewer's absorption of the work, and their subsequent projection into the world of the painting. He resists acknowledging how racially fraught Eakins's composition is and, by effect, the social and historical import of the painting's occurrence.[9] In the painting we see that Eakins is in fact obsessed with duality and juxtaposition, that which he constructs through the single vector of racial difference, from concepts of labor and leisure, sartorial extravagance and utility. At the same time, we also observe an insidious dynamic of whiteness that actively works to be imperceptible amid the artist's reliance on racial difference. Eakins's unnamed subject is placed in the composition through a function of his race as a "Blackman." While Eakins's protagonist remains the focus of Fried's absorption, the Black "help," or antihero, is the true linchpin of the picture.

Janiva Ellis's intimate knowledge of the subterranean channels of whiteness comes into focus in "Rats." As a form of clearing, Ellis momentarily attunes her brush and mind to this very paradox: the crushing and relentless invisibility of whiteness. She calls into question the other half of the picture in terms of the heightened visibility of Black bodies. And thus, the artist's new ordering of bodies and spaces within fraught and unresolved scenarios centralizes some shadow signifiers of racialized otherness: social seclusion, hypersexualization, and subjection to an invisibilized white gaze.

Notes

1.	Precious Okoyomon, "Janiva Ellis: 47 Canal," *Flash Art*, December 11, 2019, https://flash---art.com/2019/12/janiva-ellis-47-canal-new-york/.

2.	Frantz Fanon, *Wretched of the Earth* (New York: Grove Press, 2004), 3.

3.	Denise Ferreira da Silva, "Toward a Black Feminist Poethics: The Quest(ion) of Blackness Toward the End of the World," *The Black Scholar: Journal of Black Studies and Research* 44, no. 2 (2014), 81.

4.	"Sonya Renee Taylor on combating racism with action," CBS News YouTube channel, https://www.youtube.com/watch?v=GnlDj1Qii8E.

5.	Nicholas Kristof, in "A History of White Delusion," writes: "In 1962, 85 percent of white Americans told Gallup that black children had as good a chance as white kids of getting a good education. The next year, in another Gallup survey, almost half of whites said that blacks had just as good a chance as whites of getting a job. In retrospect, we can see that these white beliefs were delusional, and in other survey questions whites blithely acknowledged racist attitudes. In 1963, 45 percent said that they would object if a family member invited a black person home to dinner. This complacency among us white Americans has been a historical constant. Even in the last decade, almost two-thirds of white Americans have said that blacks are treated fairly by the police, and four out of five whites have said that black children have the same chance as white kids of getting a good education. In short, the history of white Americans' attitudes toward race has always been one of self-deception." *New York Times*, July 14, 2016, https://www.nytimes.com/2016/07/14/opinion/a-history-of-white-delusion.html.

6.	Nell Irvin Painter, *The History of White People* (New York: W.W. Norton and Company, 2010), xi.

7.	Patricia J. Williams, "Preface," in *White: Whiteness and Race in Contemporary Art*, ed. Maurice Berger, exh. cat. (Baltimore: Center for Art and Visual Culture, University of Maryland Baltimore County, 2004), 19.

8.	Michael Fried, *Realism, Writing, and Disfiguration: On Thomas Eakins and Stephen Crane* (Chicago: University of Chicago Press, 1987), 71.

9.	Berger reminds us, in *White*, that "the racial attitudes of white art historians and critics are no different from those of society at large"; this is prescient in the case of Fried's intentional avoidance of topics of racialization in Eakins's composition. Maurice Berger, "Invisible Man: An Introduction to Whiteness," in *White*, 24.

*Catchphrase Coping
Mechanism*
Oil on linen
86 × 70 in. (218.4 × 177.8 cm)

2019

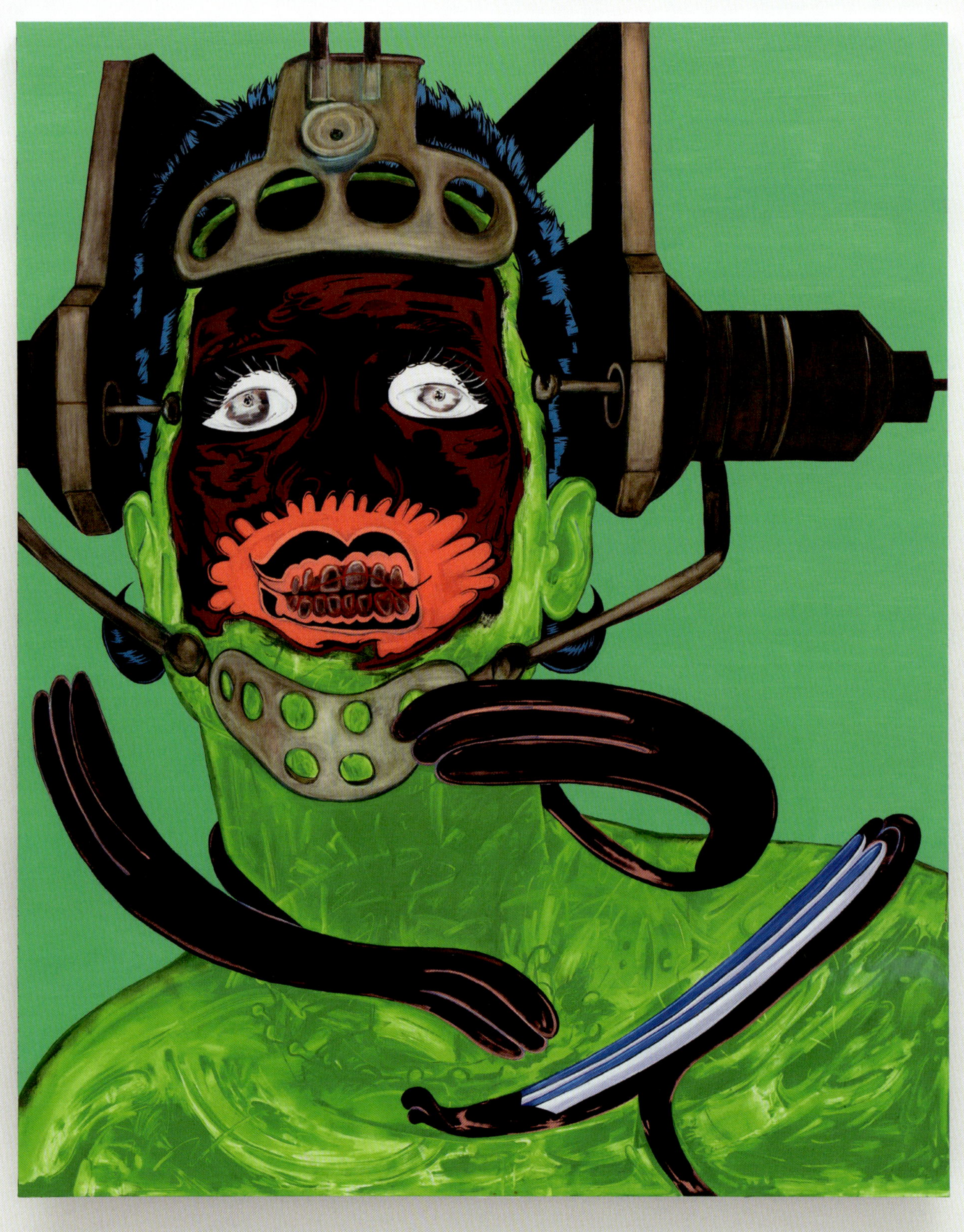

Dashland Updrown 2019
Oil on linen
98 × 80 ½ in. (248.9 × 204.5 cm)

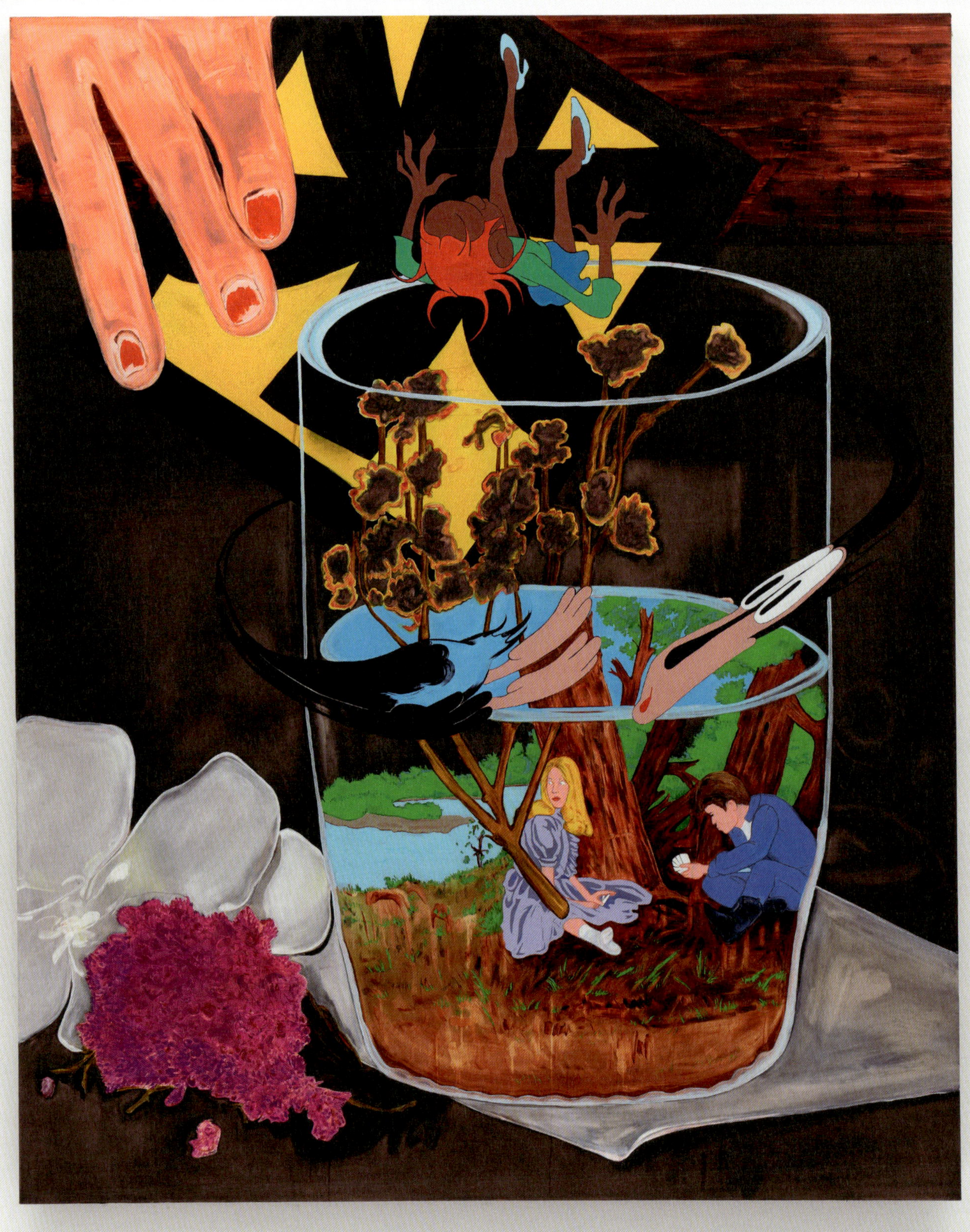

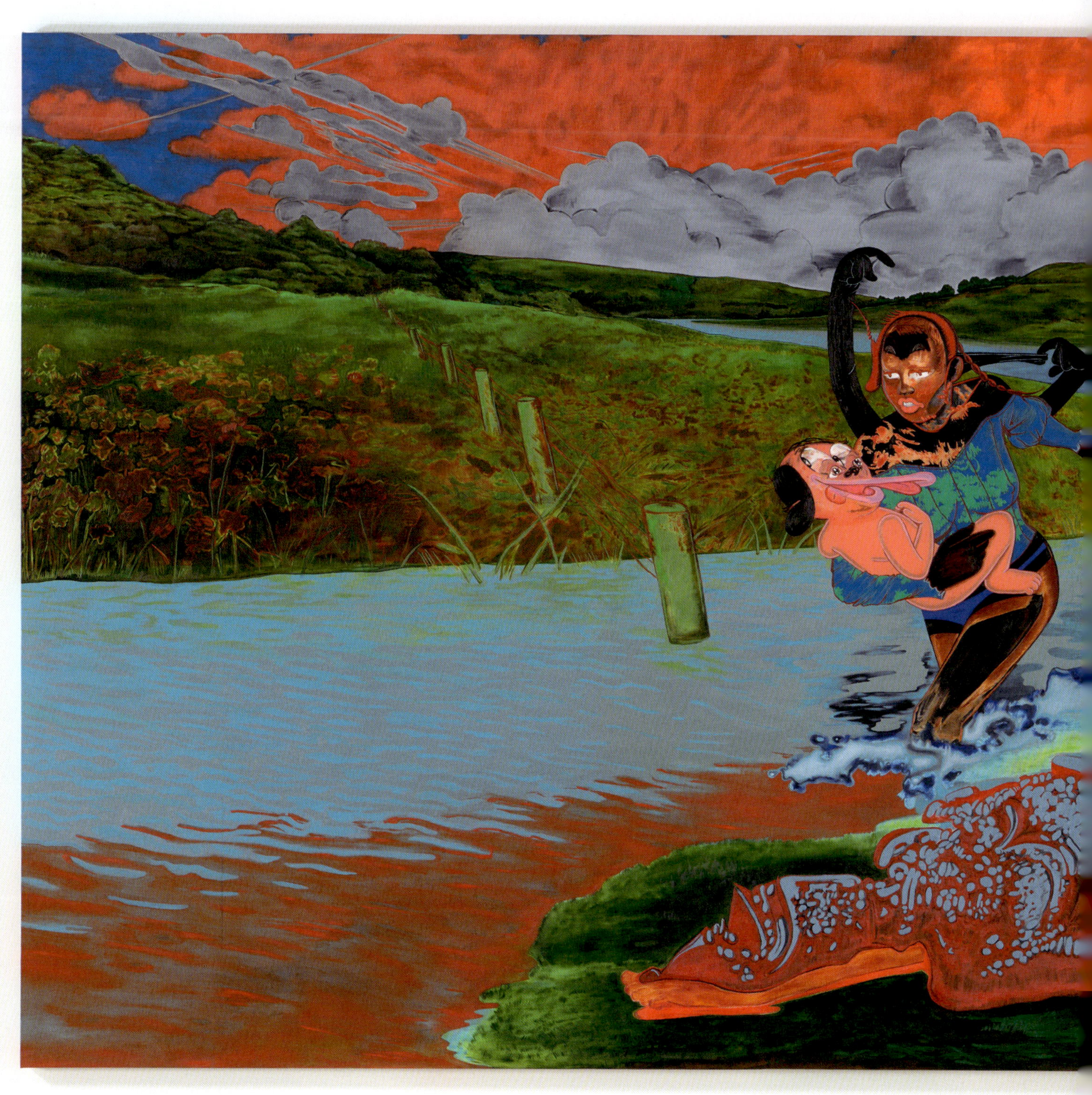

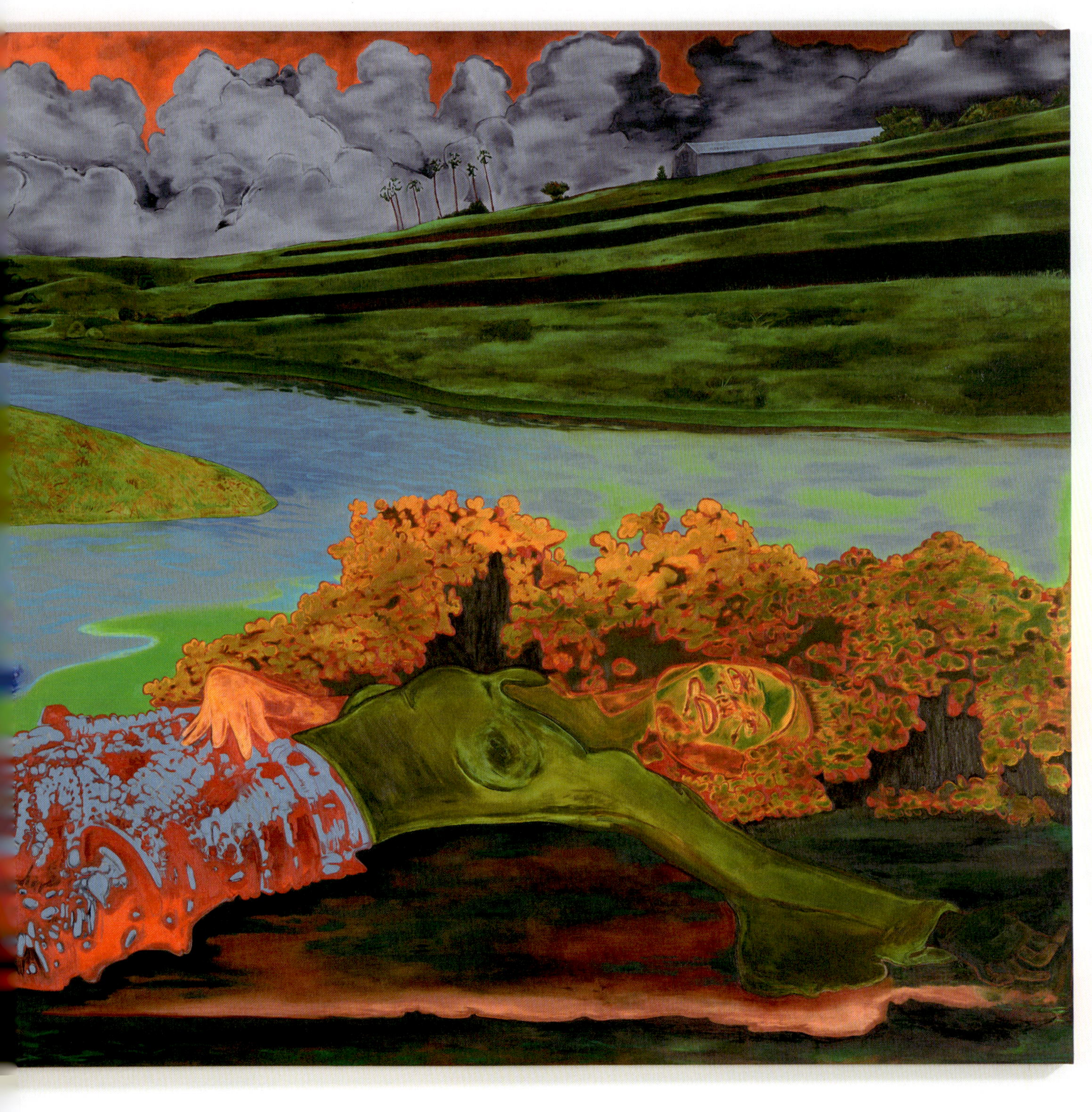

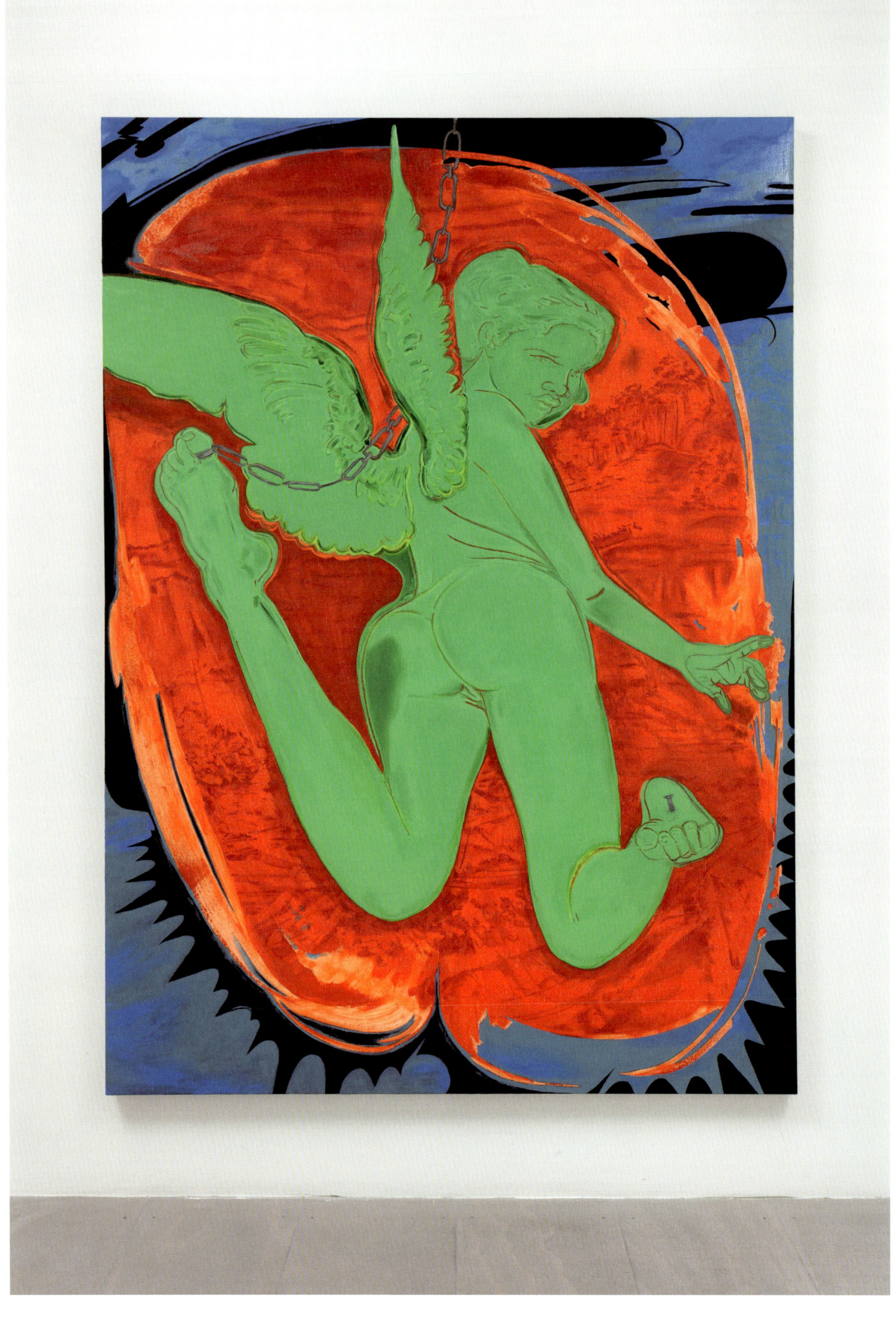

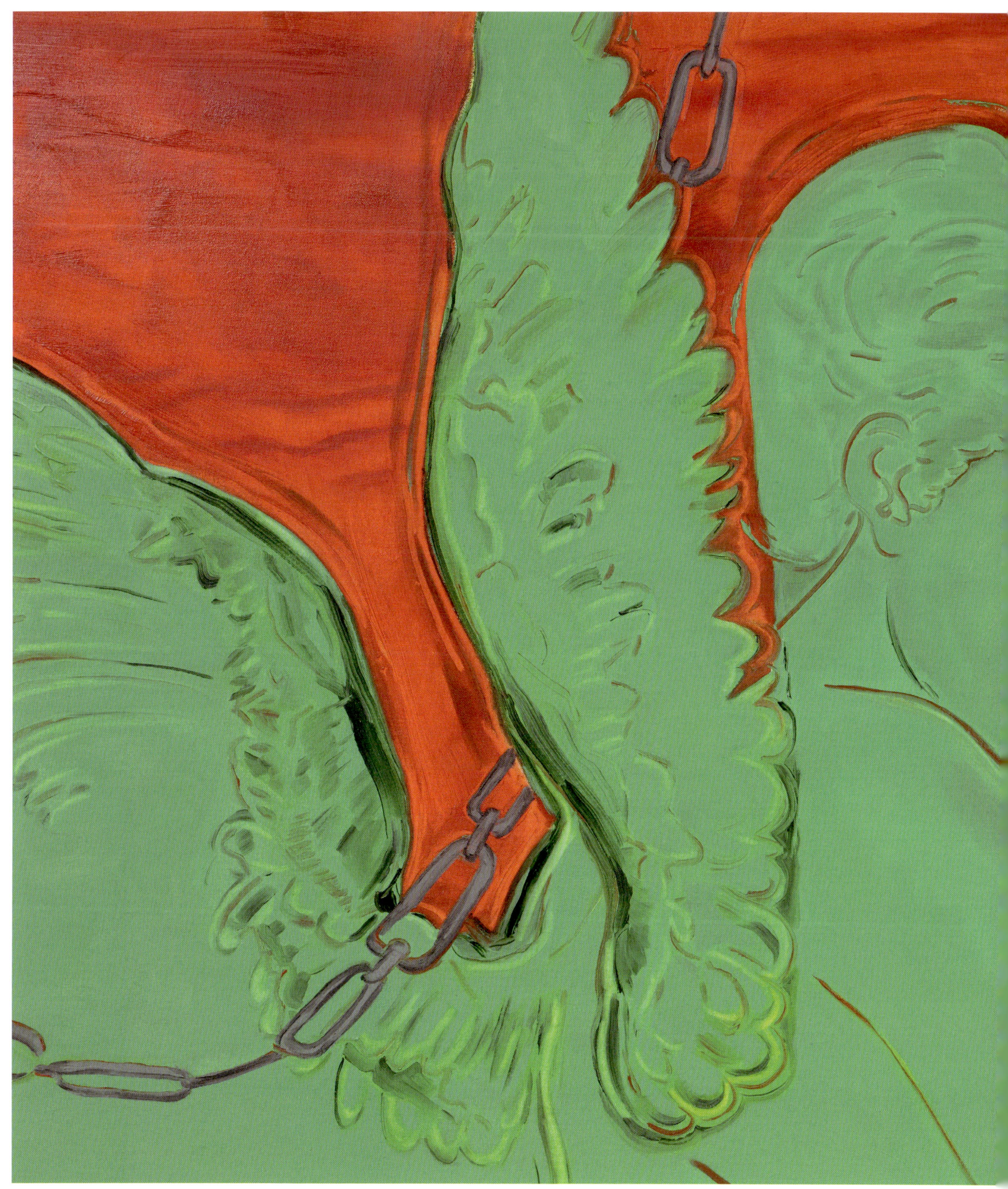

Almighty Tip Drill   2019   detail
Oil on linen
96 × 70 in. (243.8 × 177.8 cm)

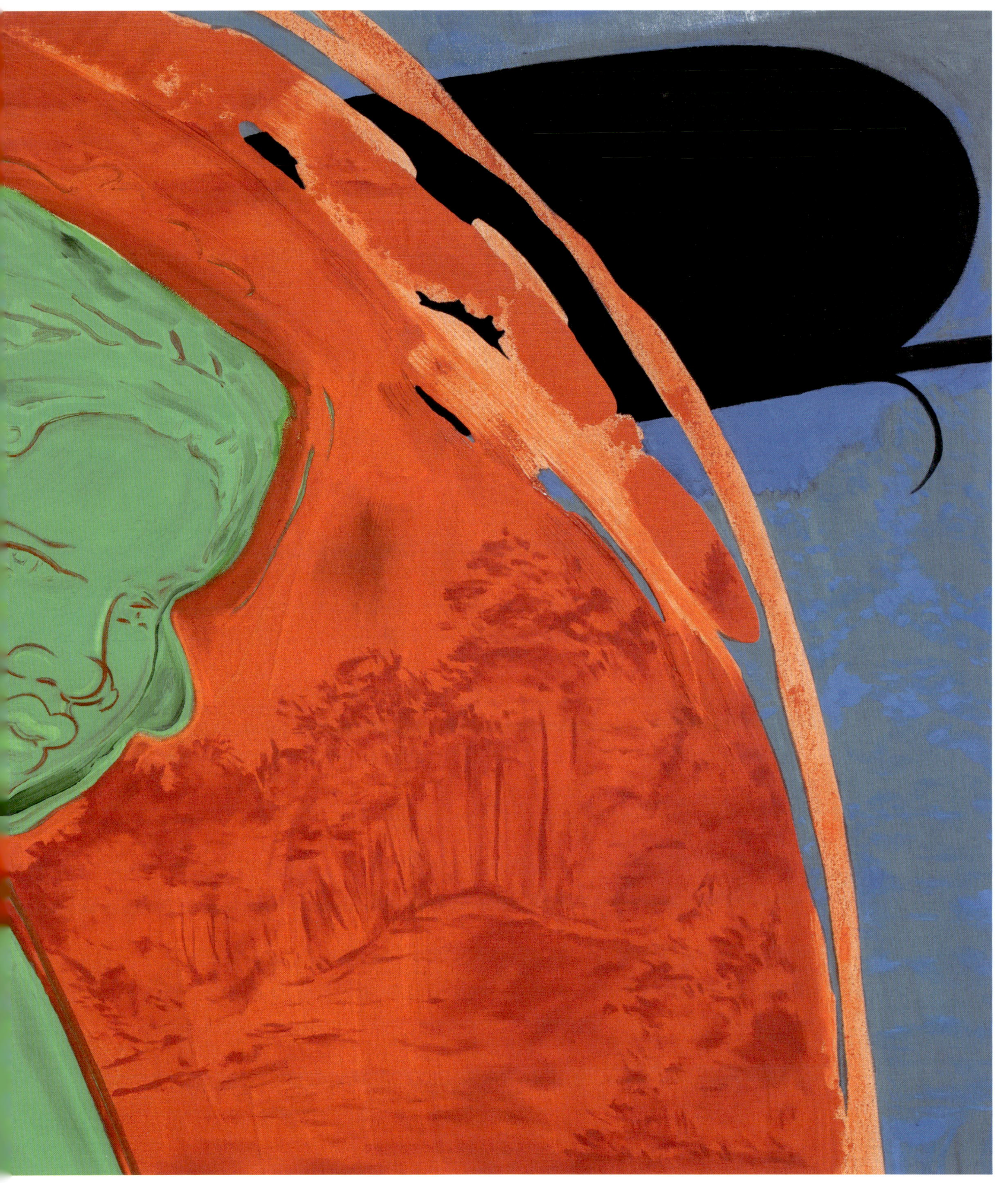

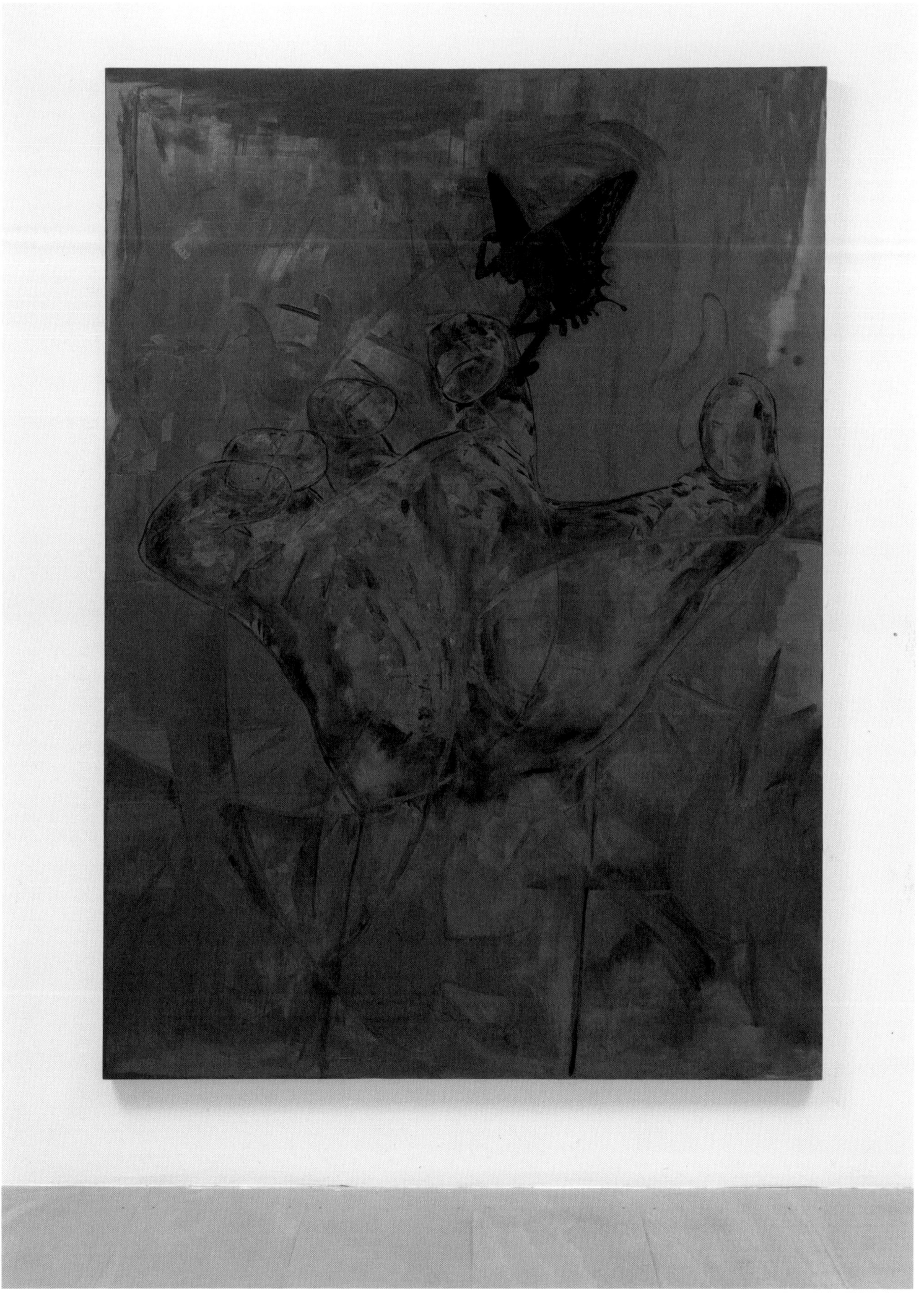

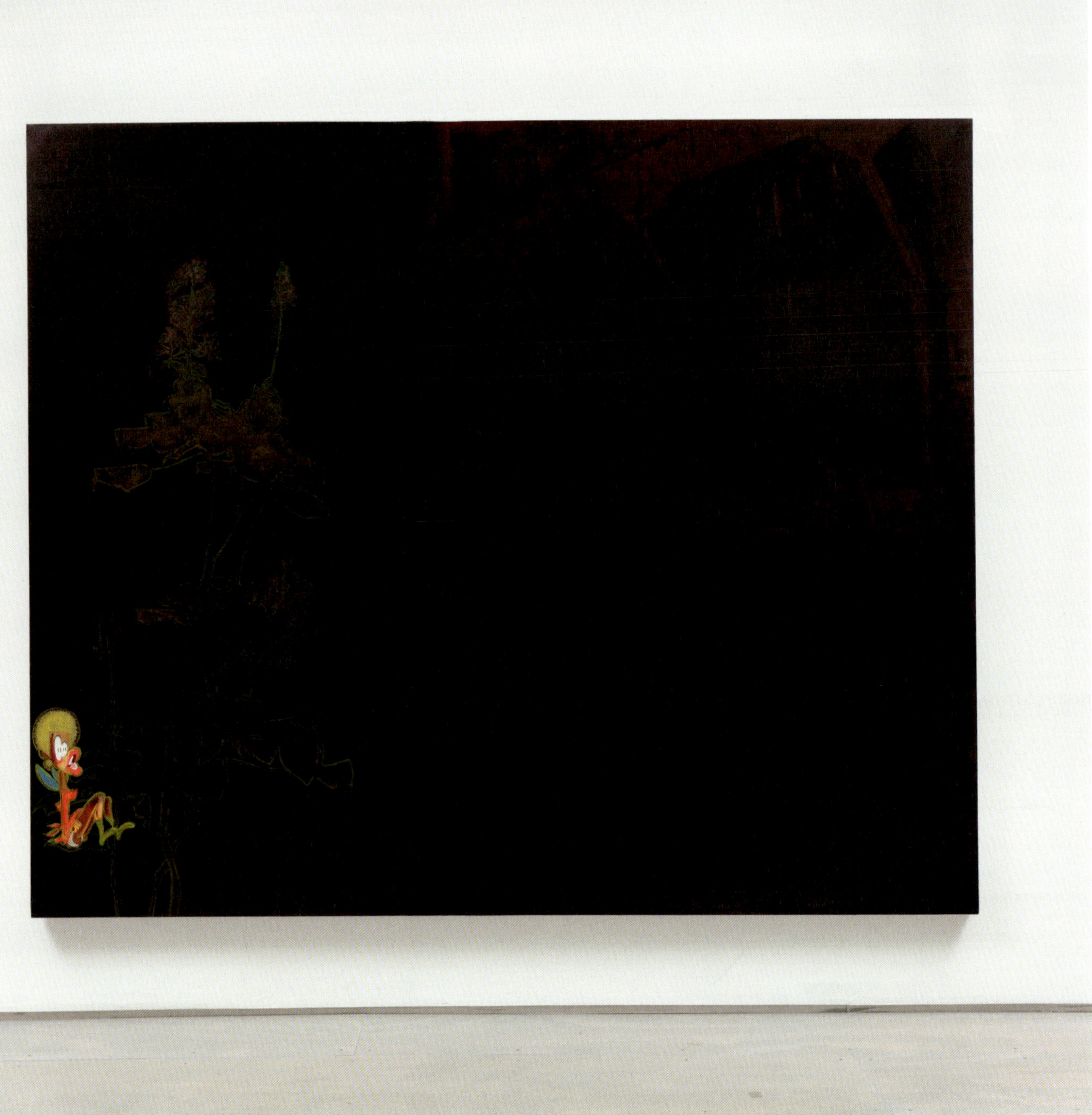

Stopgap Skank   2019
Oil on linen
96 × 70 in. (243.8 × 177.8 cm)

Shudder Home Refuge   2019
Oil on linen
80 × 98 in. (203.2 × 248.9 cm)

Shudder Home Refuge   2019   detail
Oil on linen
80 × 98 in. (203.2 × 248.9 cm)

Boys Cottages 2019
Oil on linen
70 × 76 in. (177.8 × 193 cm)

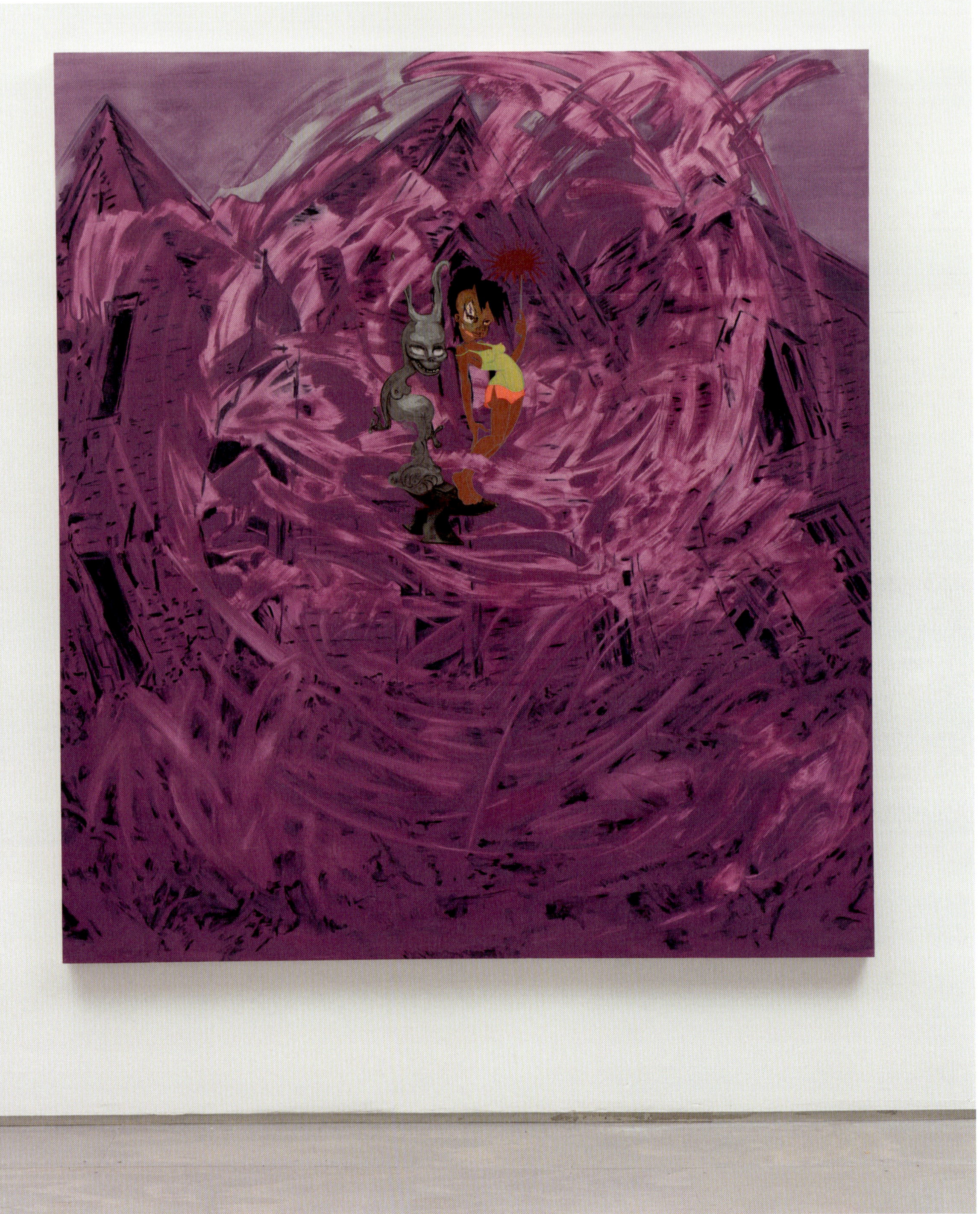

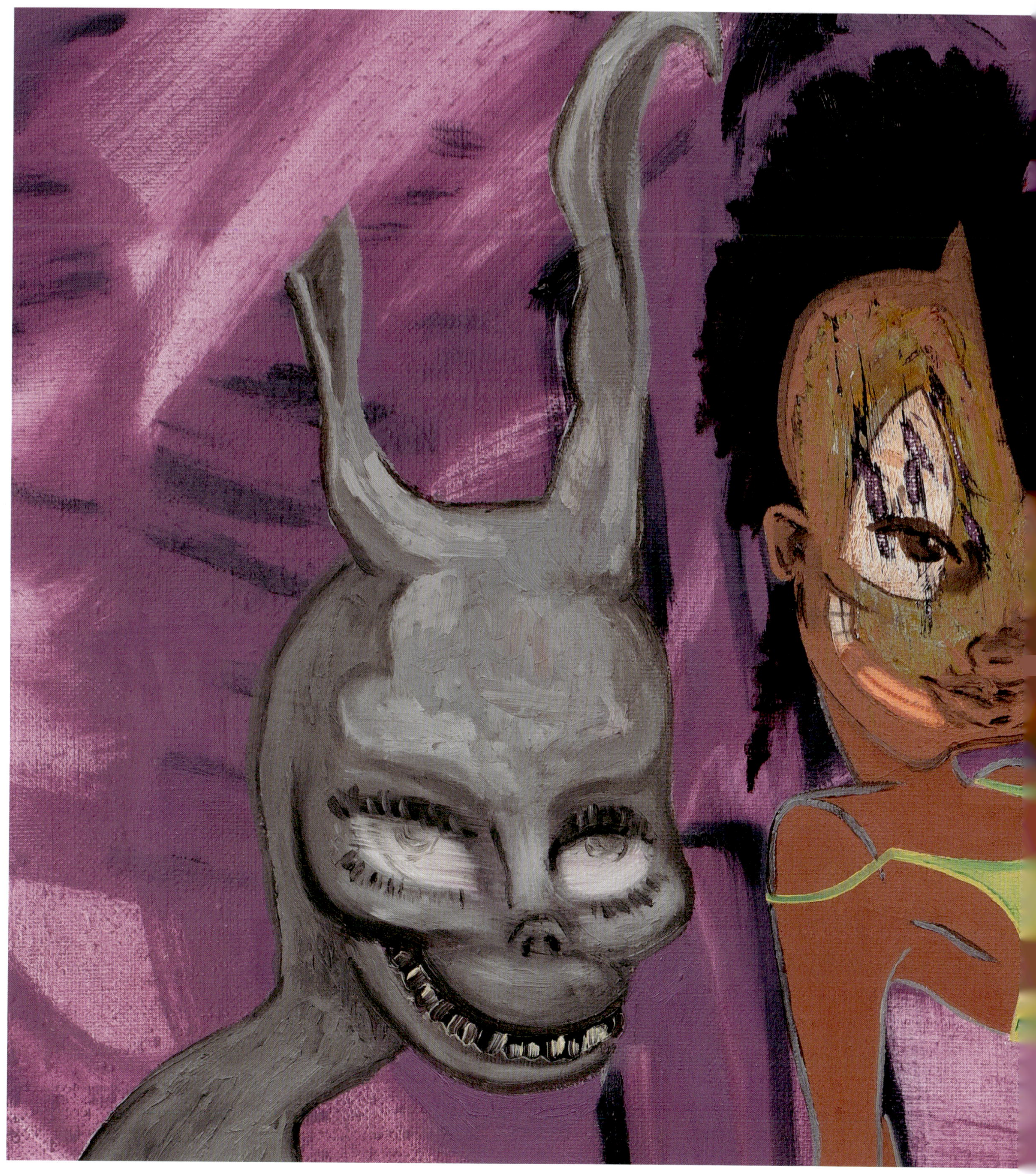

Boys Cottages 2019 detail
Oil on linen
70 × 76 in. (177.8 × 193 cm)

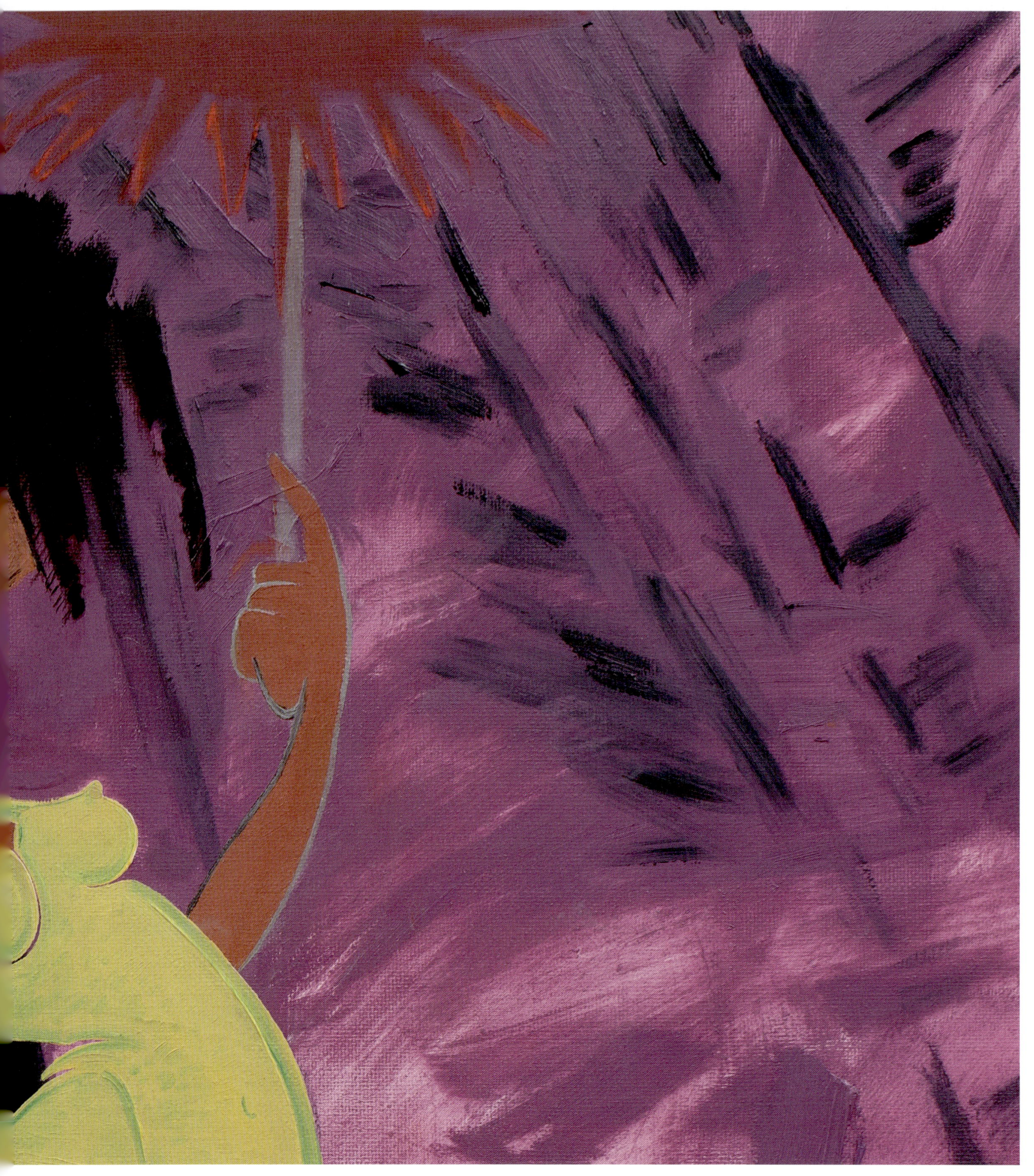

Yup Genie   2019
Oil on linen
70 × 76 in. (177.8 × 193 cm)

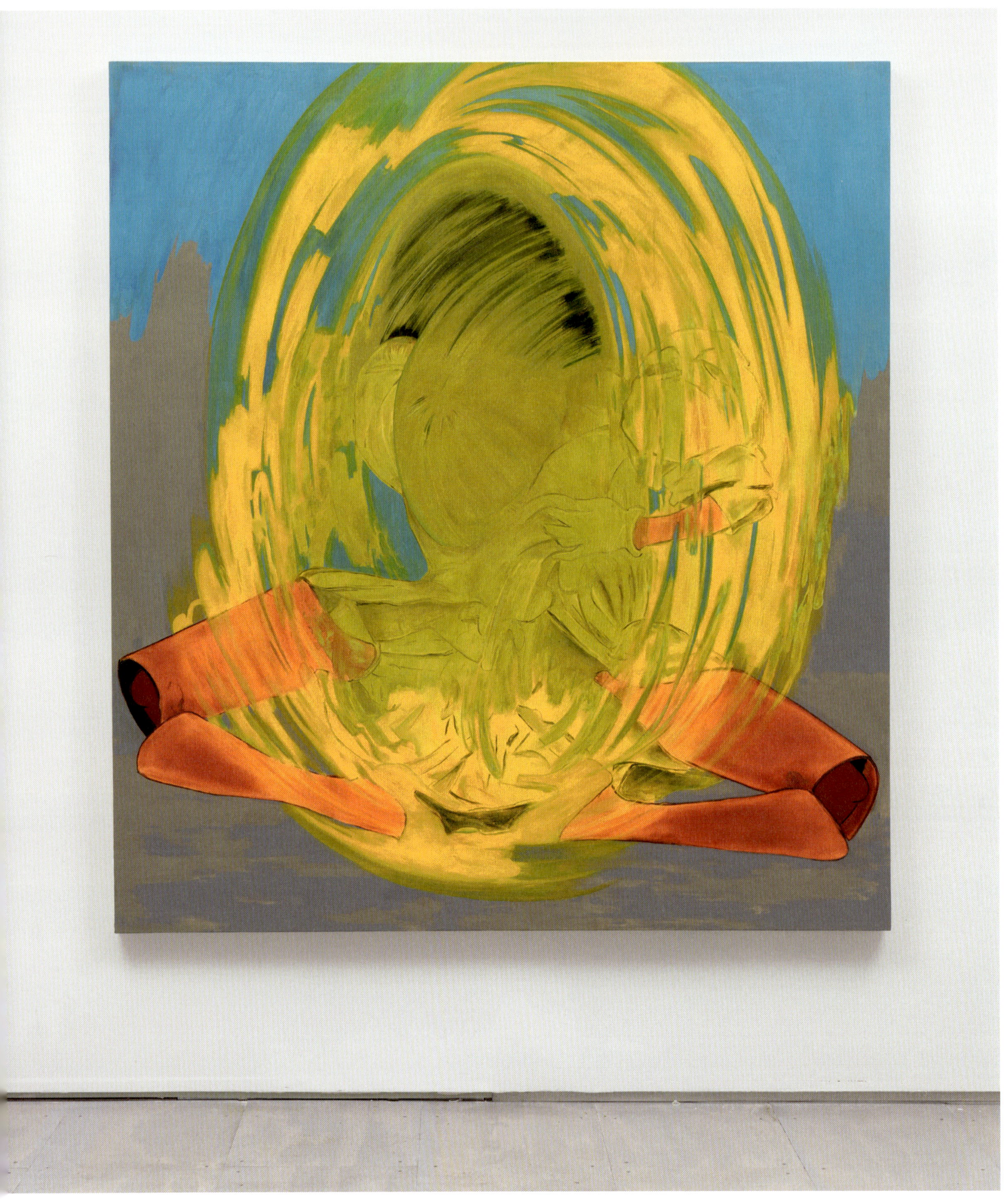

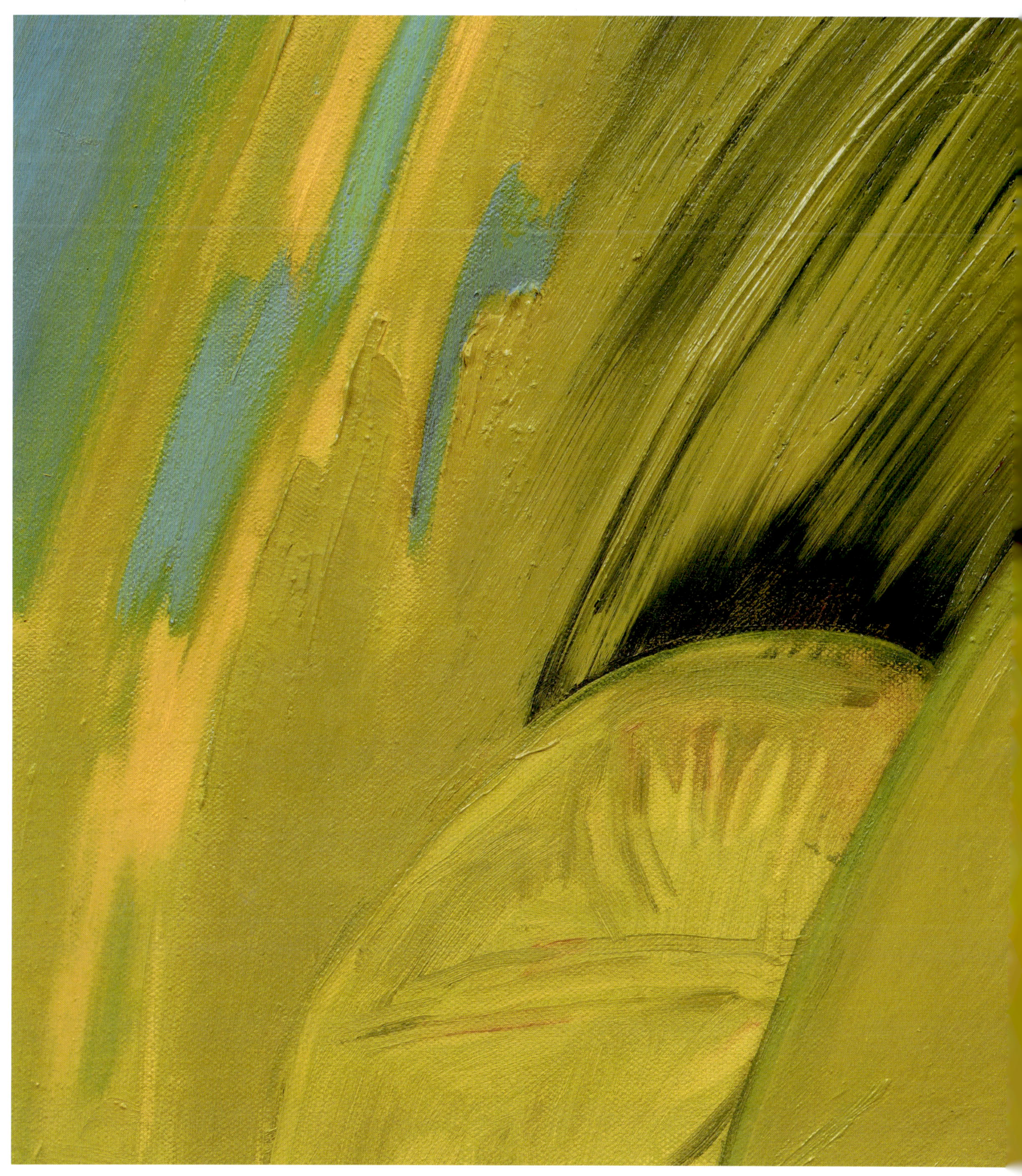

Yup Genie 2019 detail
Oil on linen
70 × 76 in. (177.8 × 193 cm)

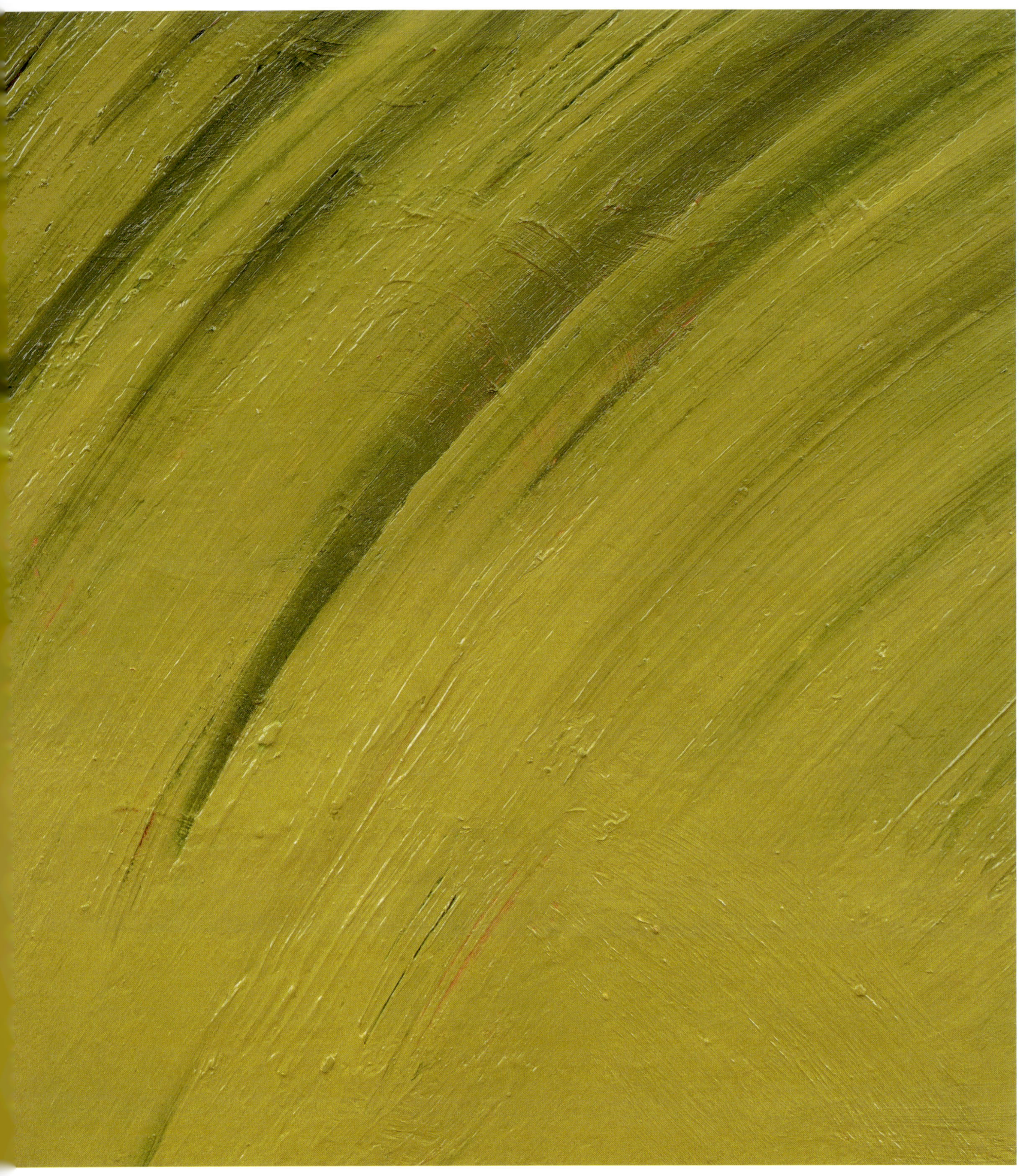

Wokey Doke   2019
Oil on linen
60 × 48 in. (152.4 × 121.9 cm)

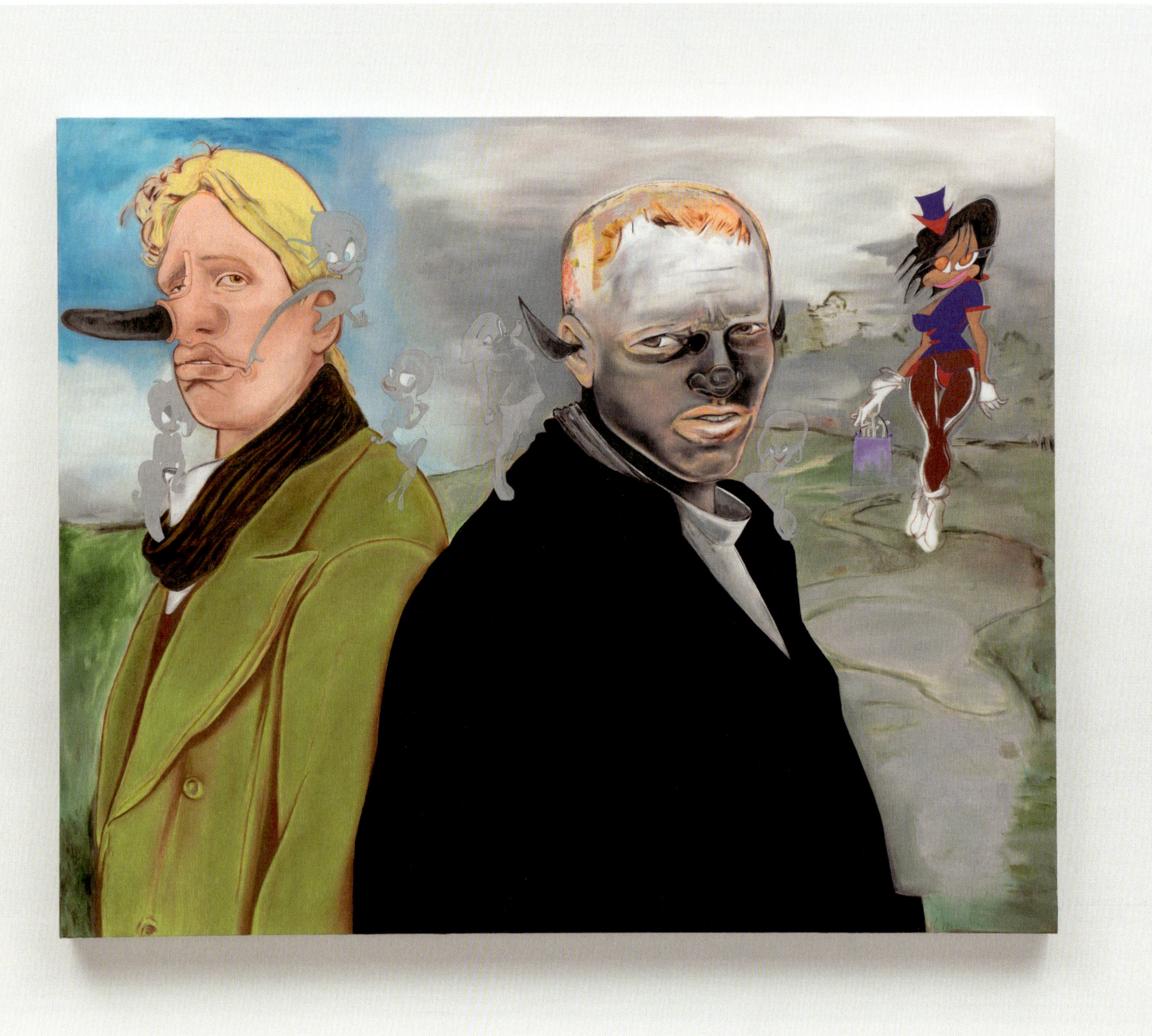

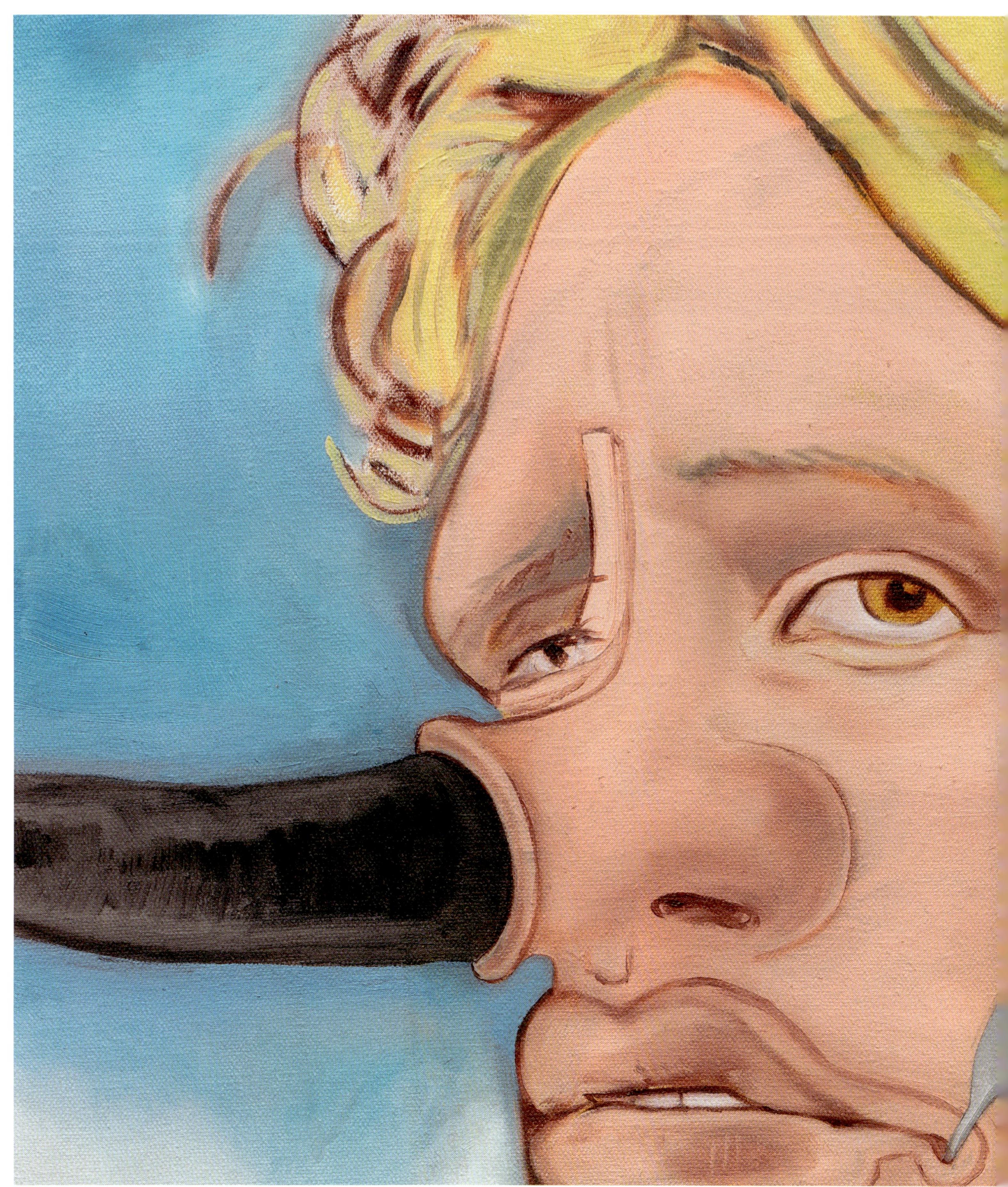

Wokey Doke   2019   detail
Oil on linen
60 × 48 in. (152.4 × 121.9 cm)

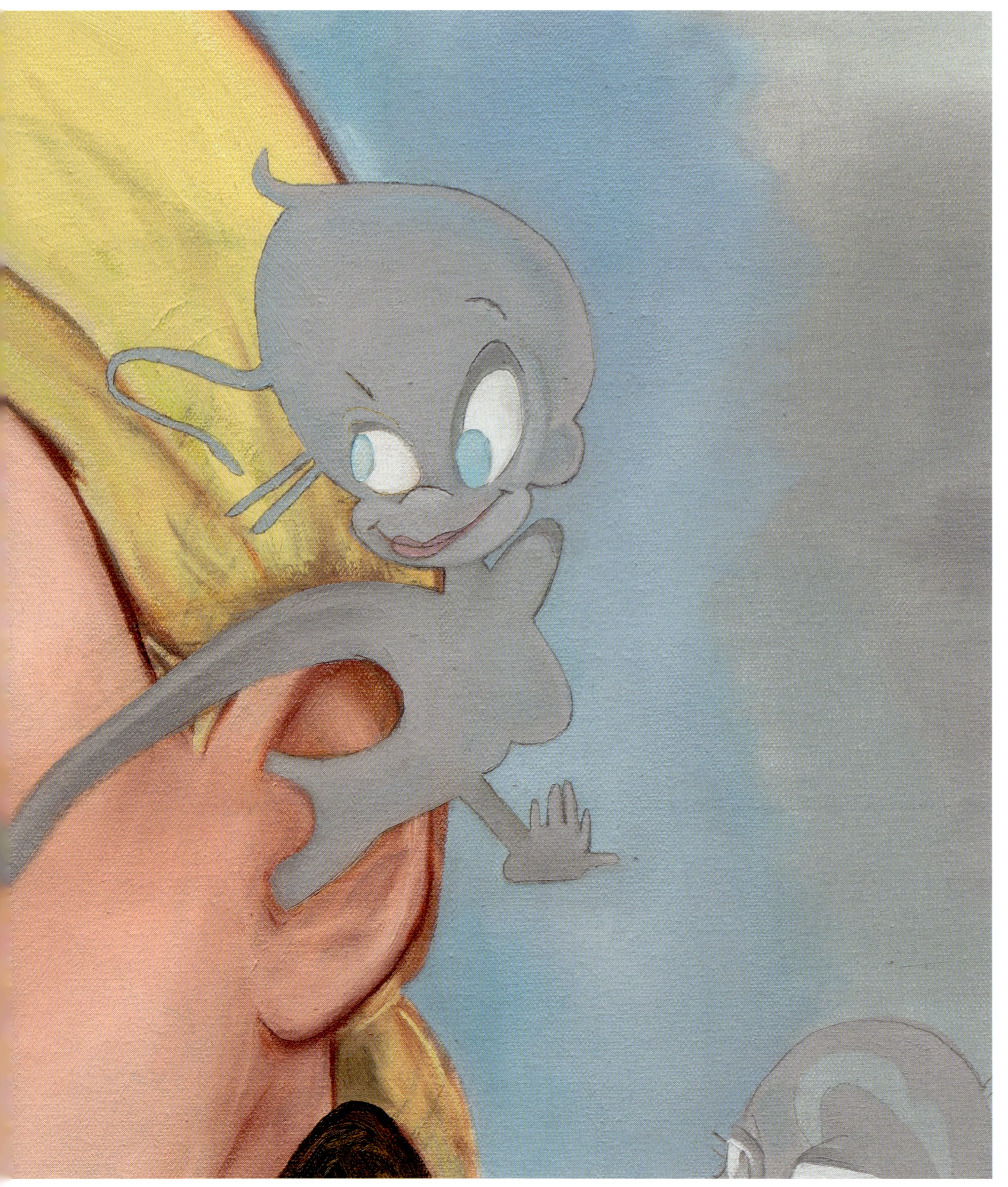

Yard Snacks		2019
Oil on linen
11 × 14 in. (27.9 × 35.6 cm)

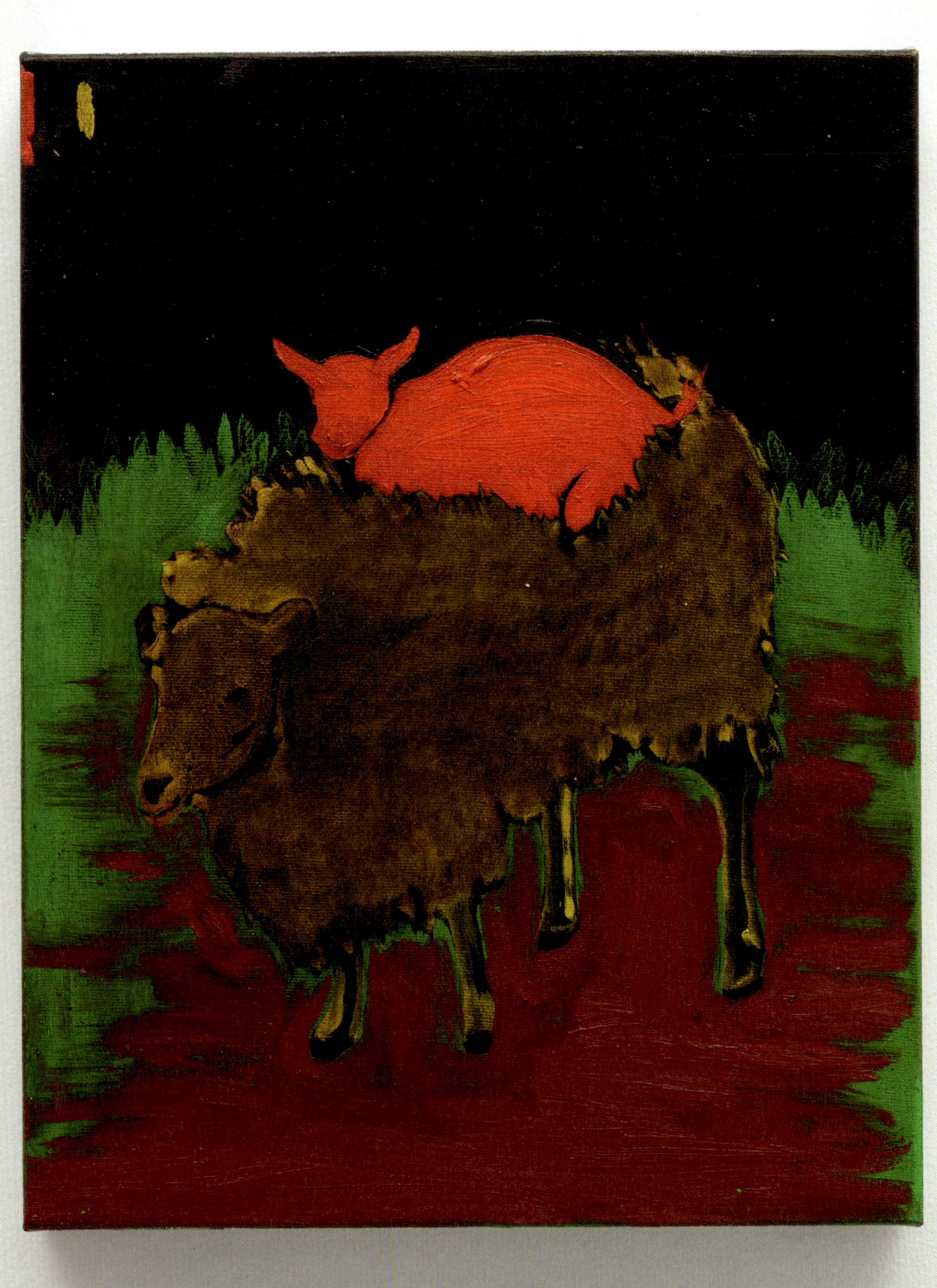

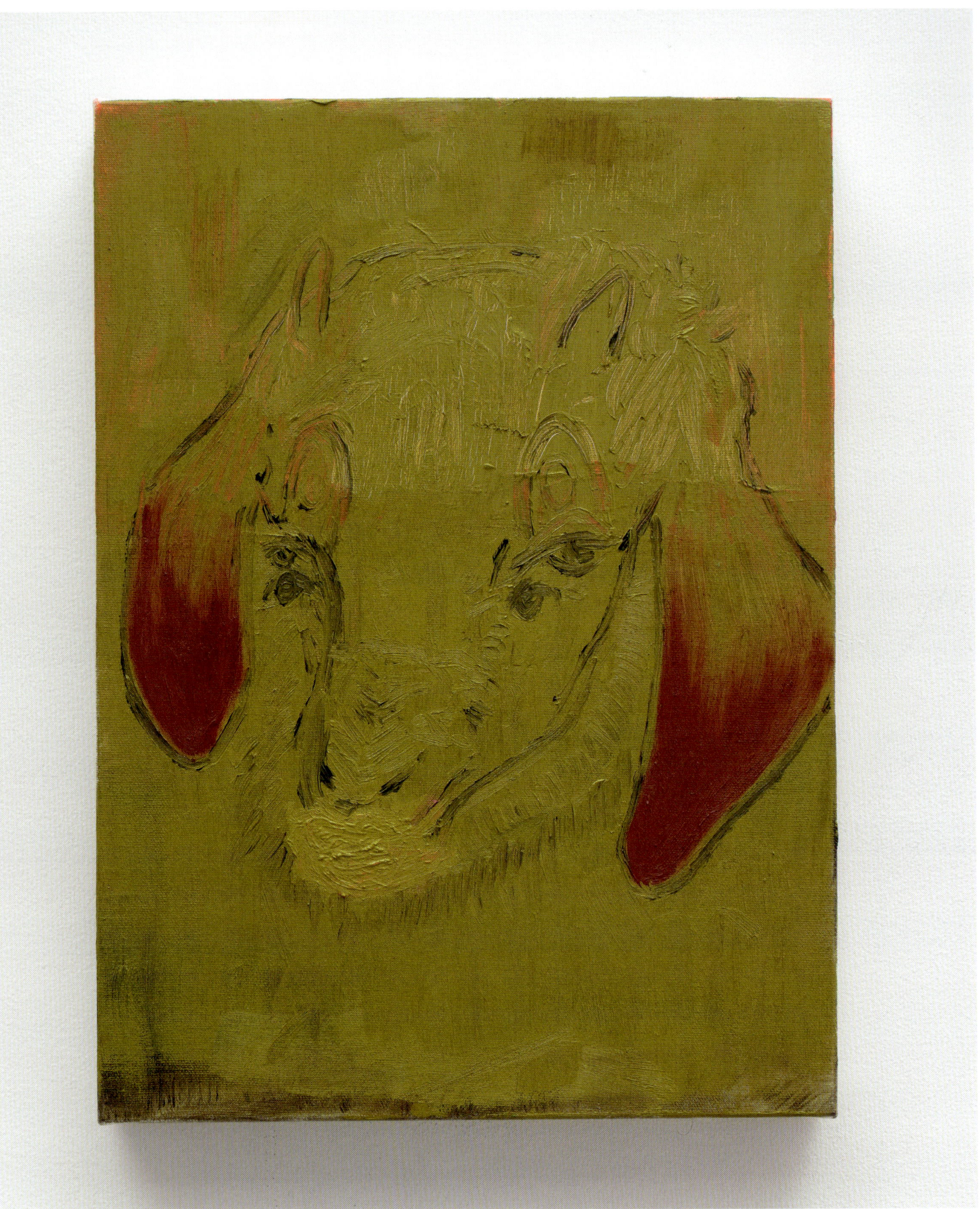

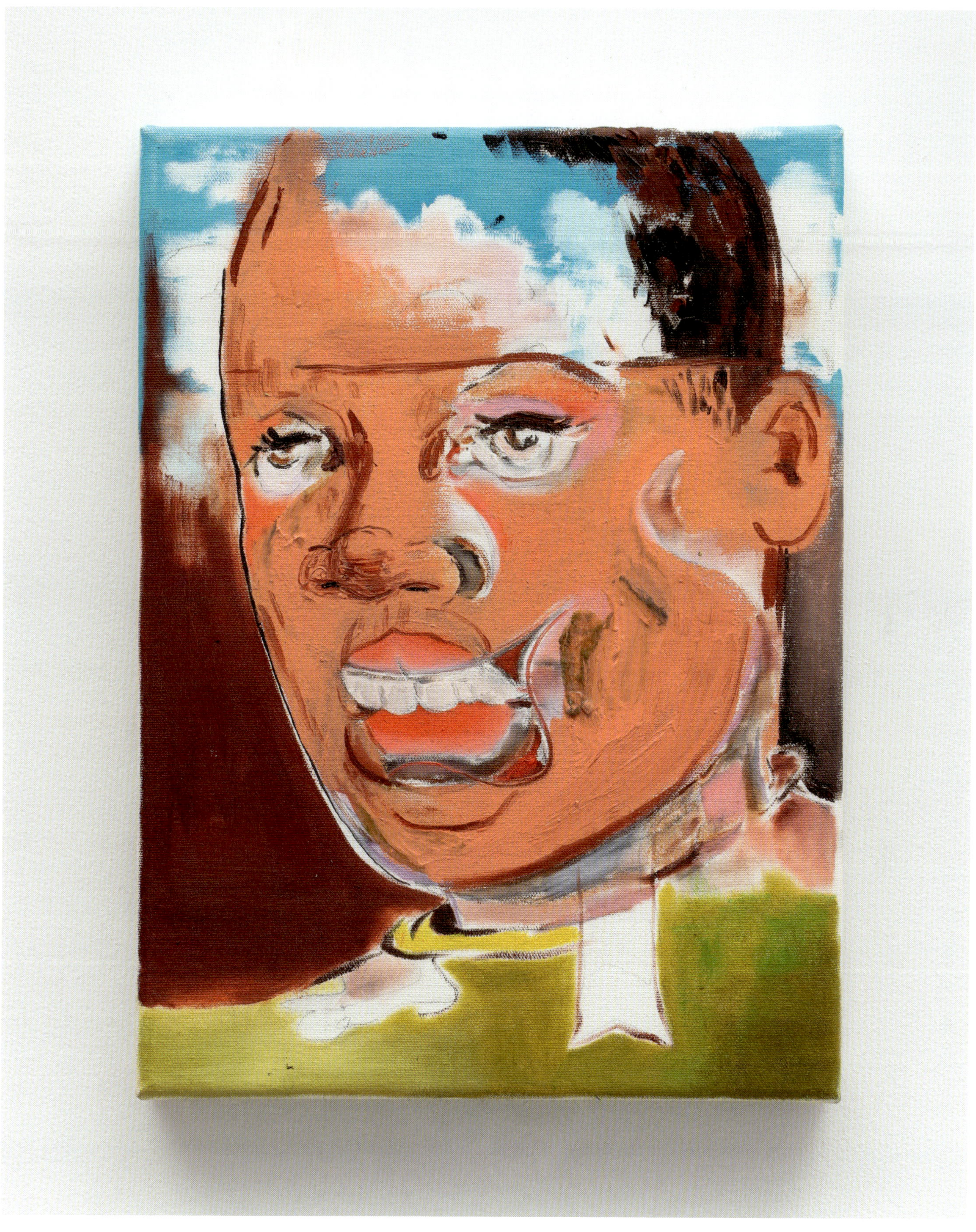

Fake Ape   2019
Oil on linen
16 × 12 in. (40.6 × 30.5 cm)

Puppy Niece   2019
Oil on linen
18 × 14 in. (45.7 × 35.6 cm)

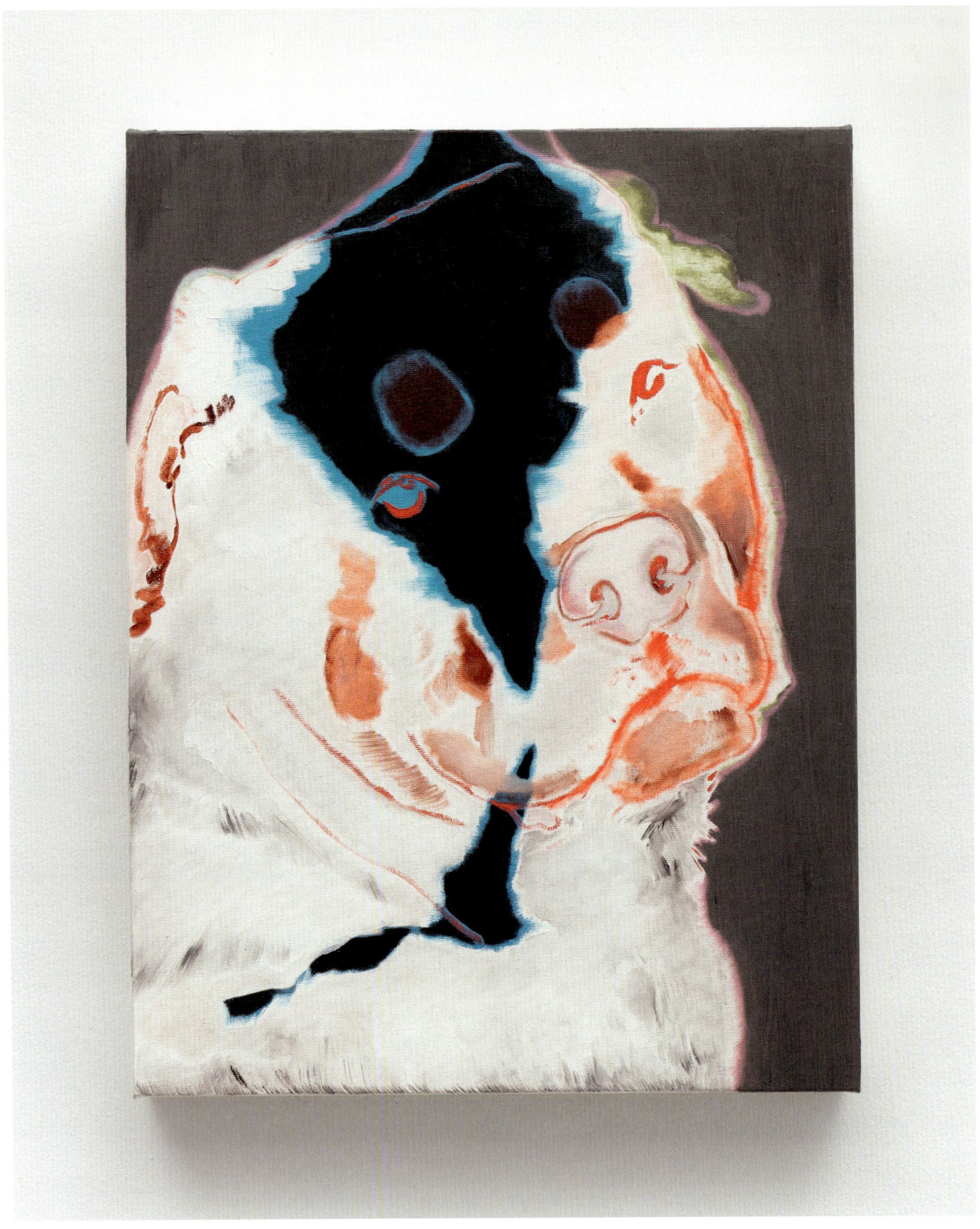

Taper Jean Girl 2019
Oil on linen
52 × 52 in. (132.1 × 132.1 cm)

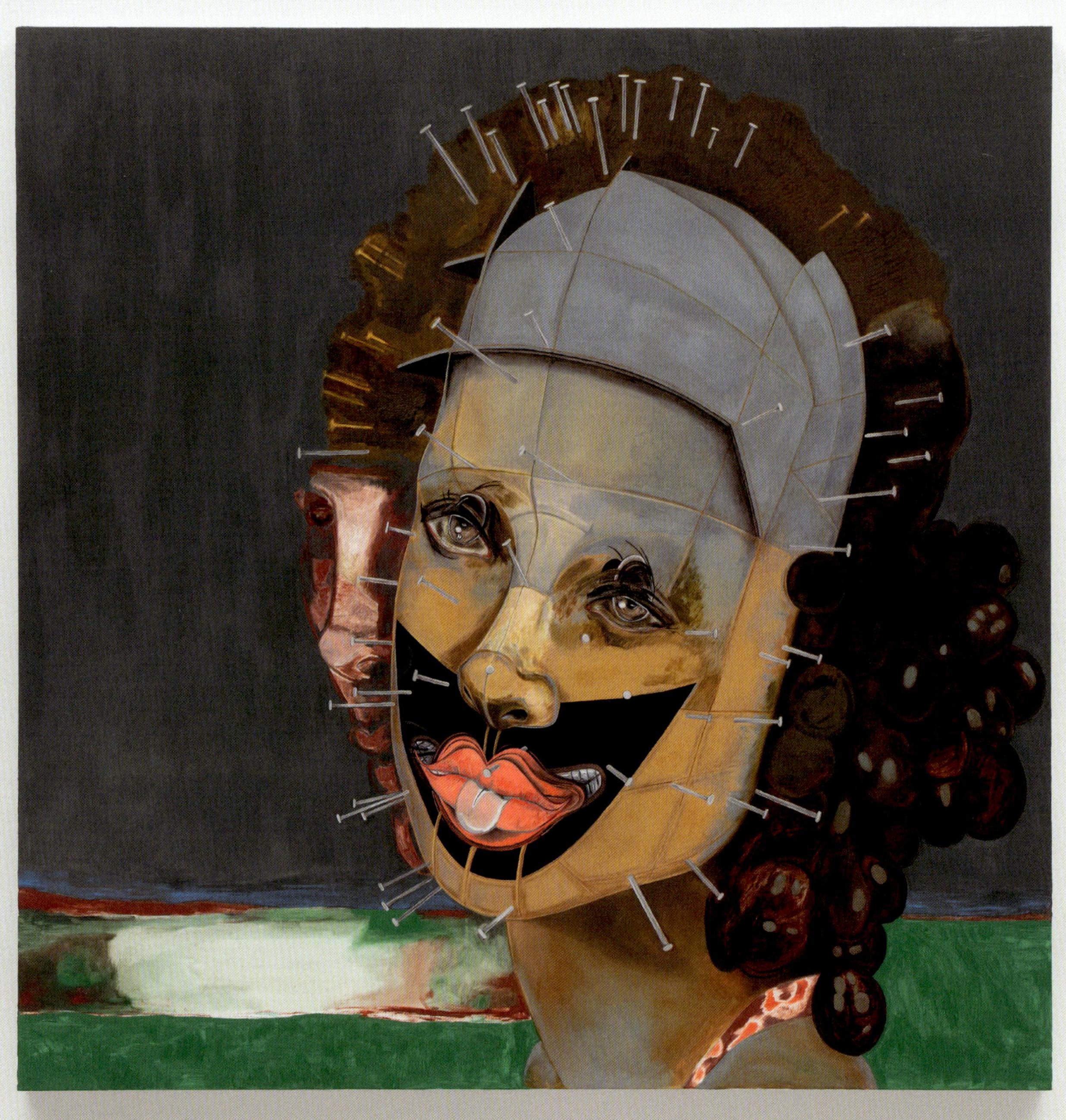

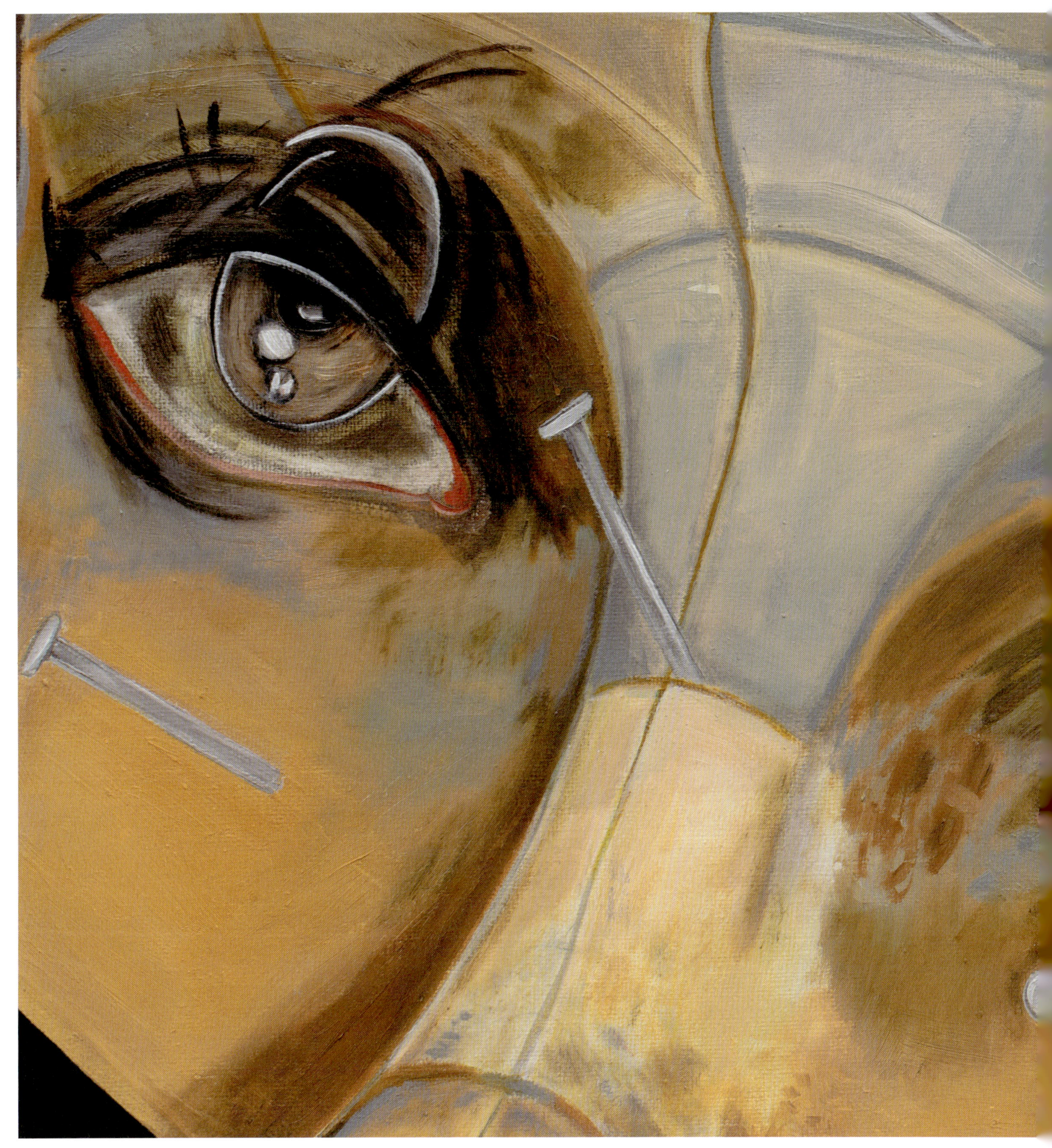

Taper Jean Girl
Oil on linen
52 × 52 in. (132.1 × 132.1 cm)

2019

detail

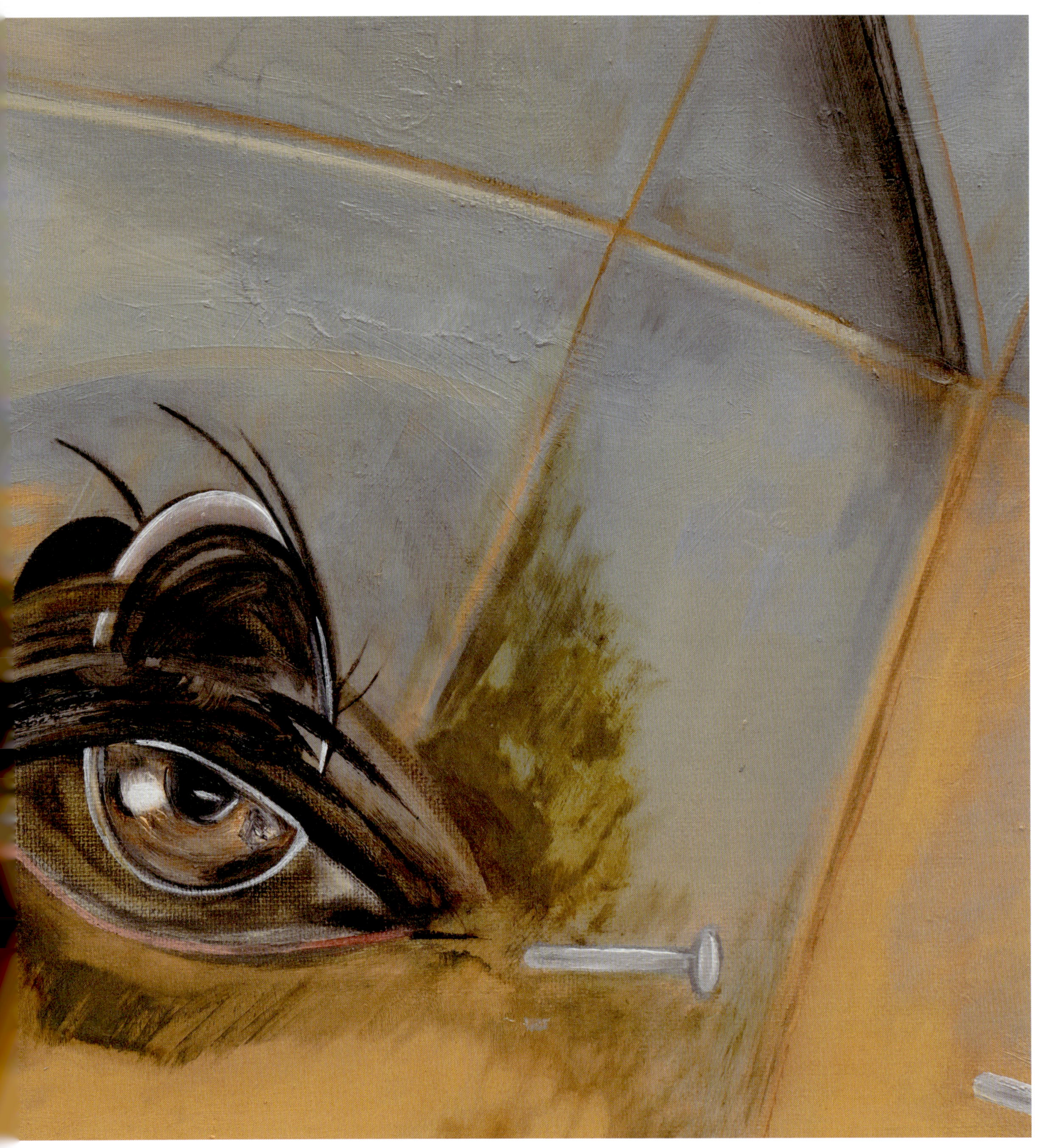

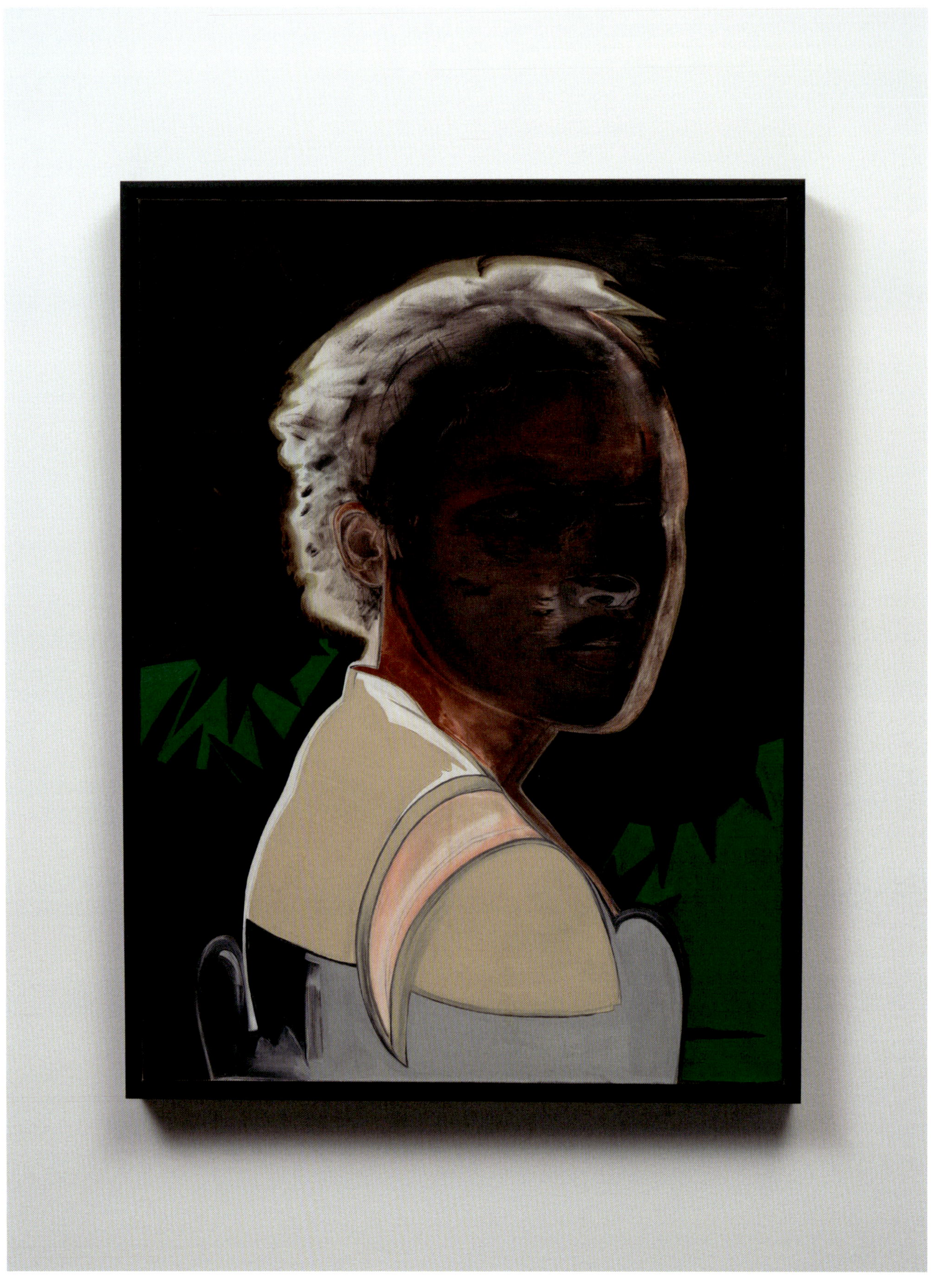

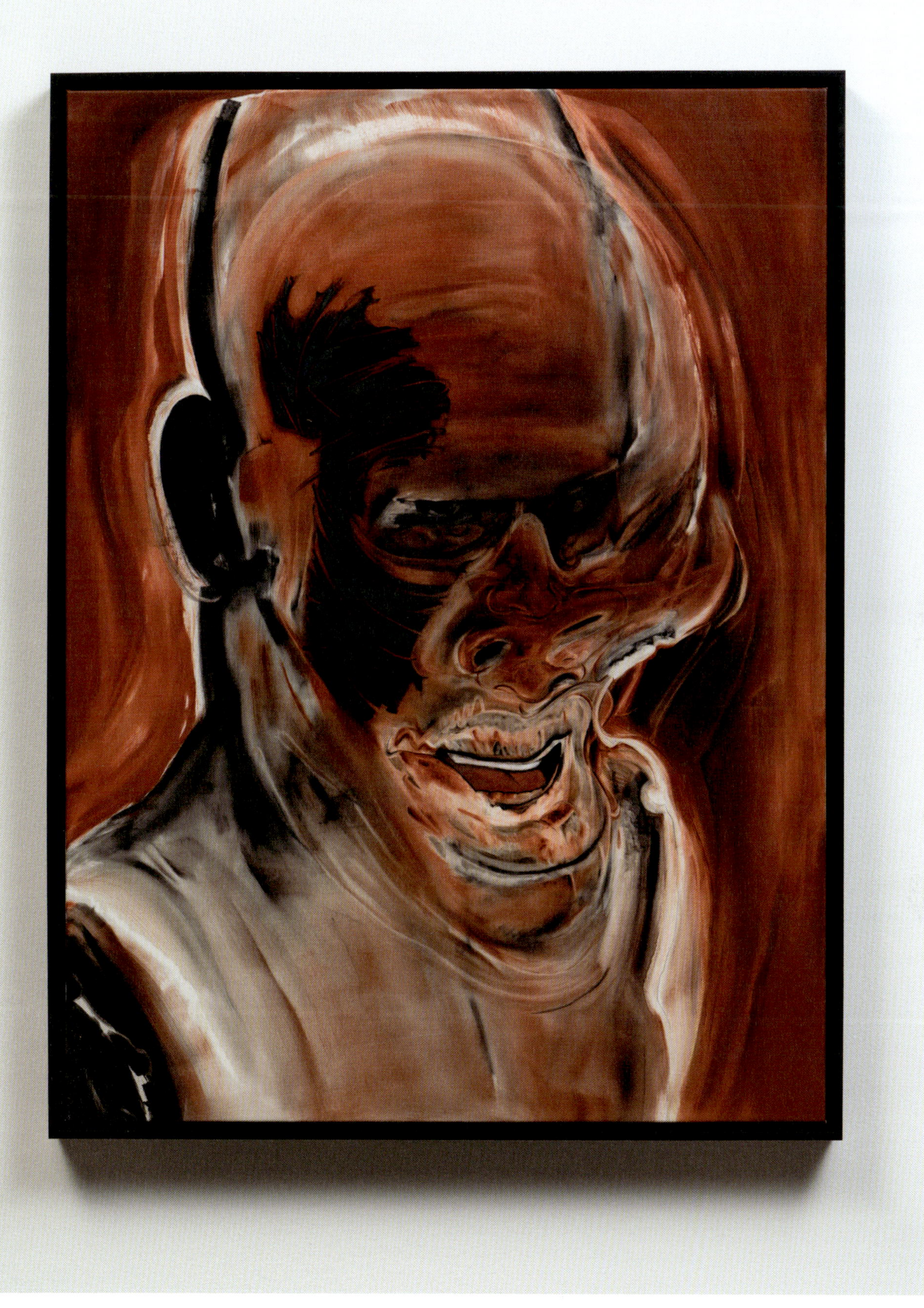

Fugue Pace   2020
Oil on canvas
48 × 36 in. (121.9 × 91.4 cm)

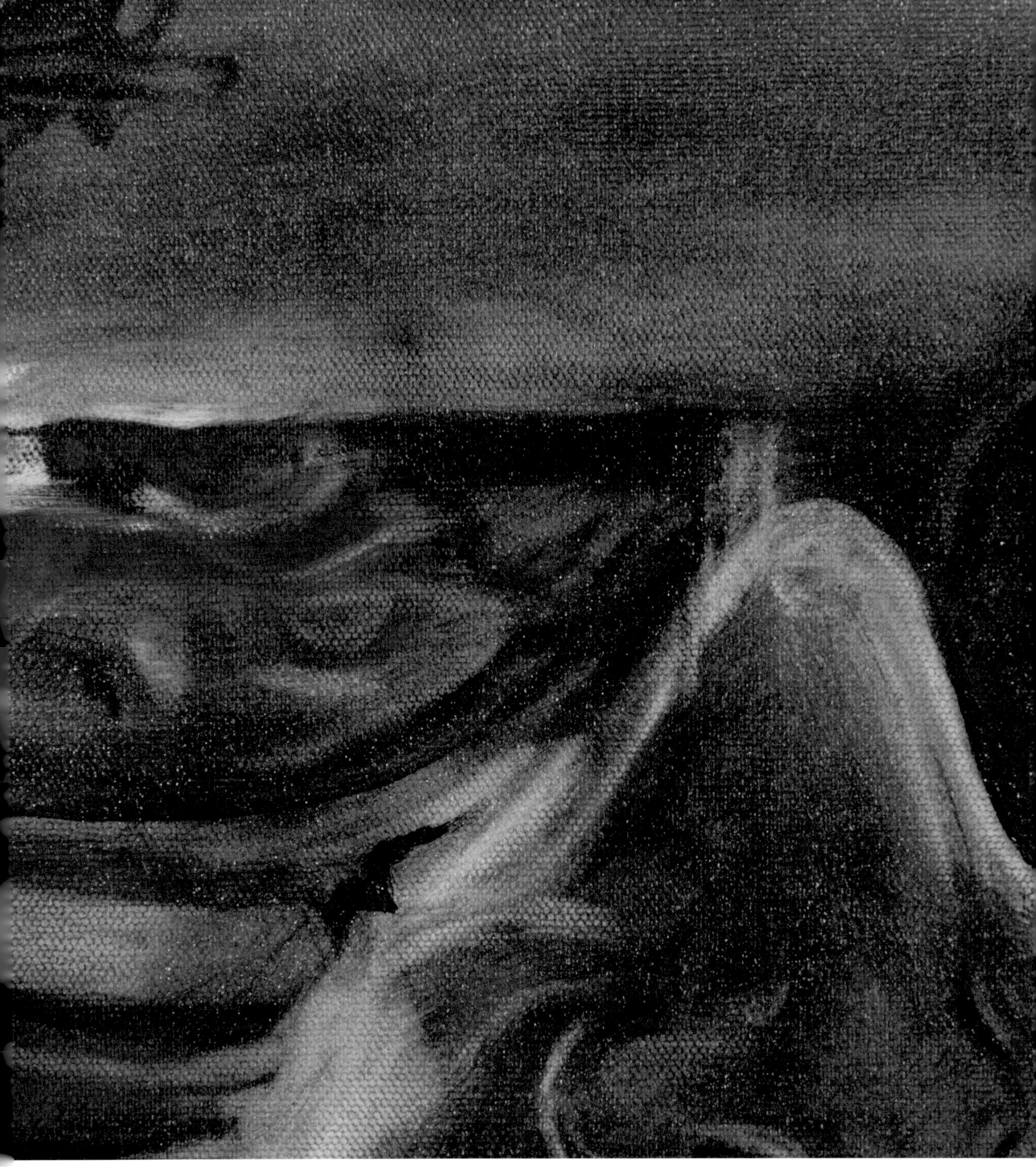

detail

The ground is blurred over in segments as thick, cabled sweeps of grays exalt the surface of Janiva Ellis's Bloodlust Halo *(2021). Knotty, spatial interlays of unfocused ground become proxies of lamentation, as a grief-filled scene takes shape at the center of the painting—a freshly packed mound of earth, delicately placed ceramic vessels, and headstones form the setting of a grave. In the background, abstract architectural structures place the scene outside of aporia, but nowhere in particular. This is both a transcription of the everyday and a precise moment recontextualized—the contours of the scene bear a direct resemblance to a 1936 photograph capturing the grave of a white child whose death arrived at the height of the Great Depression. Looming in a messy, activated orbit, the painting also centers a dense form in peachy-reds, blacks, and whites that hovers nearby the resting place. This melancholic and seemingly nonfigurative painting at first suggests a departure from Ellis's more speculative bodily expressions of Blackness, except* Bloodlust Halo *couriers complicated themes of texture, affect, and illusion often missed in her more fantastical works. The awkward and challenging locatability of Blackness in this painting is what Fred Moten elsewhere has called a thinking in Blackness. "What is overlooked in blackness," he writes, "is bound up with what has been overseen." [1] However, rather than proposing a series of practices or methods as antidote to this narrow optical hypervigilance, Moten hones in on the critical interstices of the field of Black studies. "Such investigation," he reminds us, "is best accompanied by vigilant remembrance of and commitment to the fact that blackness is present … at its own making and that all the people who are called black are given in and to that presence, which exceeds them." [2] As a fortuitous thought-partner to Moten, Ellis puts the concept of entrapment to work throughout the exhibition, naming it as both an effect of white supremacy as well as a tactic that operates inside and outside of the system to which it belongs. More than an aesthetic transcription of grief, Ellis's* Bloodlust Halo *asks where Black grief lands, since, as Claudia Rankine notes, in a recent essay, violence against Black people does not stay long in the body of the "white liberal imagination." [3] If we carefully meditate on this work, we arrive at not only the critical orientations that are Ellis's tender and active expressions of Blackness, but also at the nuanced language of Black aesthetic forms.*

Olivia K. Young: *Bloodlust Halo* is a work that almost anticipates a misconception by your viewing audience. Since this painting is not about Black death directly, let's begin with the primary impulse for this piece and what work you hope it will do in your exhibition.

Janiva Ellis: Great! So, I want a lot from painting, and I can be indecisive about how subtlety can function in a work. I started this painting off differently from some of my others. Initially, when I saw the photograph it's based on, I was struck by how staged it felt, how rigid the compositional concerns seemed in this depiction of death. This painting is based on a photograph by Walker Evans, which is called *A Child's Grave, Hale County, Alabama* [1936]; it was part of a series of images in a collaborative book that he did with James Agee—the book is called *Let Us Now Praise Famous Men* [1941]. The project was commissioned by *Fortune* magazine to document the devastation of the Great Depression in rural Alabama. And so, the book is composed of images

taken of three white tenant farmer families and the devastation they experienced as a byproduct of the depression. There's a text that accompanies it that I have not seen, so when I made this painting, I was primarily thinking about the proliferation of images that came from that book. Modernist images from the Great Depression—from Dorothea Lange to Walker Evans—were my initial understandings of what white American struggle was; cinematically operating separately from the afterlife of chattel slavery. Black history has been so isolated and contained in this country, I just thought, as a younger person, "Okay, the Great Depression is this thing where white people were really poor and we're meant to internalize that as sad." These images have come to represent the larger narrative of American struggle and white victimhood.

      So, I was thinking about representations of white struggle as a means of tailoring reality and asserting white innocence. I think the Great Depression is a moment where white vulnerability is communicated in a way that erases the violence being committed against non-white people—prior to that moment, in that moment, and since that moment. I painted the gesture above the grave thinking of the violence that is not spoken about or that I didn't learn about in tandem with this imagery. I'm thinking of the gesture as a representation of the surge in violence at that time against Black people at the hands of white people. So that's the backstory of the painting.

      I knew people might assume that this painting is about Black death. I was more thinking about white violence and representations of whiteness and how they operate in pointed ways. So, there's a gesture representing the violence that's unspoken and there's a figurative depiction of the devastation that remains centered. This image is an appropriation of what is really not specific to Walker Evans at all—this painting is about a way of thinking, a way of communicating, really, and how there's so much violence in white communication and white renditions of history.

OKY: I focused on *Bloodlust Halo* specifically because of how activating the blurring of the ground felt. This type of textural resonance directs us away from texture as tactile and guides us into other types of embodied touch and performances of intimacy as discussed by scholars such as Tina Campt and Eve Kosofsky Sedgwick.[4] Here the texture of blurring activates both within the painting and between the painting and the viewer. Elsewhere you have discussed the importance of this type of intra- and inter-compositional attention—the capacity for your work to register, distract, and obscure other elements or characters within the painting as well as between the painting and the viewers themselves. Can you talk a bit about the process of blurring parts of the ground?

JE: You're talking about this foreground in front of the grave and the layer on top. It's a grayscale painting, and then there are textural differences that create depth.

OKY: Absolutely!

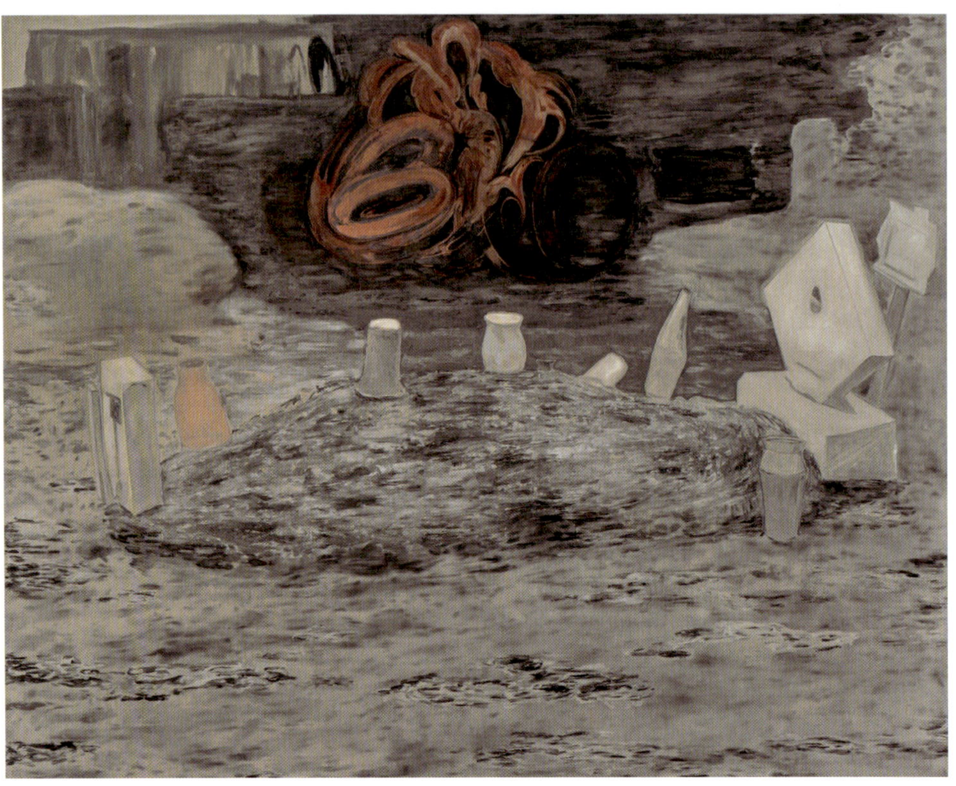

Bloodlust Halo   2021
Oil on canvas
77 × 96 in. (195.6 × 243.8 cm)

JE: I feel like the layering on top creates an illusion of play here. Just in technical terms … you know … I just find it fun—I get to laugh when I try and imitate these kinds of, you know, auteur artists that have maintained resonance in the Western canon—in the canon I was educated in. After I finished blurring the ground of this painting I stepped back and thought about Gerhard Richter and his technical blur approach. How a simple stylistic choice held so much meaning for so long within this educational process. How my subsequent blur may be interpreted as a reference to his. This painting stayed for a long time in my studio. For a long time, I hadn't painted over it and the whole painting was just blurry—it kind of served as a ghost of the photograph. And then, a few days before the work was picked up, I had to finish it! It was one of the paintings I had started the earliest but was, I think, maybe the last one I actually finished. It was in my studio just in this really blurred, unfinished state, and then I went back in, and, I don't know, I wanted to make additions, ones that felt separate from the initial blurred image but were not as exuberant and intrusive as the compositional interventions that I have created in the past. There's a sacredness to depicting devastation, but in this case, it's a lot more complex than simply evoking the sadness of a child's death. I think once images like this one become propaganda, they are flattened and oversimplified. Within white canonization, Black art and expression often get treated like propaganda. Artworks by Black people get flattened and then attempts are made to "complicate" the work to suit white logic for white understanding. And I think, similarly, art and imagery by white people can get oversimplified to remove a lot of the violence that contextualizes it, and then over-complicated to prove the artists' intelligence and emotional connectedness. In both cases, white violence is removed and emotion that centers the white imagination is applied.

OKY: Yes! The way space is used as a tool of erasure—
even the affective afterlife of an event. That makes me think of
the blurring as a type of spatial exaltation; it is both as if I could walk
above the ground on the hazed grays toward the grave—missing
the earth altogether—and/or never reach the grave at all because of
the interlay of spatial obscurity. I am interested in your practice
of confusing space and making it both of these things at the same
time. Your work gives us texture as a type of spatial poetics—but
again, not because of its grainy surface feel, but because of how it
activates and obscures. I consider this a type of critical orientation—a
grounding that you offer as a tactic. This takes us to Fred Moten's
thinking in Blackness, which, I believe, at its very core is also a spatial
inquiry. Tell me more about this practice of texture as space within your work.

JE: Yeah, I am interested in achieving depth through flatness, wheth-
er that is textural, perspective, or conceptual flatness. I'm interested in pushing against
those limitations. Thinking about traditional mechanisms of depth in painting—
which often has to do with perspective and scale—I think there are more ways than
a clinical one to create spatial depth. I want to include psychological depth in there, too.
And I think it's much harder to do that when relying on straightforward tools of representation. And so, when I think about remembering a sensation or communicating a
sensation, it's just very difficult and blurry. You know, some people are better at it
than others. I do feel like sometimes the mechanism that allows me to forget a painful
experience happens really quickly and then that pain shows up much later in an
unrelated moment. I'm interested in slowing that down. I'm interested in those things
catching up with one another. A recollection of what something felt like in real time
or in proximity to the sensation. And sometimes, in a painting, I want it to feel like something just happened or something is about to happen and you're in that in-between
space. But I also want you to know the whole story right there. I want you to know the
most intermediary part of the narrative and I also want it all to be summed up in that
moment.

OKY: Let's broaden our view for a moment and talk more
about the exhibition as a whole. What was coming up for you as
you prepared for this interview? You shared with me that this is one of
the first conversations you have had about your work since the
opening of "Rats" a few weeks ago. What emotional resonance does
this show have for you, now that it is fully installed?

JE: When I started to think intentionally about the show and even
came up with the title, "Rats," I was really trying to reorient myself and understand the
agency I have as an artist. I was confronting a lot of the ways I had avoided interro-
gating racist frameworks in conversations about my art—there was that flattening that
kept happening with how my work was being talked about by both the museum and
also by journalists prior to that. When I first started showing, I thought "what's one interview," but eventually I began processing how disorienting it had ultimately been
to feel like I wasn't creating boundaries around my work and how it was being talked

or written about. I felt like I was passively engaging with this larger agenda of packaging and flattening Blackness and Black perspective. When I started speaking with non-Black writers and curators, and their uninformed relationship to Black expressions surfaced in conversation, I realized how intentional and clear I had to be. There were certain things I thought were implied that for them were just not. For example, I thought, "Of course I'm talking about white violence and white delusion." It became clear that I couldn't assume that just because I was in an art space that the people I was talking to were not playing into that delusion and violence, too. So, I think I had a disillusioning moment both in my personal life and in my relationship to the art world/market. I felt a surge of responsibility and also felt deeply behind. There was frustration that I may not be able to say what I want to say in an institutional context. It felt silly to have this conversation in an institution in the first place, so I wanted to try an approach that felt safer.

OKY: Yes, and "Rats" is absolutely a collection of your most recent works, but at its core, it appears first to be an aesthetic manifesto, or your critical orientations for the field. Tell me about how you created that approach of safety for this exhibition.

JE: Yes, so "Rats" felt … like, cool … I do not have to be precious about this show. I can express how these art environments feel like entrapment in a lot of ways. How white mythology infests perspective, infests a larger narrative, how instead of communicating intention, we end up combatting misinterpretation before interpretation even begins, and that … that is an exhausting process and an entrapping process. As an individual, I have so much agency, so much access, and so much room to communicate. At the same time, this structure is set up with a bunch of traps to derail clarity—the clarity of Black thought and the clarity of Black perspective.

And I was thinking about the ways that Black art has been consumed over this past year—extraction that postures as appreciation, which just feels so violent. I did not want to put Black figures into that space, and at the same time, I do not want to stop painting what I want to paint because of white violence. So, I was really trying to reconcile those two inclinations: how to intentionally paint whatever I wanted while contextualizing the consequences of that since there are consequences for Black people to express ourselves freely among white people.

I think this moment is a growing pain—realizing just how much control I need to have in the communication of my work and process. To be direct, if I continue to exhibit in spaces that may have recently tried to showcase Black innovation but still operate under a white supremacist perspective of art. While many non-white people are operating in institutional art environments, the framework is largely still centering whiteness in such a strong way. So, those are the things I was thinking about.

OKY: This boundaried and thoughtfully controlled orientation toward presenting your work really comes alive in the structure of the exhibition. Can you talk about how you spatially organized your show?

JE: Yes! When you walk into the show you walk through a long wall with a doorway. I wanted to compartmentalize the show the way that art is compartmentalized in our broader communication of history. When I was thinking about the layout, I wanted to create a separate space for some of the Black figurative paintings. So, there's a smaller room in the larger gallery that has some of the Black figures, and I did this to create a more intimate emotional space for those works.

            In some ways, this show is a delousing, a necessary purge, and a chance to contextualize the environment currently framing my work. Although the broader art landscape currently centers white chronology and feels treacherous in relationship to introducing Black figures, I don't want to edit Black figuration out. Instead, going forward, I'd like to reorient my work by engaging art histories that don't center the white imagination. Ultimately, I want to contribute to the complex and expansive technologies of Black art.

In this personal account of "Rats," Ellis offers entrapment as a new analytic of Black grief. Playing with space, as she does with the arrangement of rooms and the pairing of paintings, offers protection without resolve. Playing with layers and textures suggests nuanced transcriptions of white violence without redress. "Trapped" and "infest[ing]," this discursive framework performs upon the space as much as it describes it. These complicated critical terms draw forward the overlap of art environments and histories of carcerality, while simultaneously refusing to center it as spectacle. What Ellis offers in this interview is a metamorphosized tactic of Black aesthetic survival: entrapment as an analytic of Black grief becomes a warning, a tool, an offering, and a transcription of Black artistic collaboration. A generous calling forth of what has long been understood, Ellis shows other Black artists a way forward in this new era of contemporary art.

Notes

1.   Fred Moten, "Black Op," *PMLA*, Special Topic: Comparative Racialization, 123, no. 5 (October 2008): 1745.
2.   Moten, "Black Op," 1746.
3.   Claudia Rankine, "The Condition of Black Life Is One of Mourning," in *Grief and Grievance: Art and Mourning in America*, exh. cat. (New York: Phaidon, 2020), 17.
4.   See Tina Campt, *Image Matters: Archive, Photography, and the African Diaspora in Europe* (Durham, NC: Duke University Press, 2012); Tina Campt, *Listening to Images* (Durham, NC: Duke University Press, 2017); and Eve Kosofsky Sedgwick, *Touching Feeling: Affect, Pedagogy, Performativity*, Series Q (Durham, NC: Duke University Press, 2003).

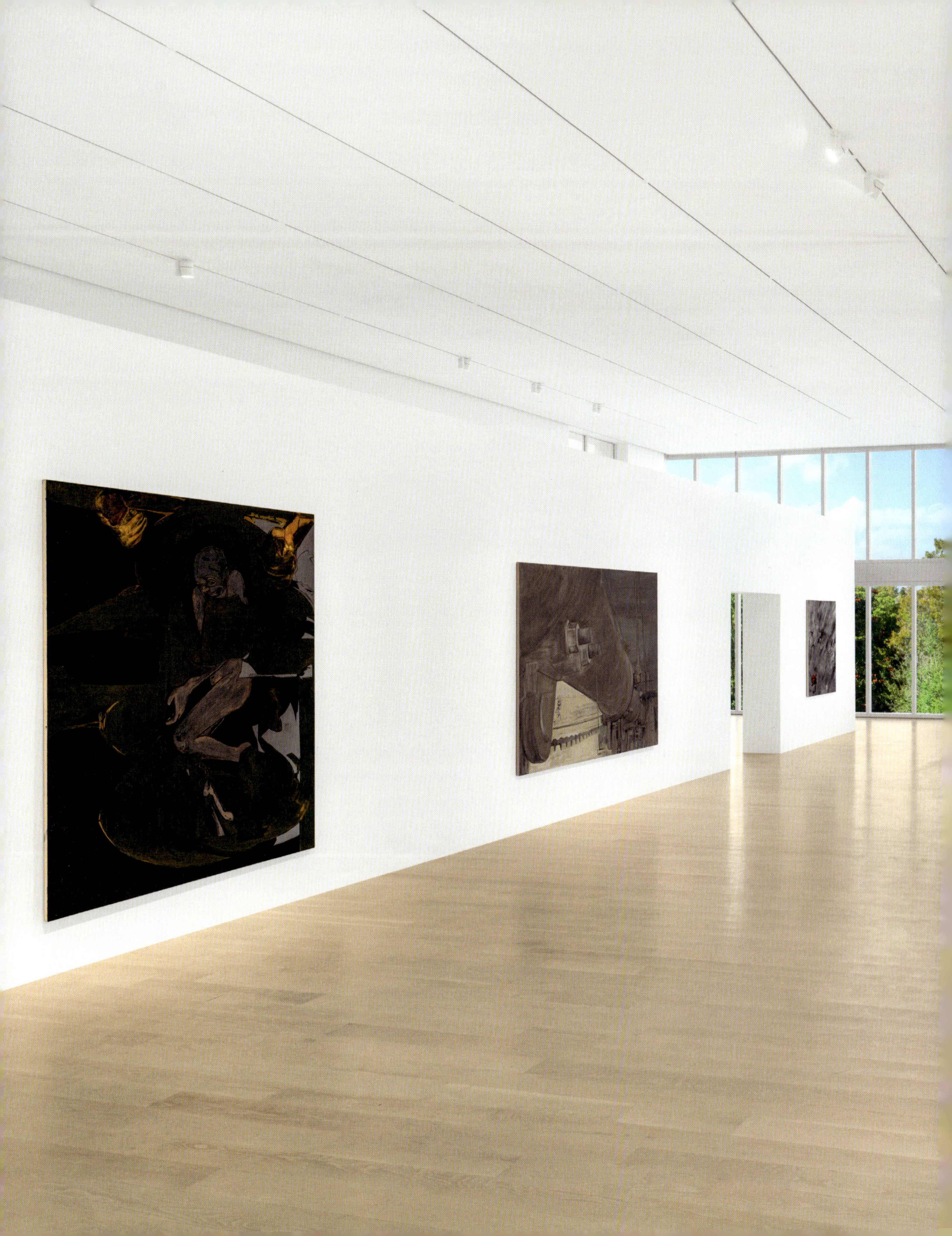

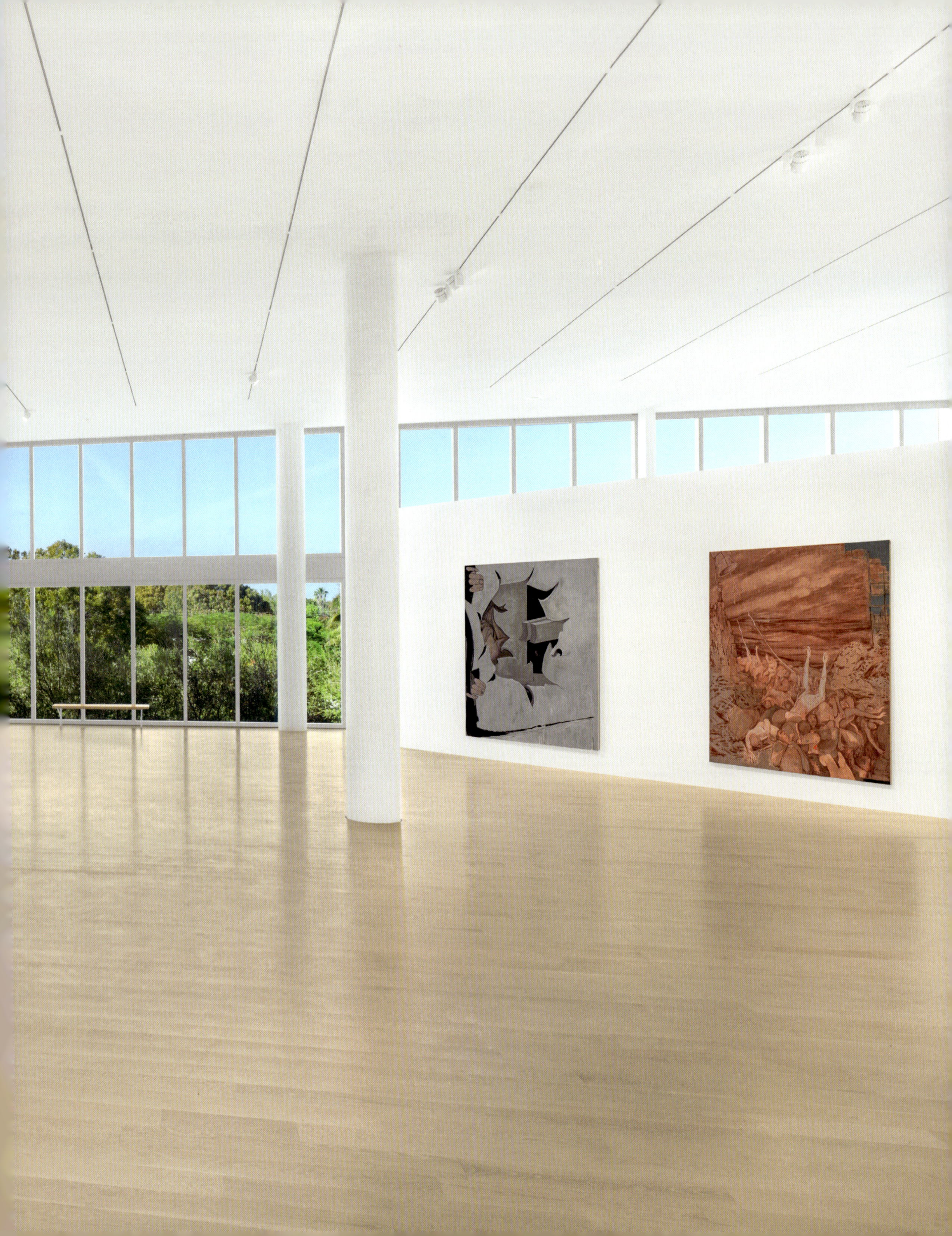

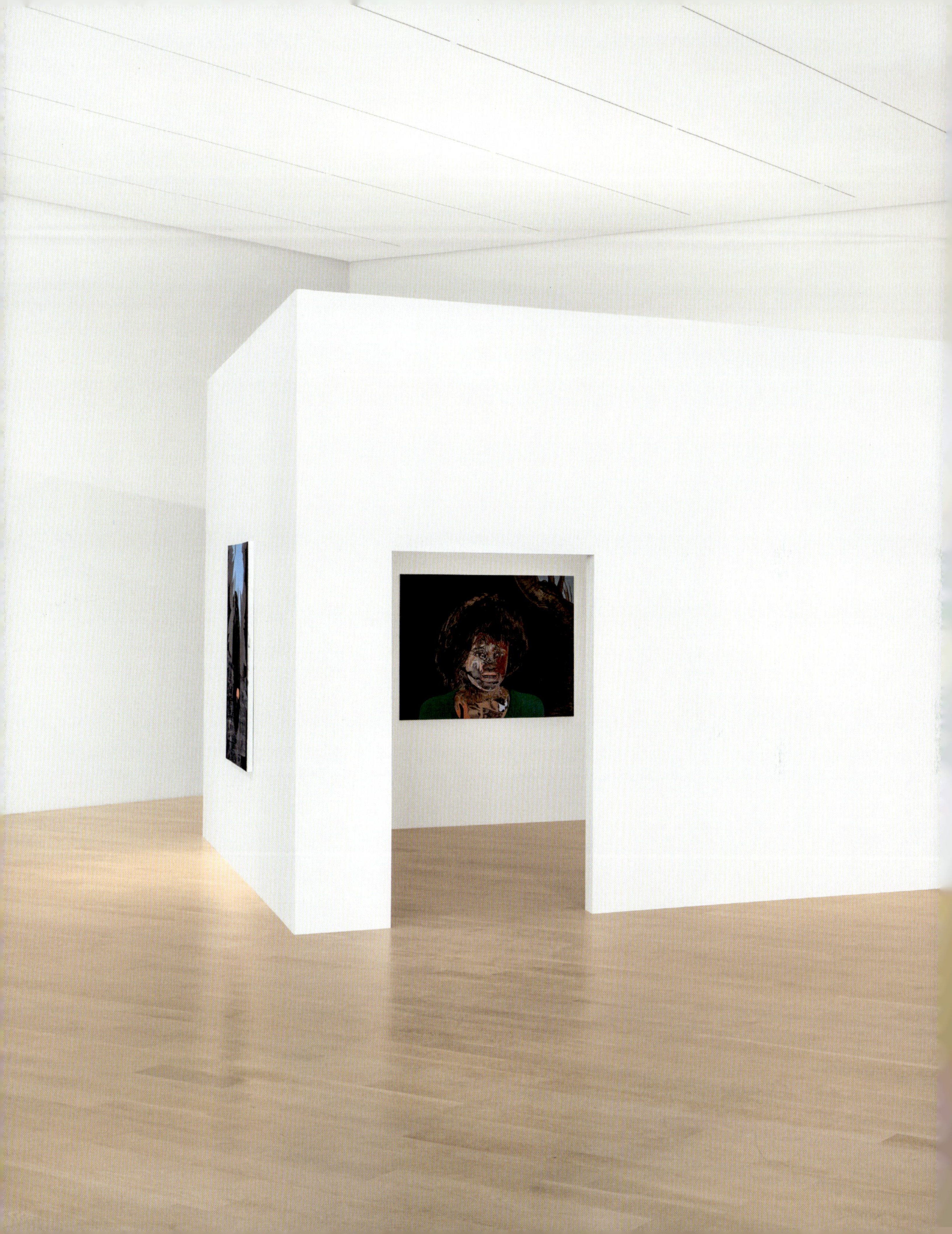

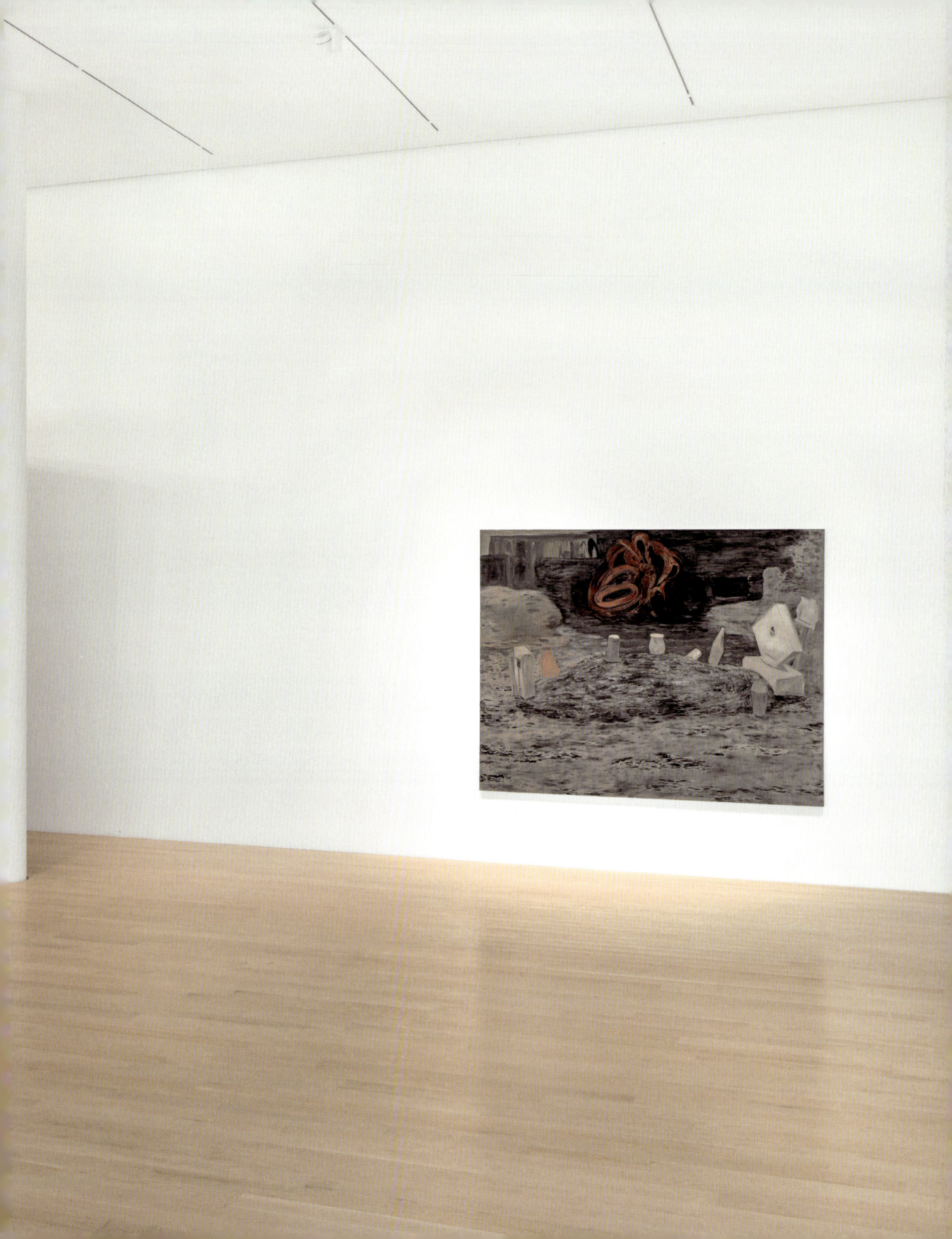

Bloodlust Halo   2021
Oil on canvas
77 × 96 in. (195.6 × 243.8 cm)

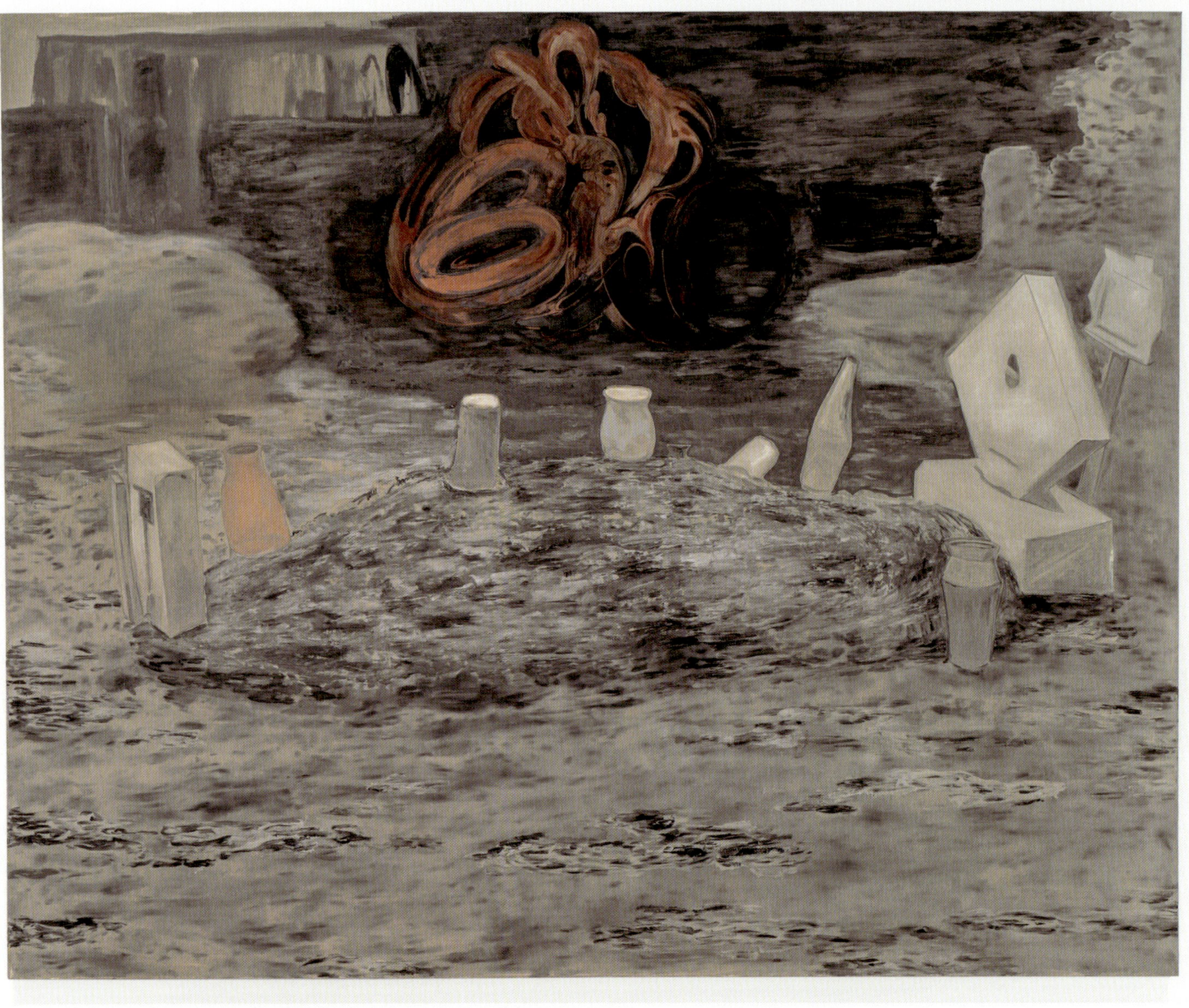

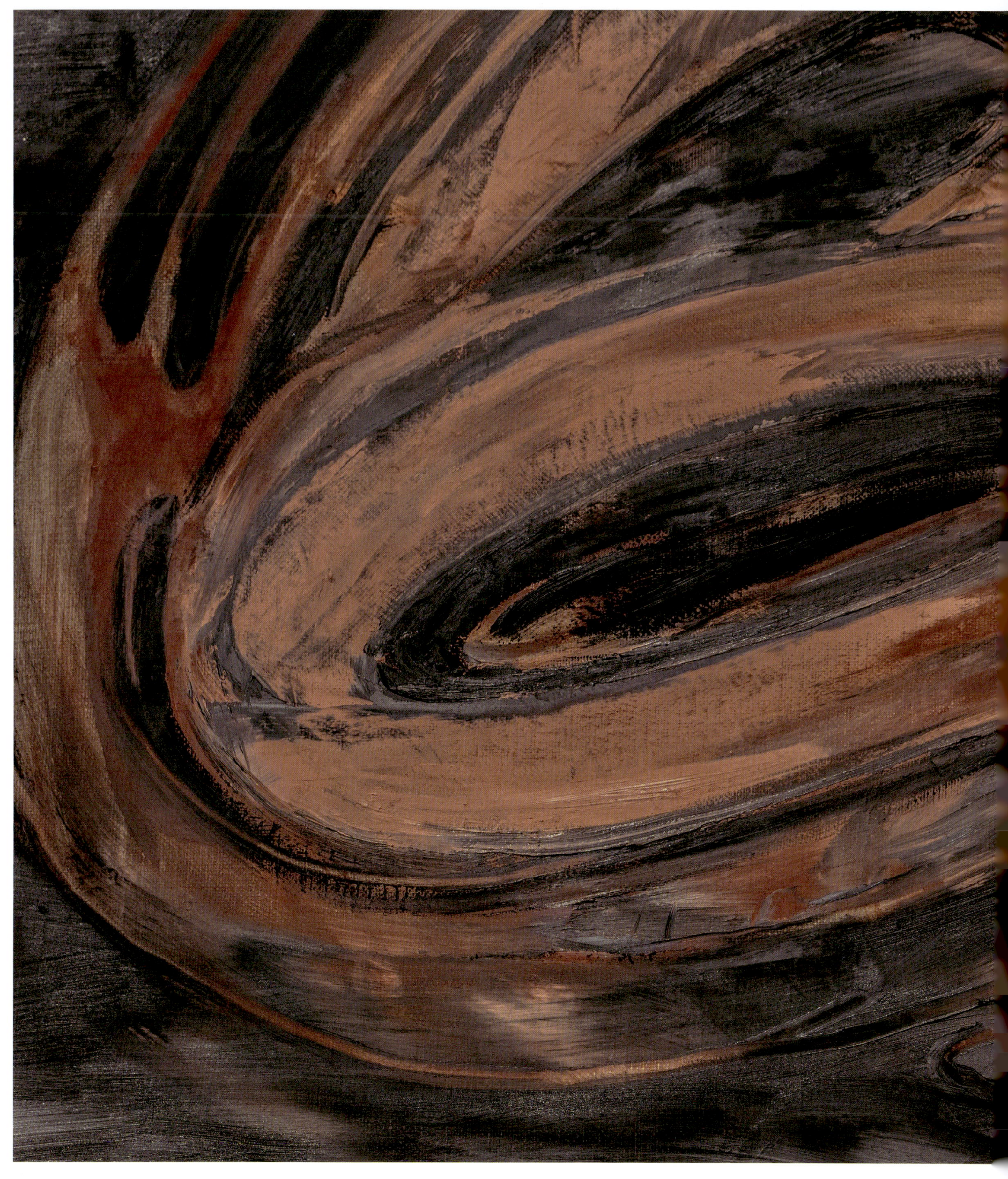

Bloodlust Halo 2021 detail
Oil on canvas
77 × 96 in. (195.6 × 243.8 cm)

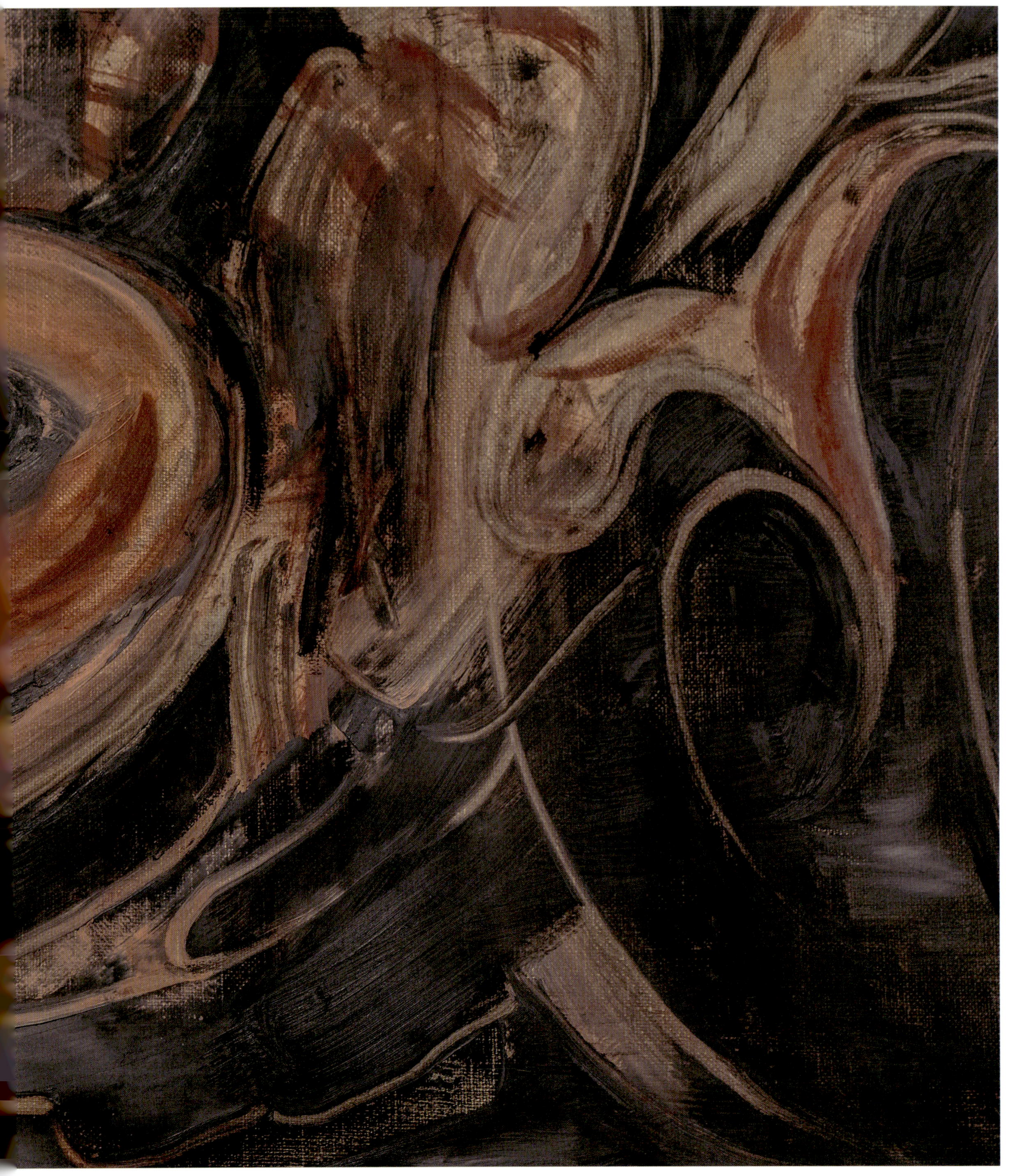

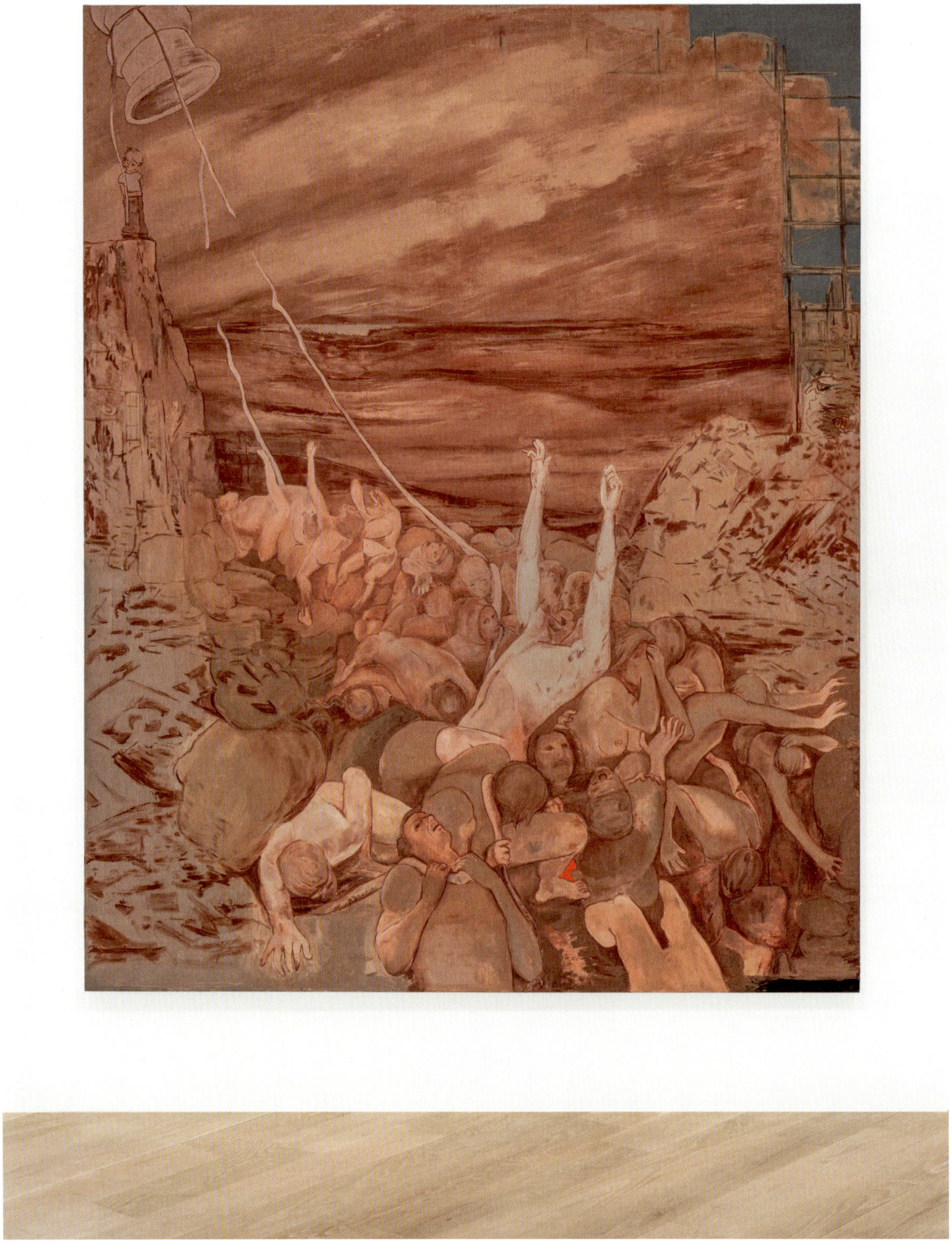

Bull Squall Bingo　　　2021
Oil on canvas
60 × 48 in. (152.4 × 121.9 cm)

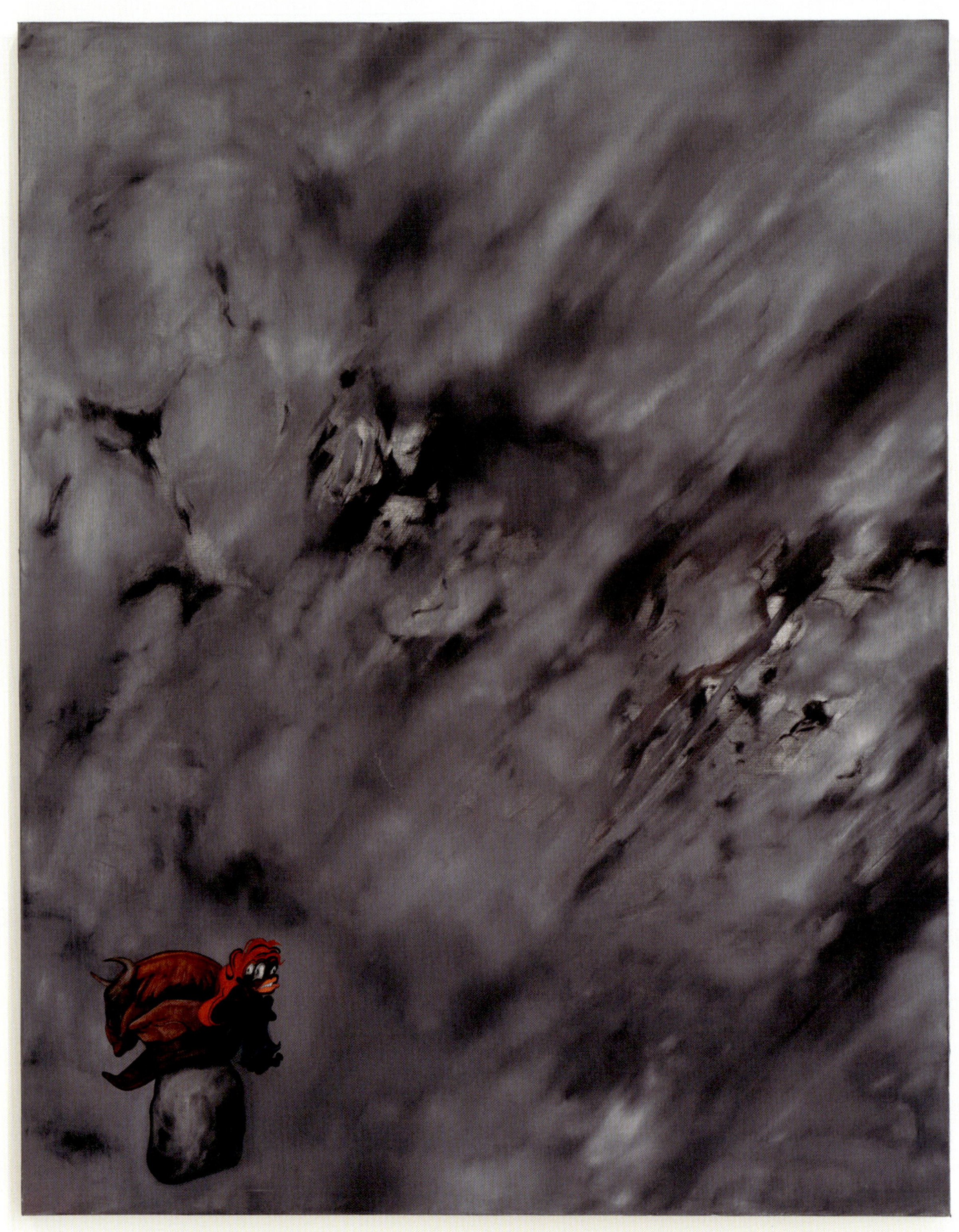

Hollow Provocation   2021
Oil on canvas
77 × 96 in. (195.6 × 243.8 cm)

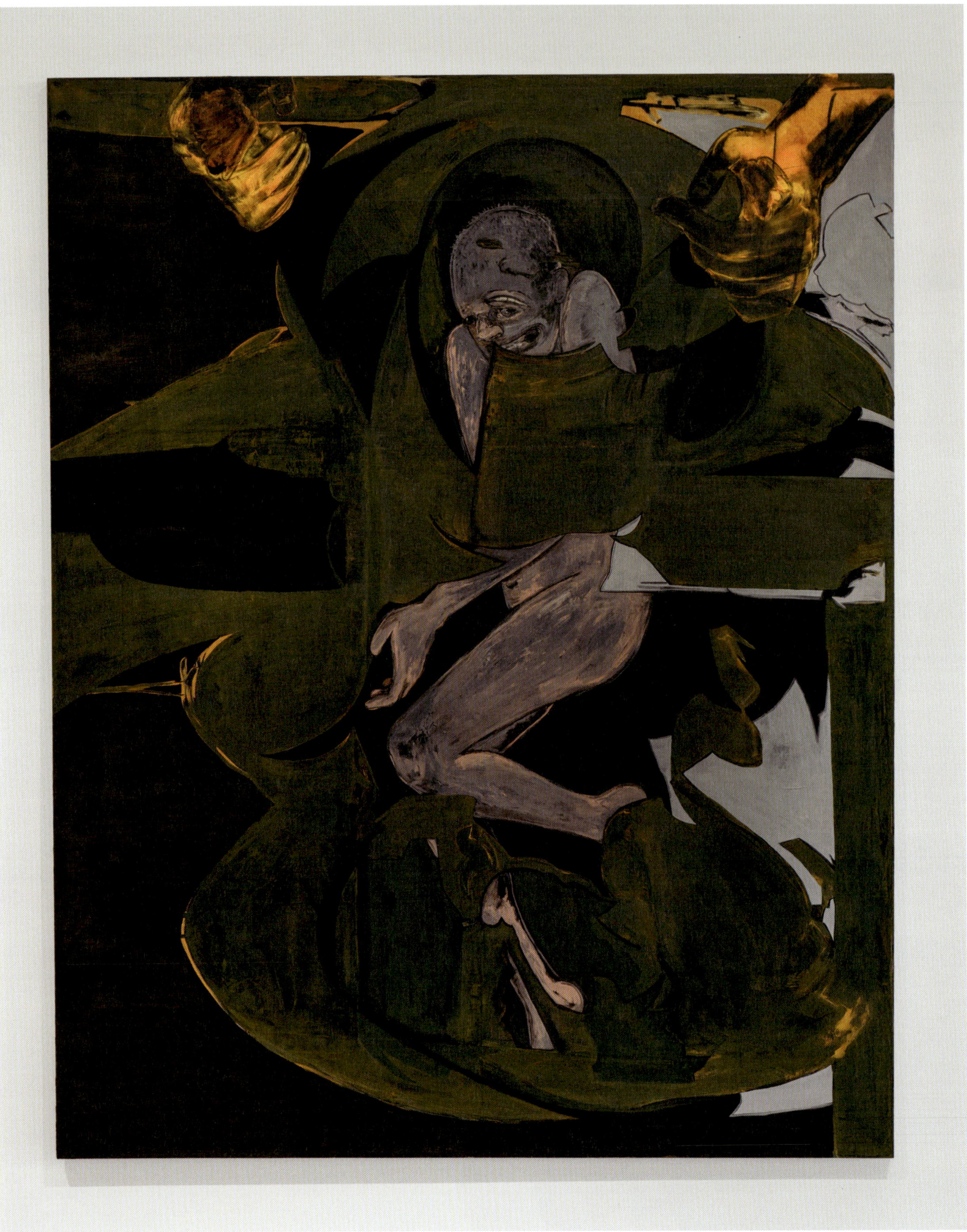

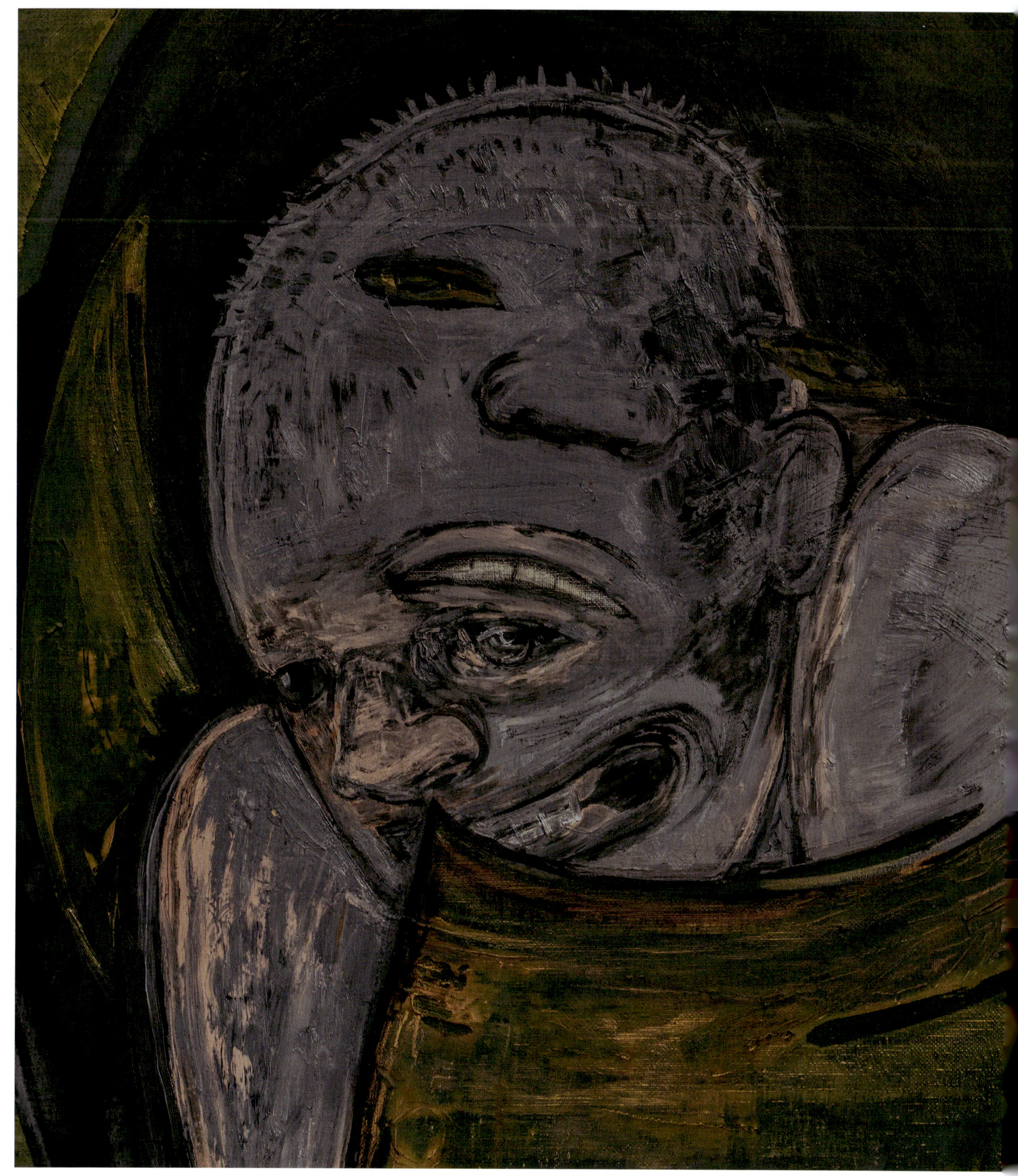

Hollow Provocation   2021   detail
Oil on canvas
77 × 96 in. (195.6 × 243.8 cm)

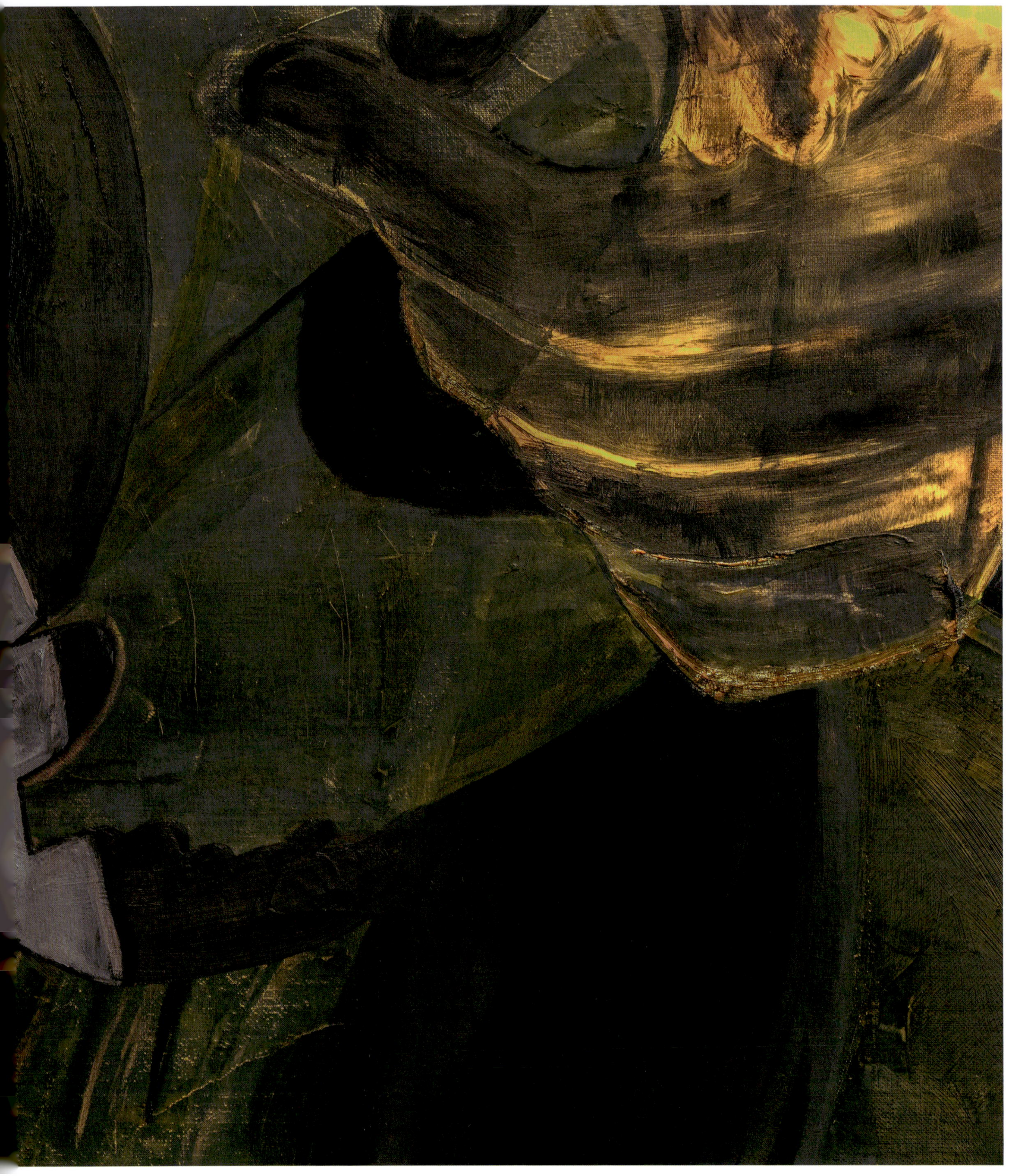

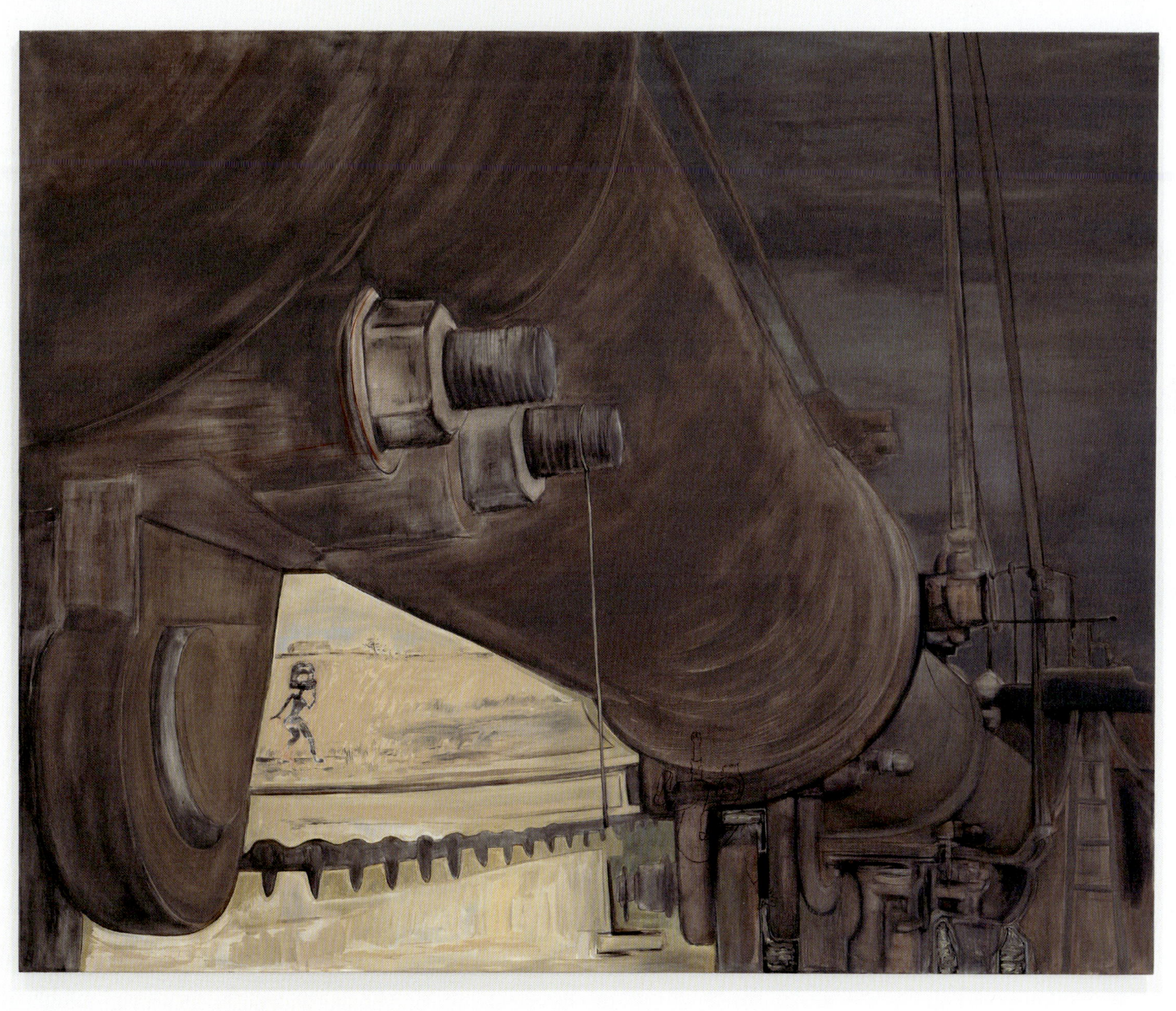

Lens Error 2021
Oil and pencil on canvas
77 × 96 in. (195.6 × 243.8 cm)

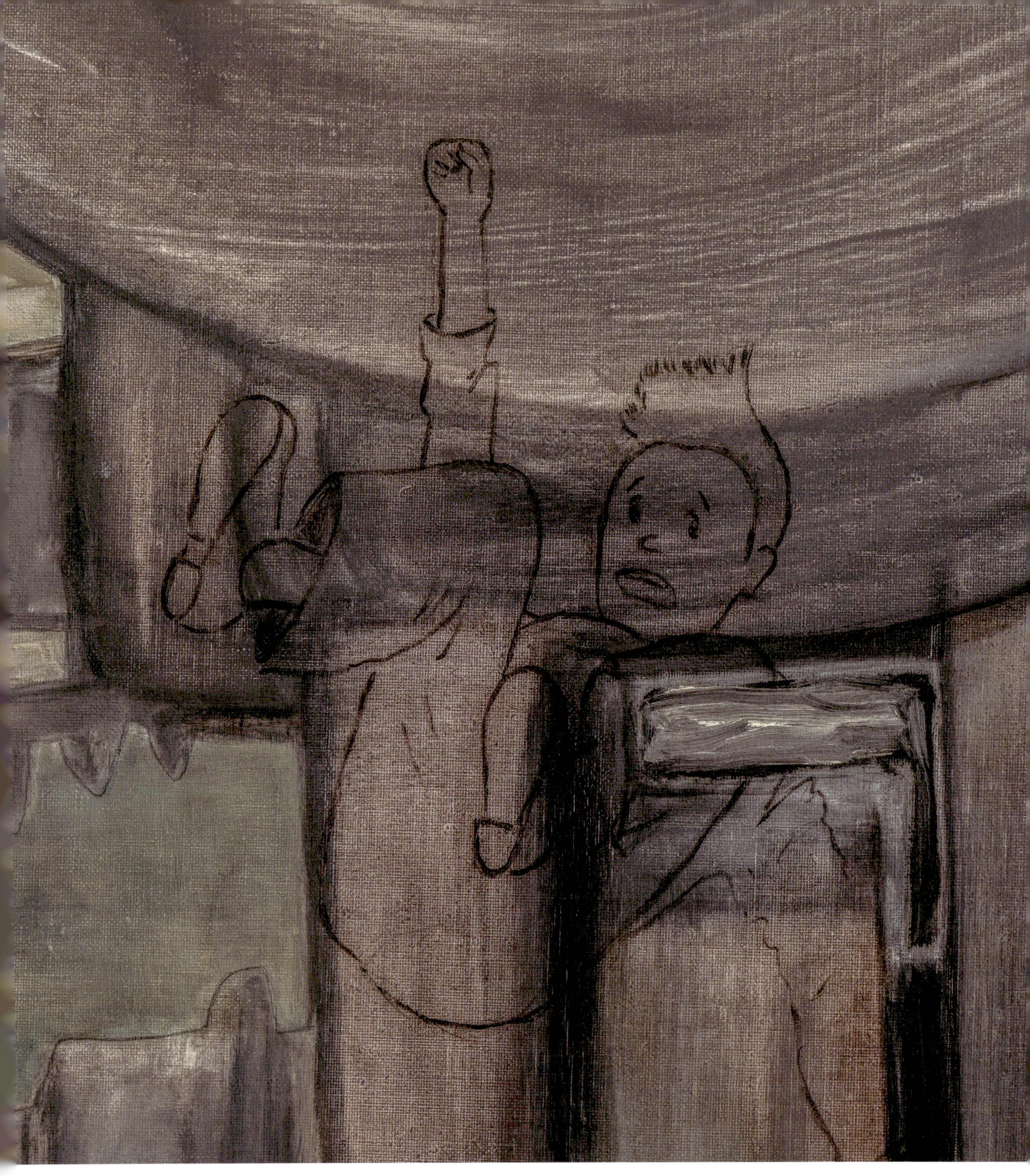

detail

From Whom the Bell Tolls   2021
Oil on canvas
96 × 77 in. (243.8 × 195.6 cm)

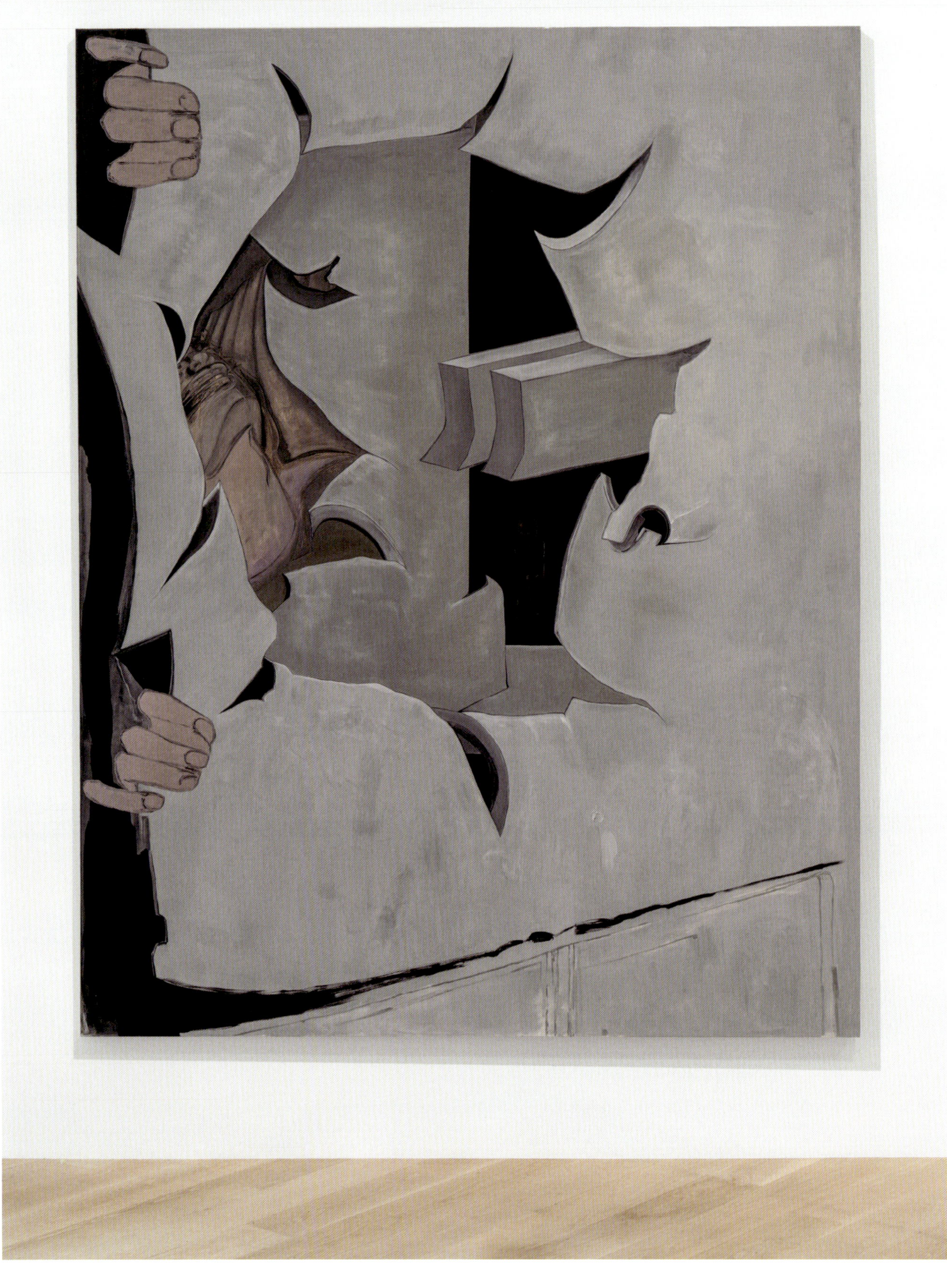

Pier in the Sphere   2021
Oil on canvas
60 × 80 in. (152.4 × 203.2 cm)

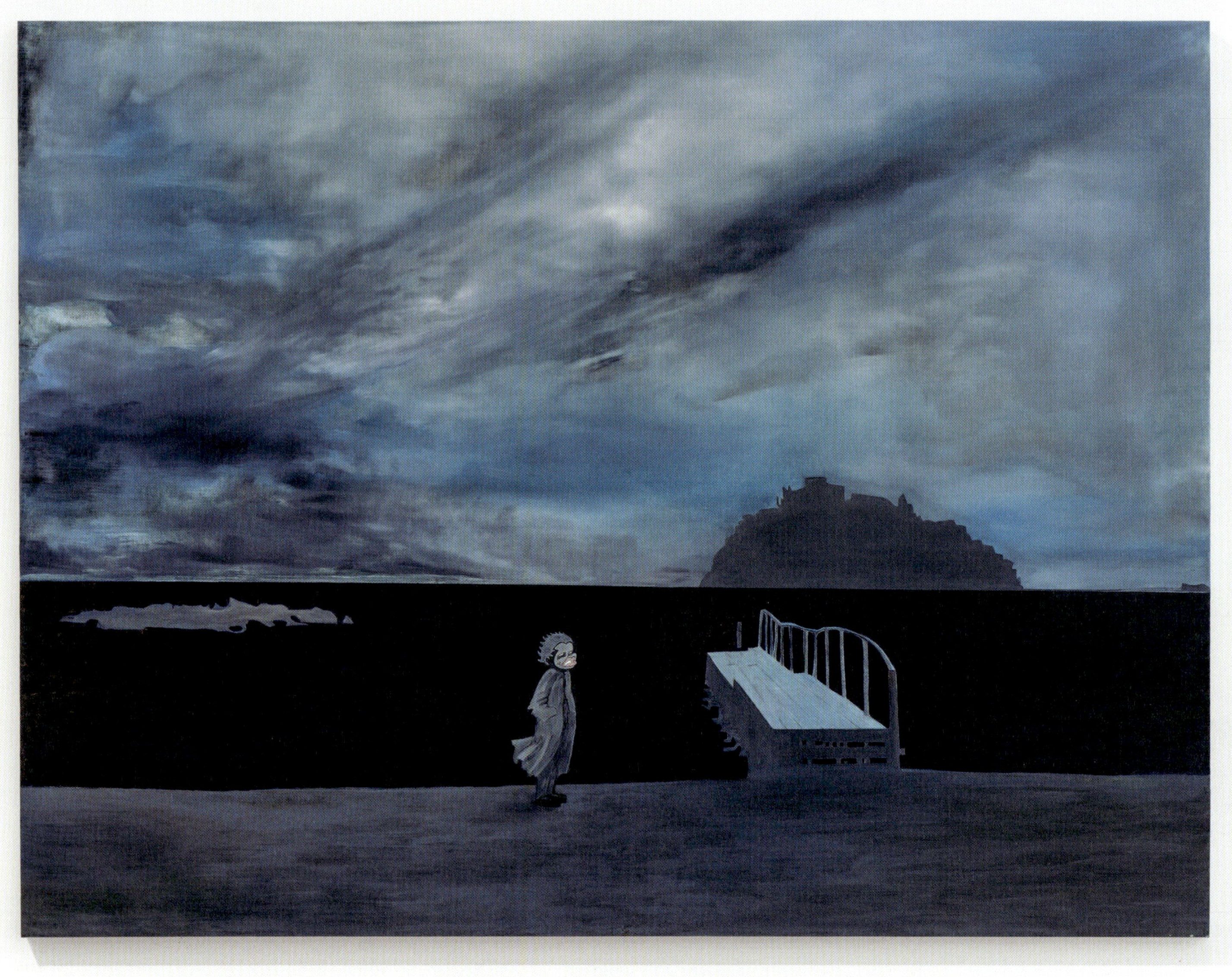

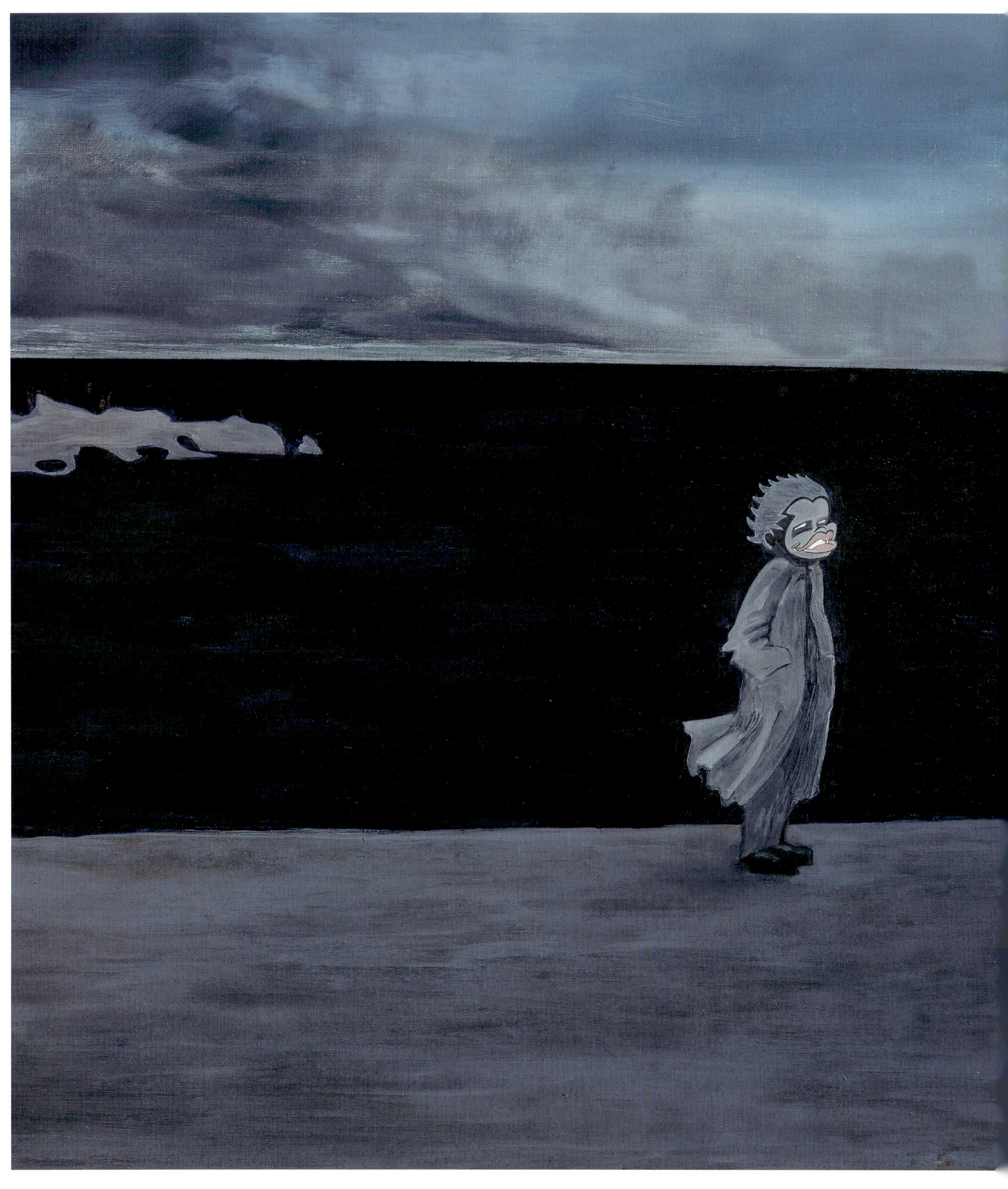

Pier in the Sphere 2021 detail
Oil on canvas
60 × 80 in. (152.4 × 203.2 cm)

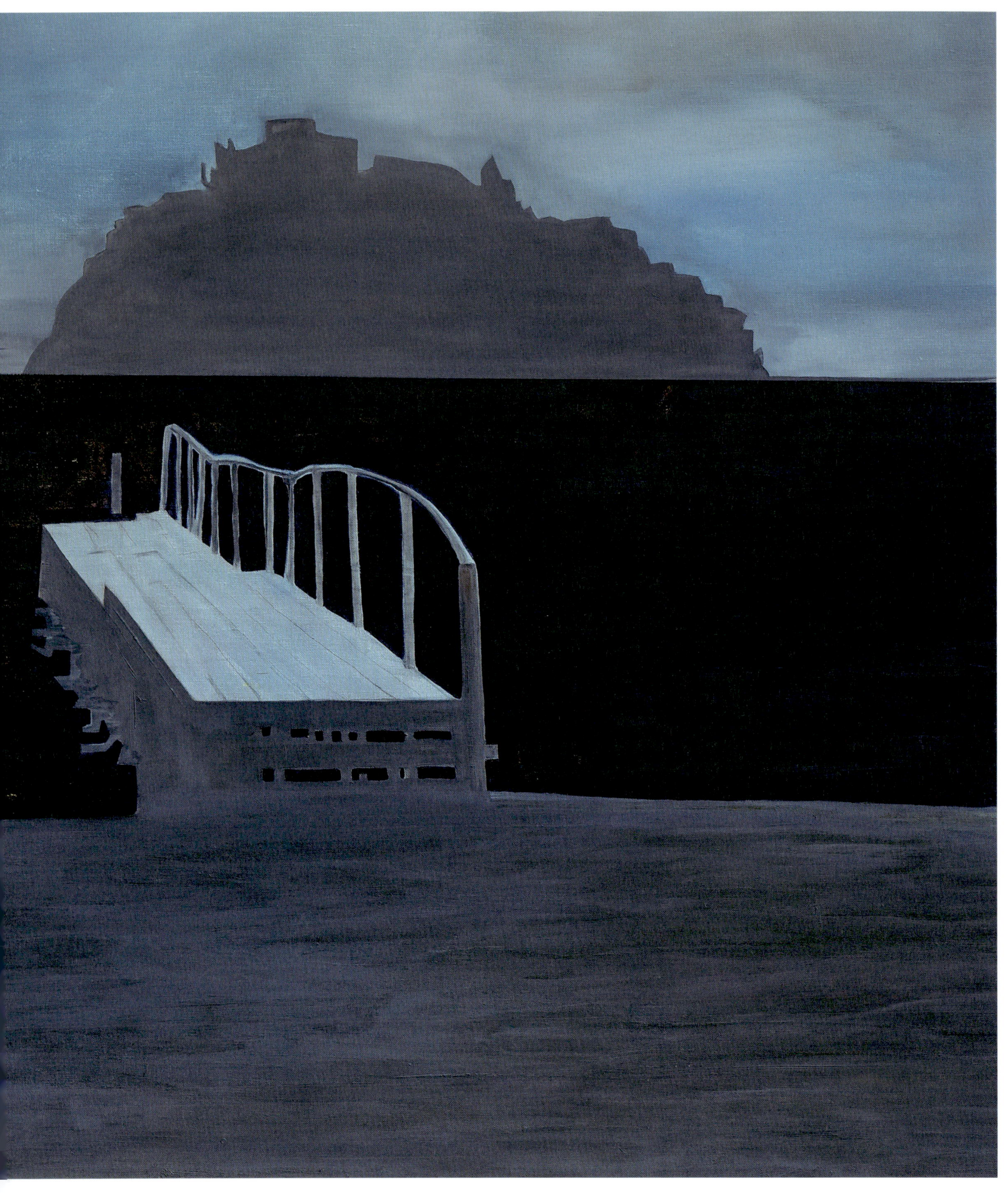

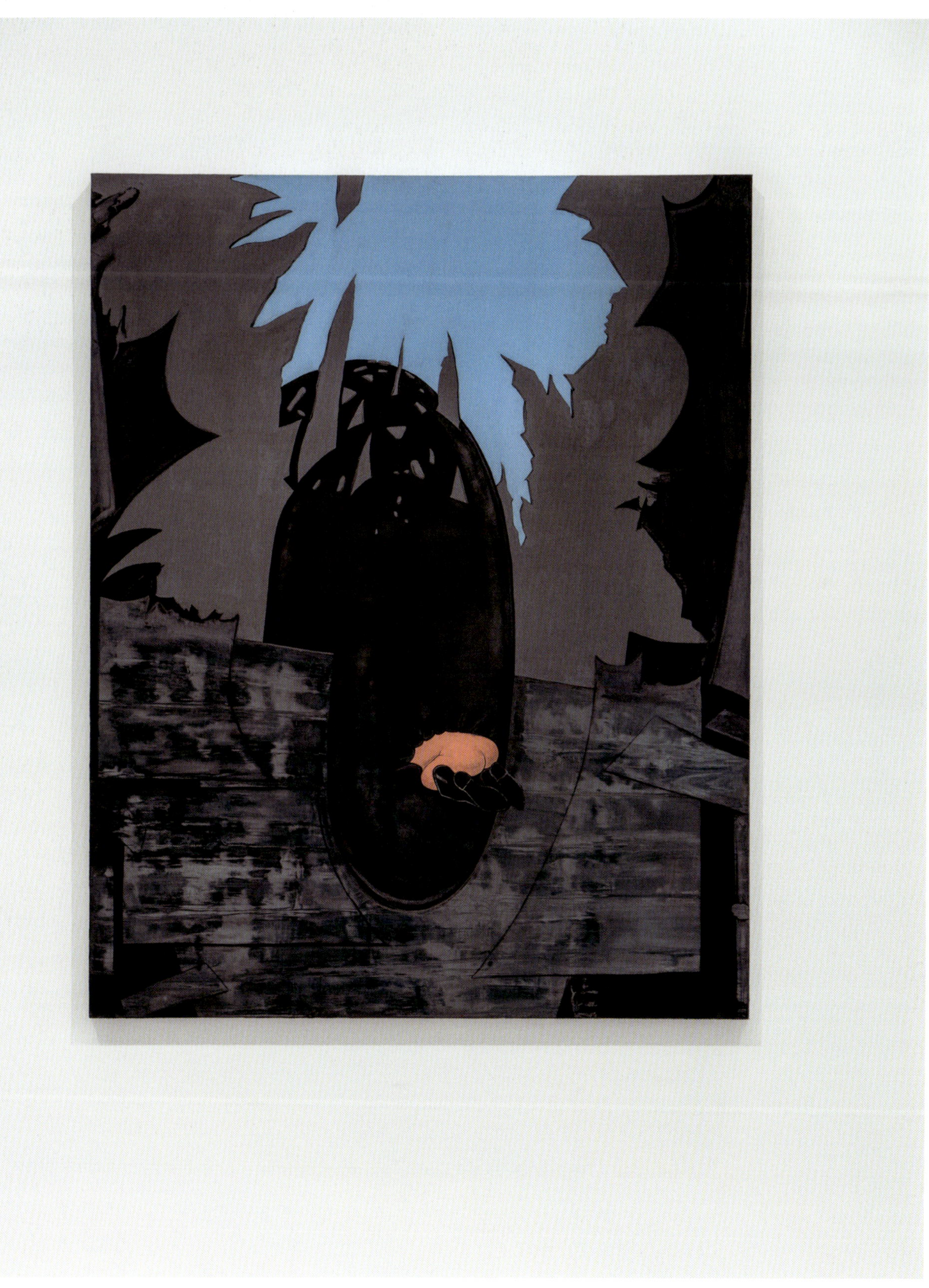

Nectar Troth   2021
Oil on canvas
48 × 60 in. (121.9 × 152.4 cm)

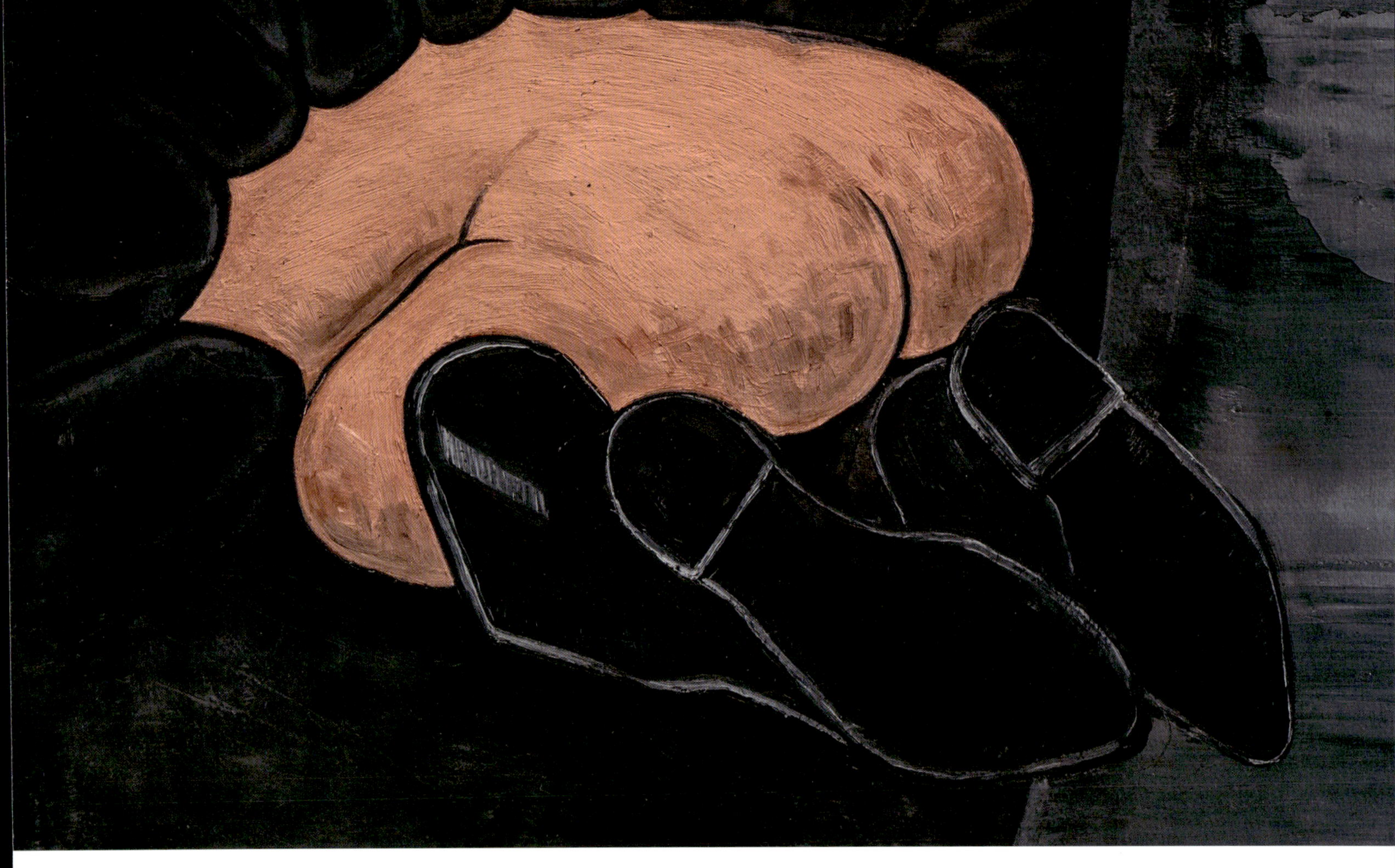

detail

Plaguing in my Face 2021
Oil and pencil on canvas
60 × 48 in. (152.4 × 121.9 cm)

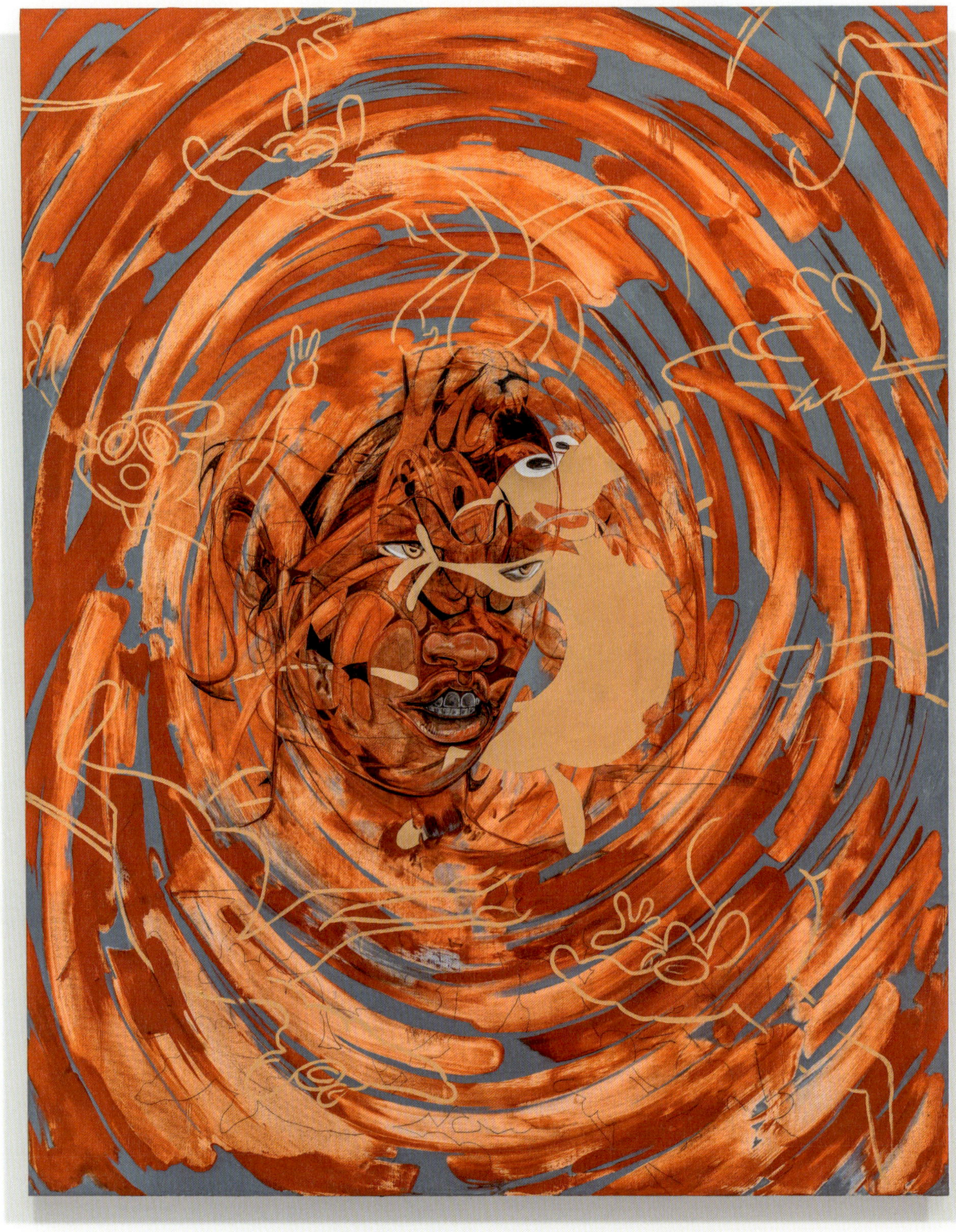

Vacant Faith   2020
Oil on canvas
60 × 48 in. (152.4 × 121.9 cm)

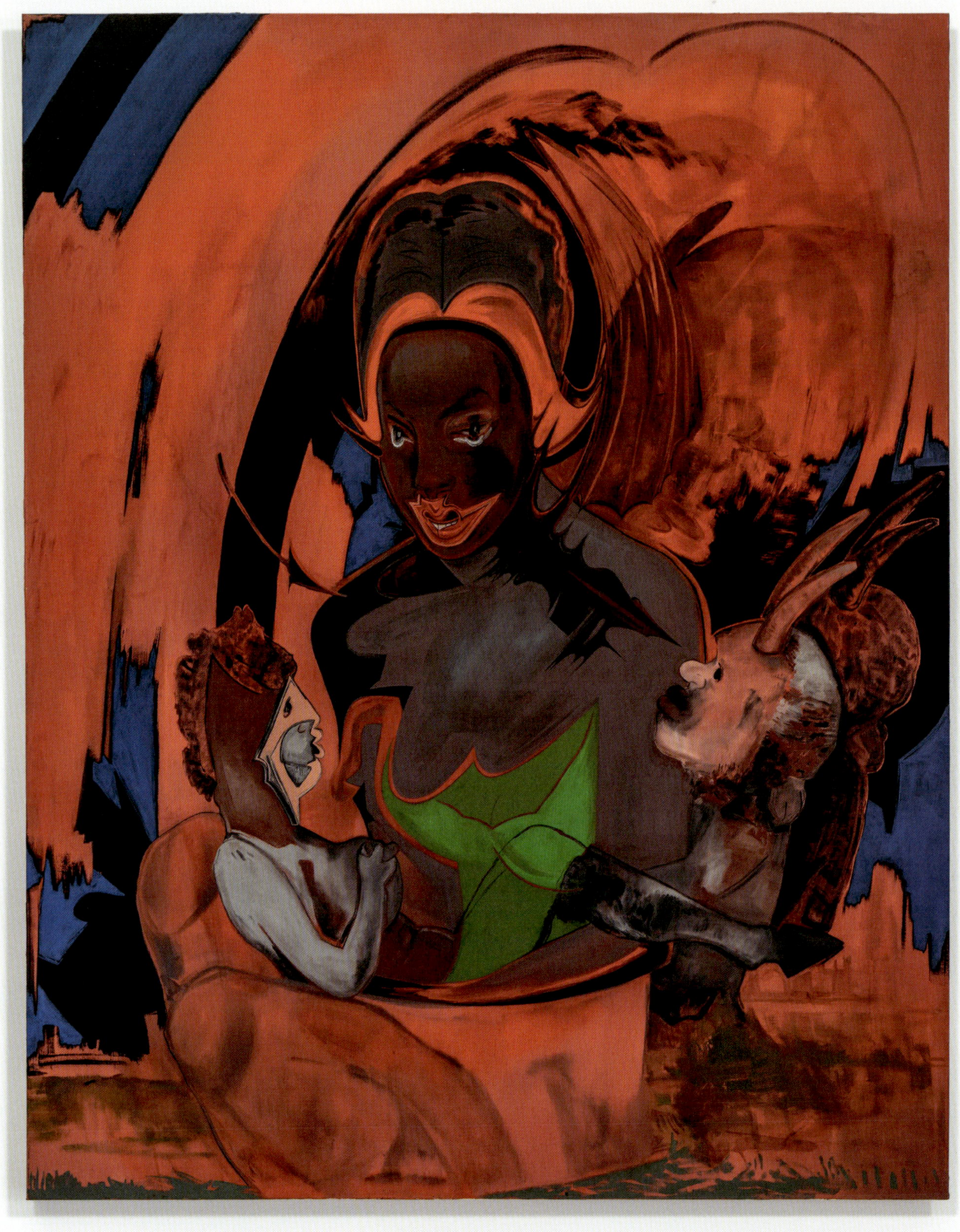

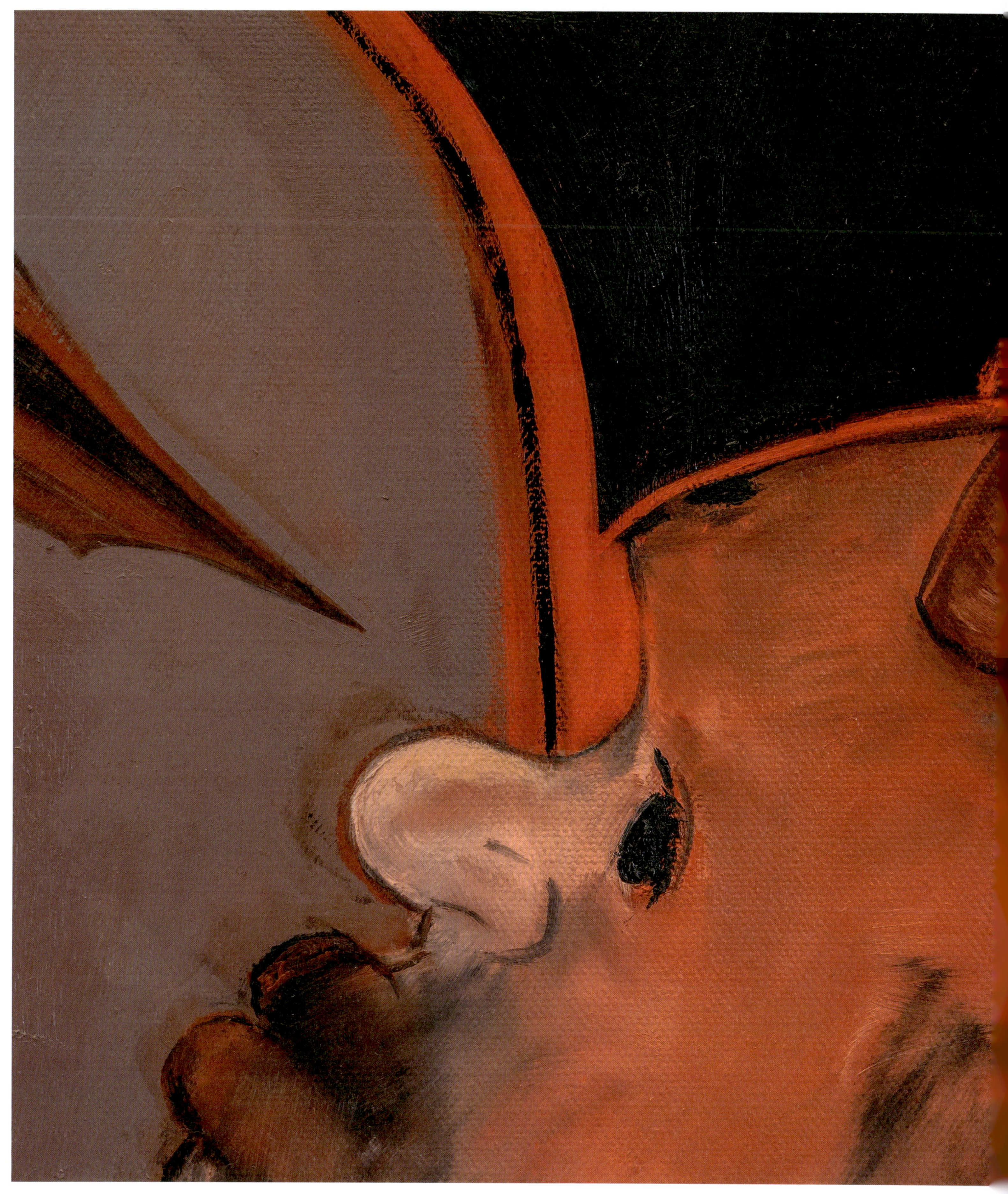

Vacant Faith
Oil on canvas
60 × 48 in. (152.4 × 121.9 cm)

2020

detail

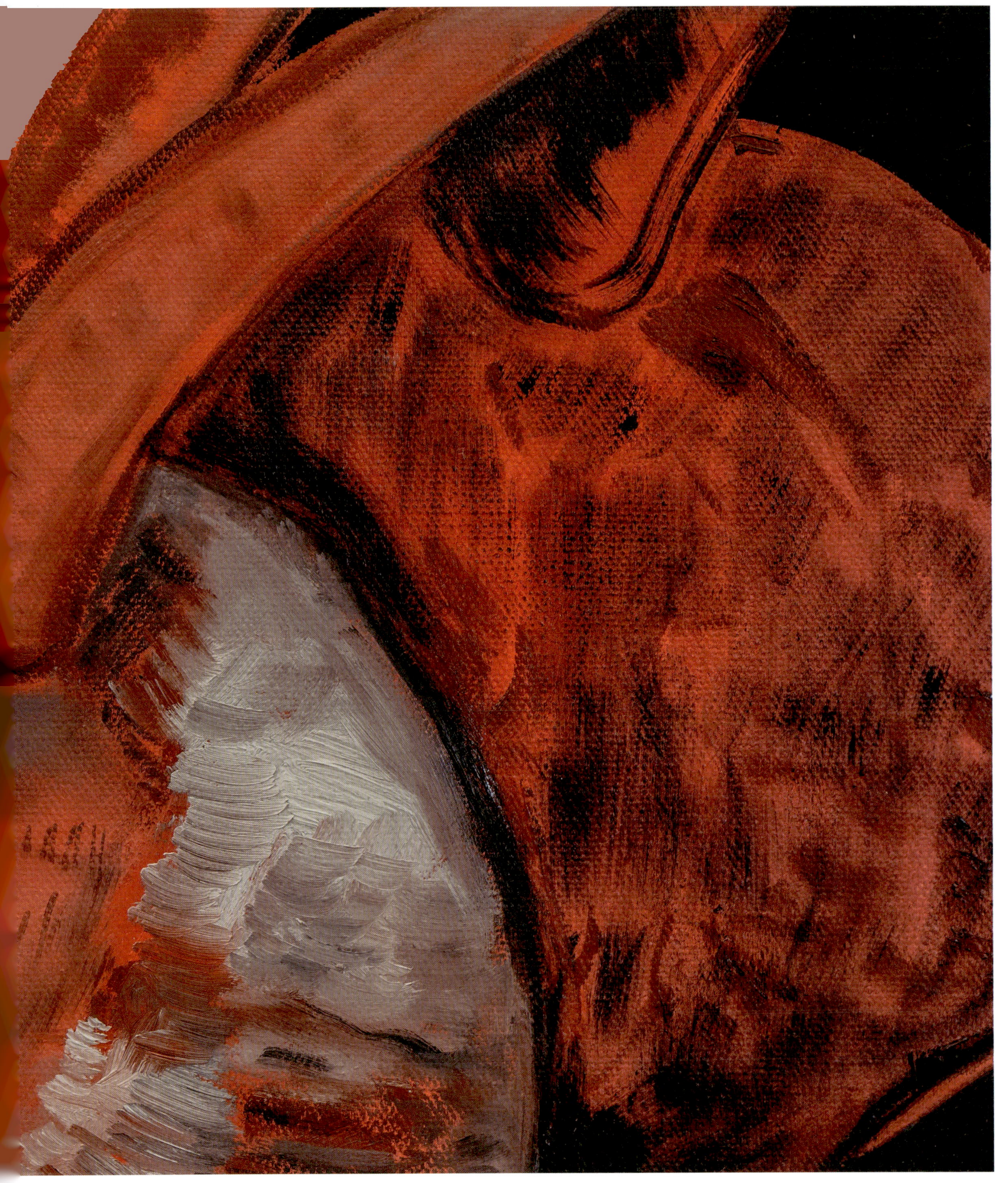

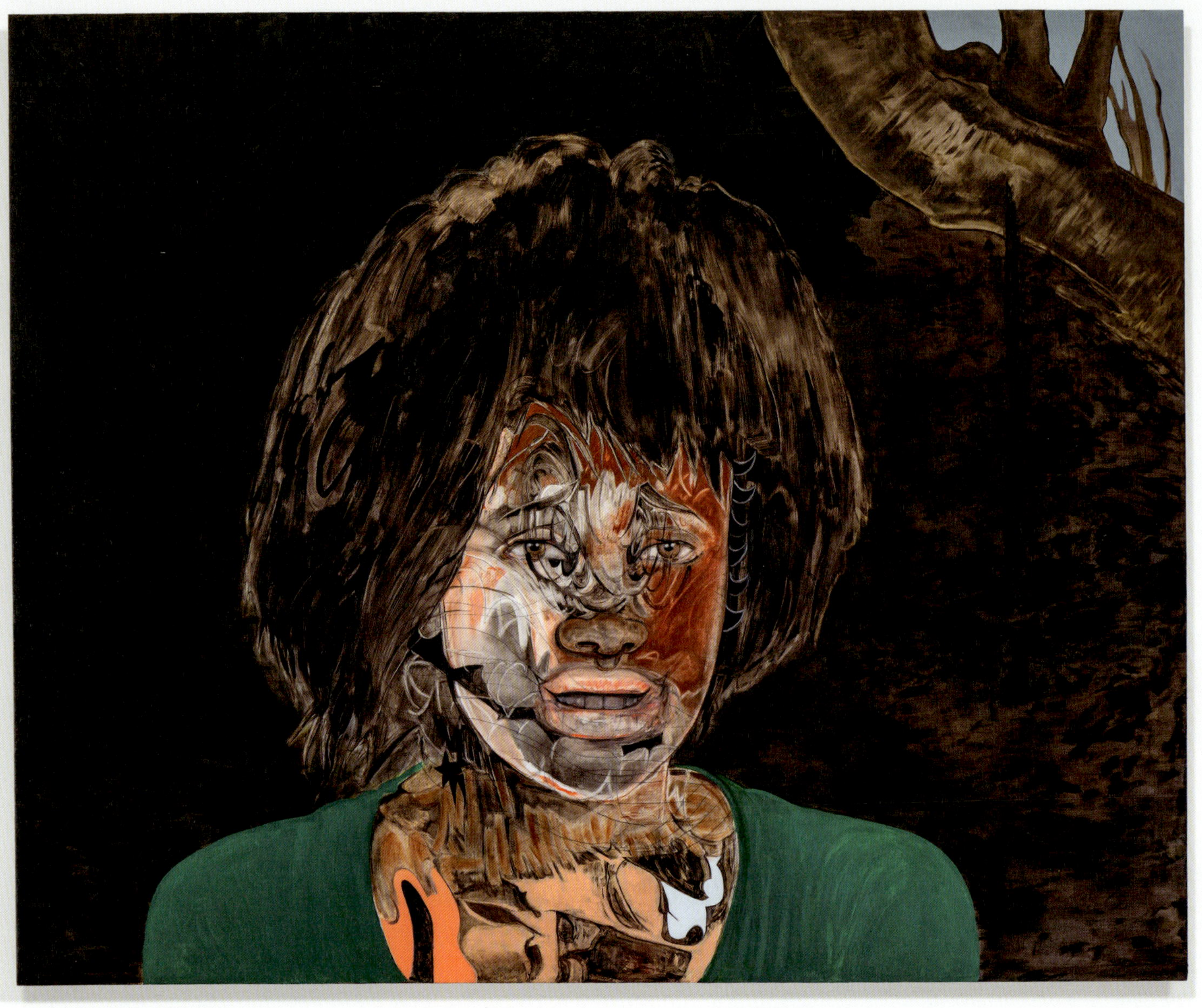

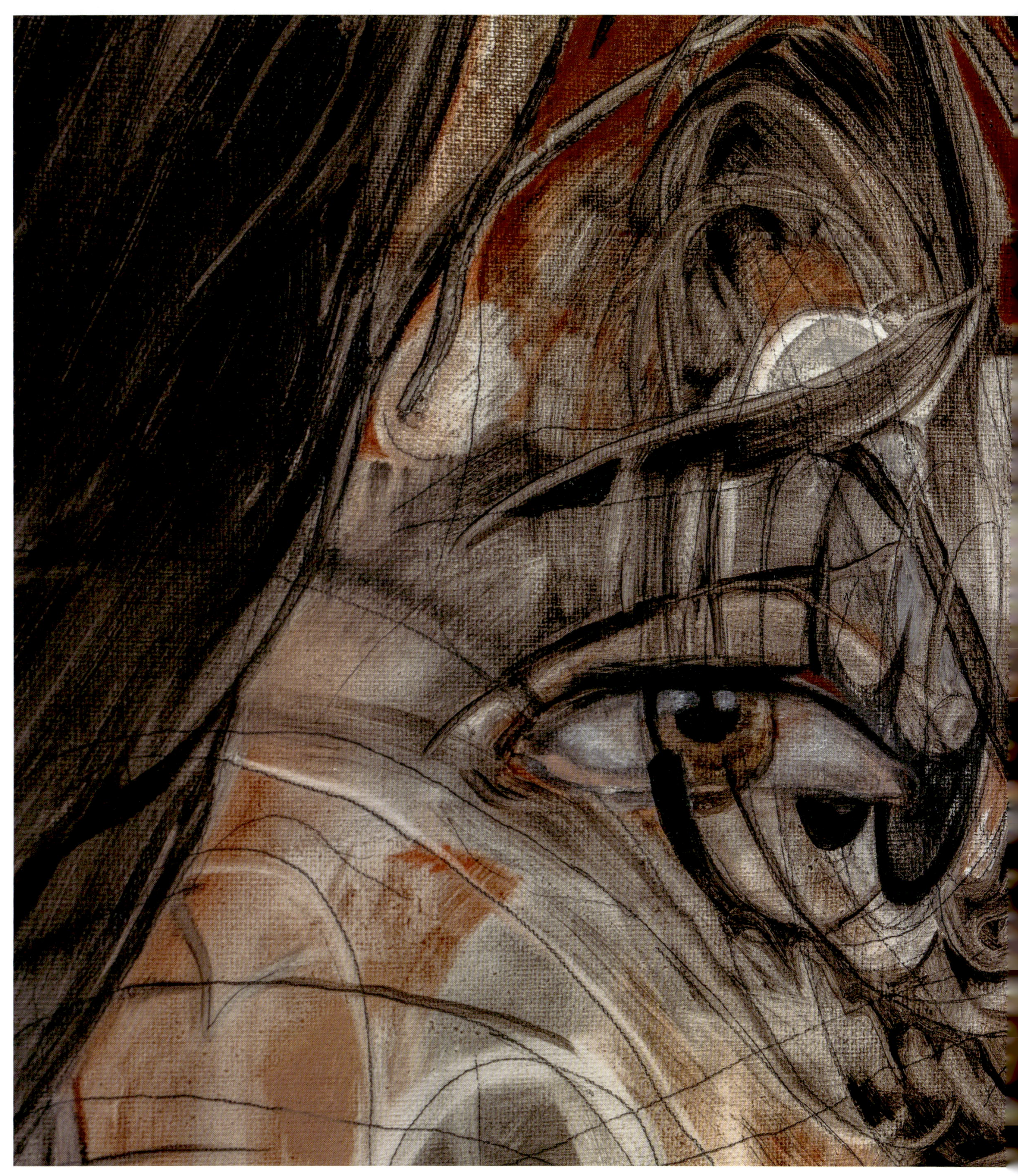

Lemon Squeezy   2021   detail
Oil and pencil on canvas
48 × 60 in. (121.9 × 152.4 cm)

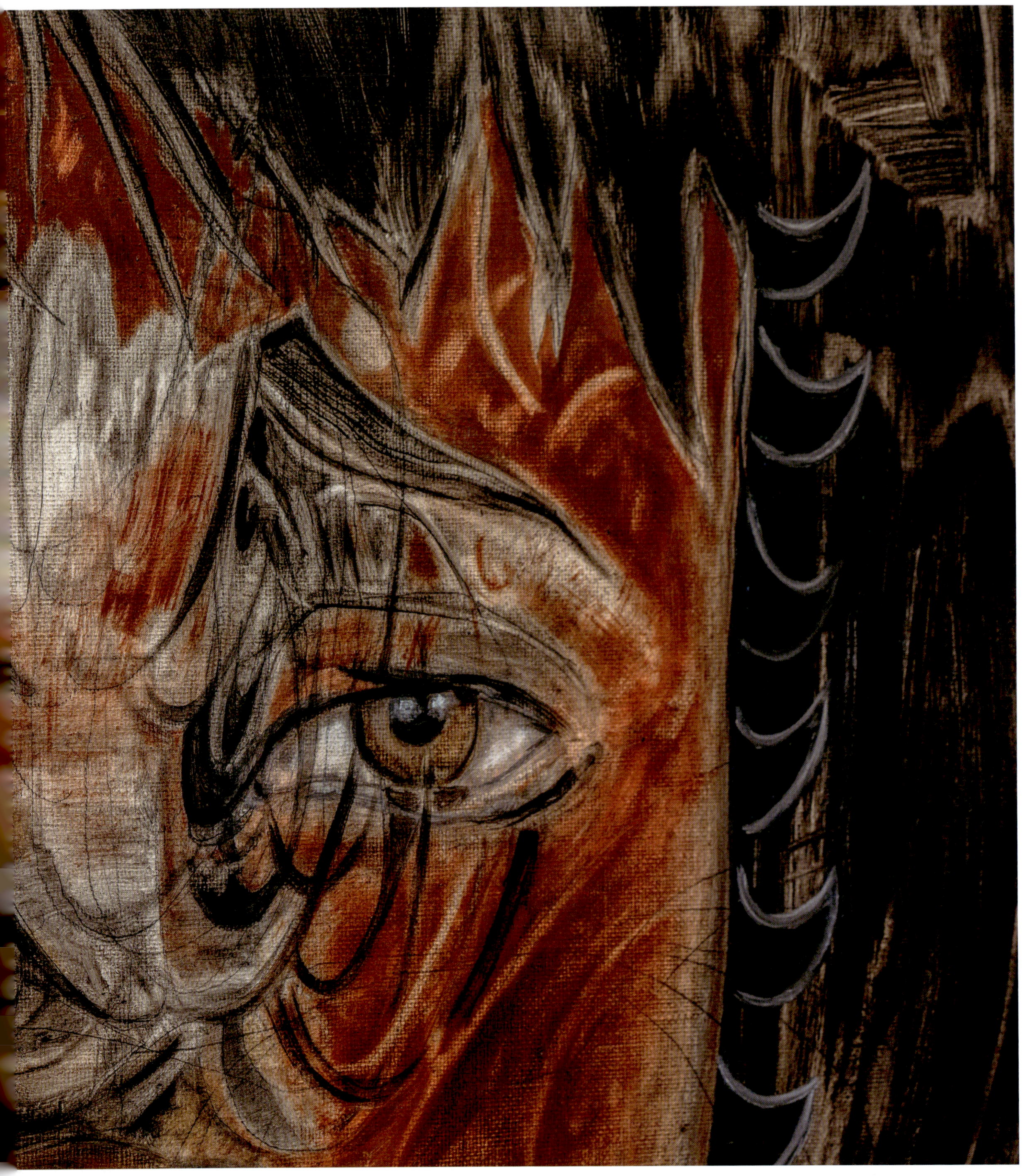

Something in the Way 2019
Oil and pencil on canvas
14 × 18 in. (35.6 × 45.7 cm)

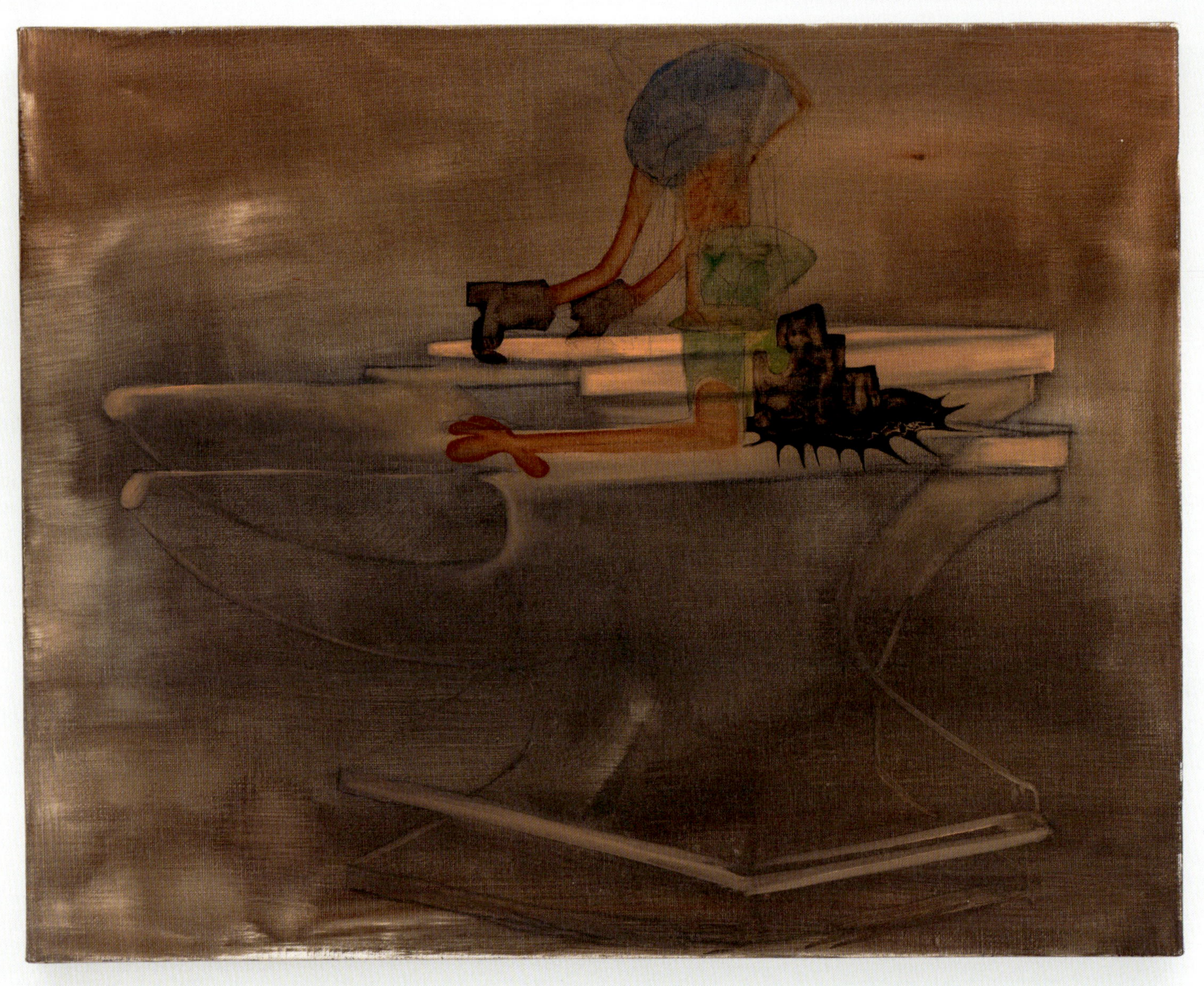

List of Works

pp. 12–13
Scambient Pet 2017
Oil on canvas
70 × 40 in. (177.8 × 101.6 cm)

pp. 14–15
Something Anxiety 2017
Oil on panel
60 × 60 in. (152.4 × 152.4 cm)

pp. 16–17
Open Pour Reality 2017
Oil on canvas
35 ½ × 35 ½ in. (90.2 × 90.2 cm)

pp. 18–19
Co-Panic.ing 2017
Oil on canvas
30 × 22 ½ in. (76.2 × 57.2 cm)

pp. 20–21
*Memorializing My
Industry In Sculpture* 2017
Oil on canvas
47 ½ × 34 ½ in. (120.7 × 87.6 cm)

pp. 22–23
Hi-ho The Derry-o 2017
Oil on canvas
27 ½ × 24 in. (69.9 × 61 cm)

p. 24
Duck Duck Deuce 2017
Oil on canvas
23 × 19 in. (58.4 × 48.3 cm)

p. 25
Runk'd 2017
Oil on canvas
14 ½ × 10 in. (36.8 × 25.4 cm)

pp. 26–27
Fire Walk With Me 2 2017
Oil on canvas
12 × 9 in. (30.5 × 22.9 cm)

p. 28
Abrandoment 2017
Oil on canvas
11 ½ × 8 in. (29.2 × 20.3 cm)

pp. 29–31
Bloodlust Halo 2017
Oil on canvas
40 × 30 in. (101.6 × 76.2 cm)

pp. 32–33
The Okiest Doke 2017
Oil on canvas
40 × 30 in. (101.6 × 76.2 cm)

p. 34
Gaze Cage 2017
Oil on canvas
24 × 24 in. (61 × 61 cm)

p. 35
*Cotton Eyed Misery
Business* 2017
Oil on canvas
36 × 24 in. (91.4 × 61 cm)

pp. 36–37
Doubt Guardian 2 2017
Oil on canvas
60 × 48 in. (152.4 × 121.9 cm)

pp. 38–39
Thrill Issues 2017
Oil on canvas
95 × 77 in. (241.3 × 195.6 cm)

pp. 40–41
*Curb Check Regular,
Black Chick* 2018
Oil on canvas
70 × 76 in. (177.8 × 193 cm)

pp. 42–43
Keebler's Revenge 2018
Oil on canvas
40 × 48 in. (101.6 × 121.9 cm)

pp. 44–45
Doubt Guardian 2018
Oil on canvas
48 × 48 in. (121.9 × 121.9 cm)

pp. 46–47
Thumper Tantrum 2018
Oil on canvas
20 × 16 in. (50.8 × 40.6 cm)

pp. 48–49
Bimini Boop Bullaby 2018
Oil on canvas
30 × 24 in. (76.2 × 61 cm)

pp. 50–55
A Devotion Deficit 2018
Oil on canvas
72 × 48 in. (182.9 × 121.9 cm)

pp. 56–57
Bramble's Briar Patch 2018
Oil on canvas
40 × 30 in. (101.6 × 76.2 cm)

pp. 58–63
*Full-Fledged Safari
Syndrome* 2018
Oil on canvas
48 × 59 ½ in. (121.9 × 151.1 cm)

pp. 64–65
Playful But Bites 2018
Oil on canvas
20 × 16 in. (50.8 × 40.6 cm)

pp. 66–67
Scripture for the Enemy 2018
Oil on canvas
48 × 36 in. (121.9 × 91.4 cm)

pp. 68–71
*Rube Boy Leisure
Obstacle* 2018
Oil on canvas
36 × 42 in. (91.4 × 106.7 cm)

pp. 72–73
Prescribed Ambush 2018
Oil on canvas
42 × 36 in. (106.7 × 91.4 cm)
Institute of Contemporary
Art, Miami. Museum
purchase with funds from
the Simkins Family

p. 74
None of Our Dreams 2018
Are Pipe
Oil on canvas
36 × 30 in. (91.4 × 76.2 cm)

p. 75
Thought Iron Frontier 2018
Oil on canvas
46 × 40 in. (116.8 × 101.6 cm)

pp. 76–77
Fire Walk with Me 2018
Oil on canvas
23 × 35 in. (58.4 × 88.9 cm)

pp. 86–87
Catchphrase Coping 2019
Mechanism
Oil on linen
86 × 70 in. (218.4 × 177.8 cm)

pp. 88–89
Dashland Updrown 2019
Oil on linen
98 × 80 ½ in. (248.9 × 204.5 cm)

pp. 90–91
Uh Oh, Look Who 2019
Got Wet
Oil on canvas
108 ¼ × 240 in. (275 × 609.6 cm)
Whitney Museum of
American Art, New York.
Museum purchase, with
funds from the Director's
Discretionary Fund and
anonymous donors

pp. 92–95
Almighty Tip Drill 2019
Oil on linen
96 × 70 in. (243.8 × 177.8 cm)

p. 96
Stopgap Skank 2019
Oil on linen
96 × 70 in. (243.8 × 177.8 cm)

pp. 97–99
Shudder Home 2019
Refuge
Oil on linen
80 × 98 in. (203.2 × 248.9 cm)

pp. 100–03
Boys Cottages 2019
Oil on linen
70 × 76 in. (177.8 × 193 cm)

pp. 104–07
Yup Genie 2019
Oil on linen
70 × 76 in. (177.8 × 193 cm)

pp. 108–11
Wokey Doke 2019
Oil on linen
60 × 48 in. (152.4 × 121.9 cm)

pp. 112–13
Yard Snacks 2019
Oil on linen
11 × 14 in. (27.9 × 35.6 cm)

pp. 114–15
Poof 2019
Oil on linen
16 × 12 in. (40.6 × 30.5 cm)

p. 116
Fake Ape 2019
Oil on linen
16 × 12 in. (40.6 × 30.5 cm)

p. 117
Puppy Niece 2019
Oil on linen
18 × 14 in. (45.7 × 35.6 cm)

pp. 118–21
Taper Jean Girl 2019
Oil on linen
52 × 52 in. (132.1 × 132.1 cm)

pp. 122–23
Stop Keep 2020
Oil on canvas
40 × 30 in. (101.6 × 76.2 cm)

pp. 124–25
Fugue Pace 2020
Oil on canvas
48 × 36 in. (121.9 × 91.4 cm)

pp. 140–43
Bloodlust Halo 2021
Oil on canvas
77 × 96 in. (195.6 × 243.8 cm)

pp. 144–45
The Alleyest Oop 2021
Oil on canvas
96 × 77 in. (243.8 × 195.6 cm)

pp. 146–47
Bull Squall Bingo 2020
Oil on canvas
60 × 48 in. (152.4 × 121.9 cm)

pp. 148–51
Hollow Provocation 2021
Oil on canvas
77 × 96 in. (195.6 × 243.8 cm)

pp. 152–53
Lens Error 2021
Oil and pencil on canvas
77 × 96 in. (195.6 × 243.8 cm)

pp. 154–55
From Whom the 2021
Bell Tolls
Oil on canvas
96 × 77 in. (243.8 × 195.6 cm)

pp. 156–59
Pier in the Sphere 2021
Oil on canvas
60 × 80 in. (152.4 × 203.2 cm)

pp. 160–61
Nectar Troth 2021
Oil on canvas
48 × 60 in. (121.9 × 152.4 cm)

pp. 162–63
Plaguing in my Face 2021
Oil and pencil on canvas
60 × 48 in. (152.4 × 121.9 cm)

pp. 164–67
Vacant Faith 2020
Oil on canvas
60 × 48 in. (152.4 × 121.9 cm)

pp. 168–71
Lemon Squeezy 2021
Oil and pencil on canvas
48 × 60 in. (121.9 × 152.4 cm)

pp. 172–73
Something in the Way 2021
Oil and pencil on canvas
14 × 18 in. (35.6 × 45.7 cm)

Contributors

Jessica Bell Brown is the Associate Curator for Contemporary Art at the Baltimore Museum of Art. Brown previously held roles at Gracie Mansion Conservancy, New York; Creative Time, New York; Brooklyn Academy of Music; and the Museum of Modern Art, New York. A Ph.D. candidate in modern and contemporary art at Princeton University, her writing has appeared in various publications including *Flash Art*, *Artforum*, *Art Papers*, and the *Brooklyn Rail*.

Olivia K. Young, Ph.D., is an interdisciplinary scholar of African diaspora studies whose interests are contemporary art, visual culture, Black cultural history, queer theory, Black feminisms, performance studies, and disability studies. Young is an Assistant Professor of African Diasporic Art in the Department of Art History and the Center of African and African American Studies (CAAAS) at Rice University, Houston. Young is a graduate of the Department of African Diaspora Studies at the University of California, Berkeley, with a designated emphasis in women, gender, and sexuality. In 2020–21, Young was a University of California President's Postdoctoral Fellow in the Department of African American Studies at the University of California, Los Angeles, and in 2019–20 they were a Patricia and Phillip Frost Predoctoral Fellow at the Smithsonian American Art Museum.

Staff

Executive
Alex Gartenfeld
    Artistic Director
Juan Ledesma
    Executive Assistant

Administrative
Julie Fliegenspan
    Operations Manager
Allison Matherly
    Finance Coordinator

Curatorial
Gean Moreno
    Director
    Knight Foundation Art +
    Research Center
Stephanie Seidel
    Curator
Amanda Morgan
    Assistant Curator
    Exhibitions and Publications
Donna Honarpisheh
    Assistant Curator
    Knight Foundation Art +
    Research Center
Nathalie Chybik
    Research Assistant
Asia Perrotti
    Research Assistant

Development
Paula Campolieto
    Senior Development
    Manager
Kali Kahn
    Development Officer
    Institutional and Corporate
    Giving
Sophia Neitsch
    Membership Coordinator
Claire Karalla
    Development Assistant

Education
Lisa Fernandez
    Director of Education and
    Community Engagement
Alyssa Panganiban
    Education Programs
    Coordinator
Morel Doucet
    Curriculum and Tour
    Coordinator
Itzel Basualdo
    Youth Programs Coordinator
Logan Moises
    Accessibility Assistant
Jessica Helsinger
    Teaching Assistant

Exhibitions
Kerri Kneer
    Director of Exhibitions,
    Collections, and Visitor
    Experience
Isabella Rodriguez
    Assistant Registrar
Katherine Fleitman
    Exhibitions Assistant
Mikhail Yusufov
    Preparator

External Affairs
Courtney Casci
    Director of External Affairs
Andrew McLees
    Senior Marketing Manager
Diana Eusebio
    Marketing Assistant
    Press and Social Media
Anthony Anaya
    Graphic Designer
Daniela Granadillo
    Digital Producer

Facilities
Fabio Ortega
    Facility Manager
Kenia Gaitan
    Custodian

Production
Nicole Rodriguez
    Events Manager
Victor Princiotta
    Production Coordinator

Visitor Services
Bianca Cipriani
    Visitor Services Manager
Joshua Byrnes
    Assistant Visitor Services
    Manager
Sandra Vanegas
    Assistant Visitor Services
    Manager
Gianneli Canda
    Senior Gallery Associate

Visitor Services
Malú Anavitarte
Cyrus Blot
Samuel Cardona
Anika Huda
Raphael Jean
Amanda Marquez
Alexis Morales
Gabriel Morejon
Brianna Smith

Installation Team
O'Neil Bardin III
David Brieske
Merritt Cates
Dennis Fuller
Pebble Jaffe
Phillip Karp
Jason Morrison
Daniel A. Taveras
    Hernandez

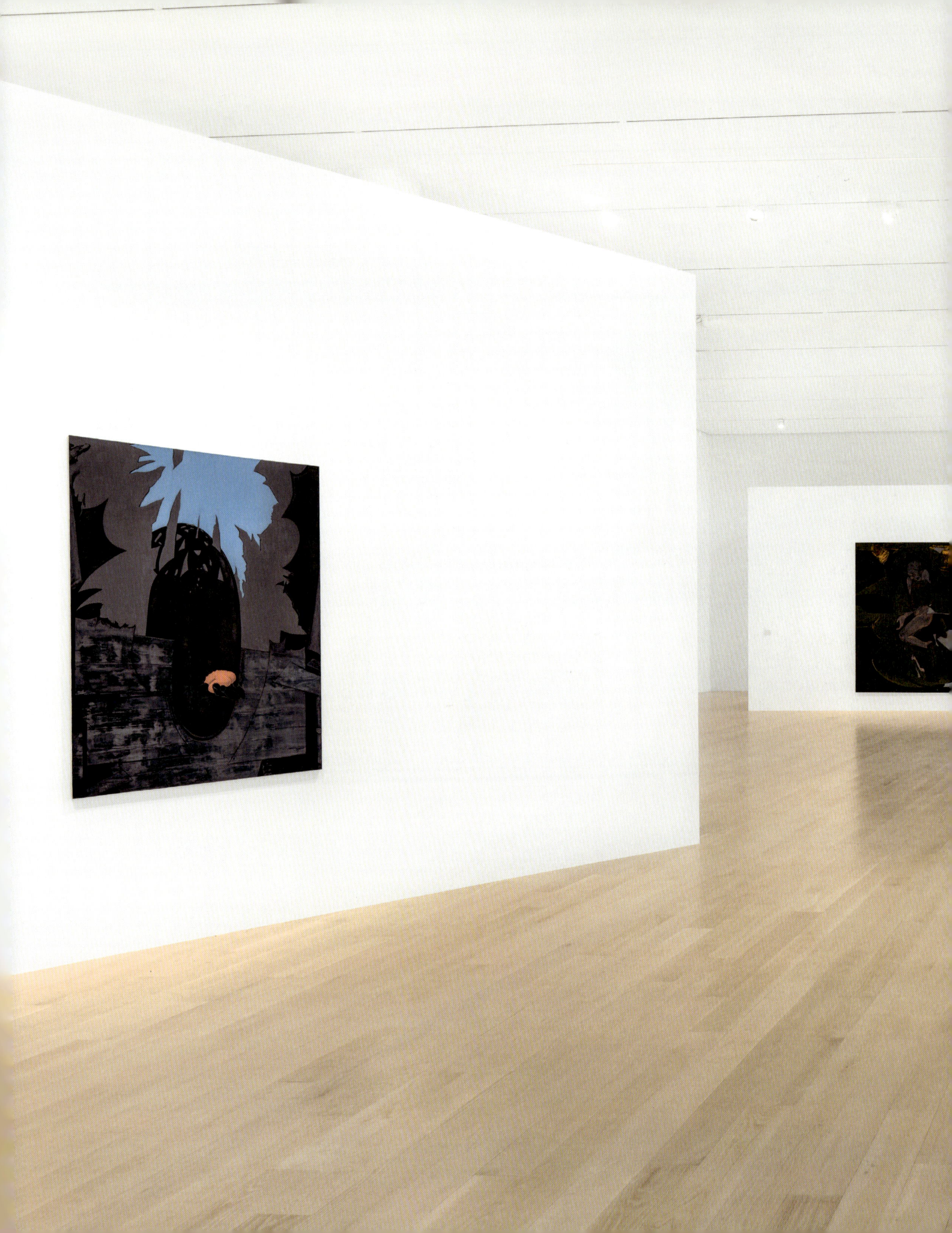

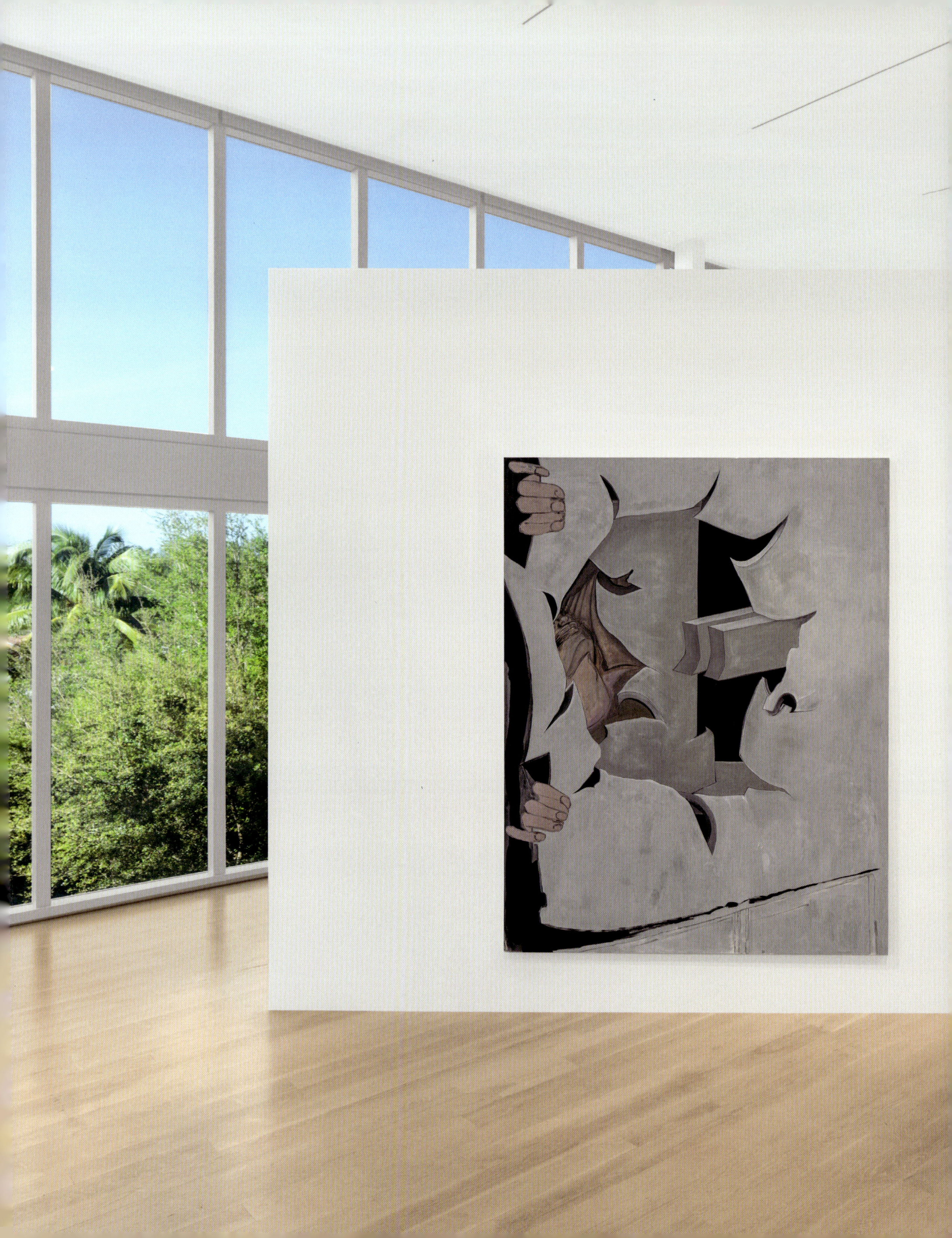

Published on the occasion of the exhibition "Janiva Ellis: Rats," organized by the Institute of Contemporary Art, Miami, February 25–September 12, 2021

Curated by Alex Gartenfeld, Artistic Director, and Stephanie Seidel, Curator

Published in 2022 by the Institute of Contemporary Art, Miami, and DelMonico Books • D.A.P.

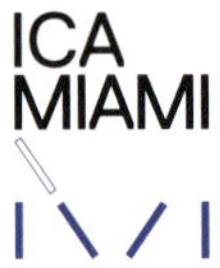

ICA
MIAMI

Institute of Contemporary Art, Miami
61 NE 41st Street
Miami, FL 33137
icamiami.org

DelMonico Books available through
ARTBOOK | D.A.P.
75 Broad Street, Suite 630
New York, NY 10004

artbook.com
delmonicobooks.com

Editors: Alex Gartenfeld and Stephanie Seidel
Publications assistant: Amanda Morgan
Copy editor: Kara Pickman, Pickman Editorial
Design: Eric Hu Studio
Production: die Keure
Printed in Belgium

Exhibitions at the Institute of Contemporary Art, Miami, are generously supported by the Knight Contemporary Art Fund at The Miami Foundation.

KF KNIGHT FOUNDATION

Additional support for "Janiva Ellis: Rats" is provided by Ray Ellen and Allan Yarkin; 47 Canal, New York; and the Miami Design District.

All artworks by Janiva Ellis © the artist.

Photo credits by page number:

Unless otherwise noted, all images: Photos: Zachary Balber; 13–28, 34–49, 73–74, 77, 87–89, 93–121: Photos: Joerg Lohse. Courtesy the artist and 47 Canal, New York; 29–31, 123–25: Photos: Jeff McLane. Courtesy the artist and 47 Canal, New York; 33: Photo: Ed Mumford. Courtesy the artist and 47 Canal, New York; 51–65, 69–71: Photos: Tim Bowditch. Courtesy the artist and 47 Canal, New York; 67: Photo: Sean Logue. Courtesy the artist and 47 Canal, New York; 75: Photo: Dawn Blackman. Courtesy the artist and 47 Canal, New York; 90–91: Photo: Ron Amstutz. Courtesy the artist; 47 Canal, New York; and the Whitney Museum of American Art, New York

Library of Congress Control Number: 2021950381

ISBN: 978-1-63681-026-3

Acknowledgments
Daphna Bentata, Jamie Kenyon, Margaret Lee, Oliver Newton, Ed Nicoll, David Simkins, Ray Ellen Yarkin

We are thankful to Jessica Bell Brown and Olivia K. Young for their enlightening contributions and to Eric Hu for his engaging design. Janiva Ellis would like to thank Kelela Mizanekristos, Adee Roberson, Junglepussy, Carolyn Lazard, Ezili Jean Williamceau, Gaby Thompson, Ade J. Omotosho, Kandis Williams, and Sonya Renee Taylor, whose insights supported her and her thinking for this show.

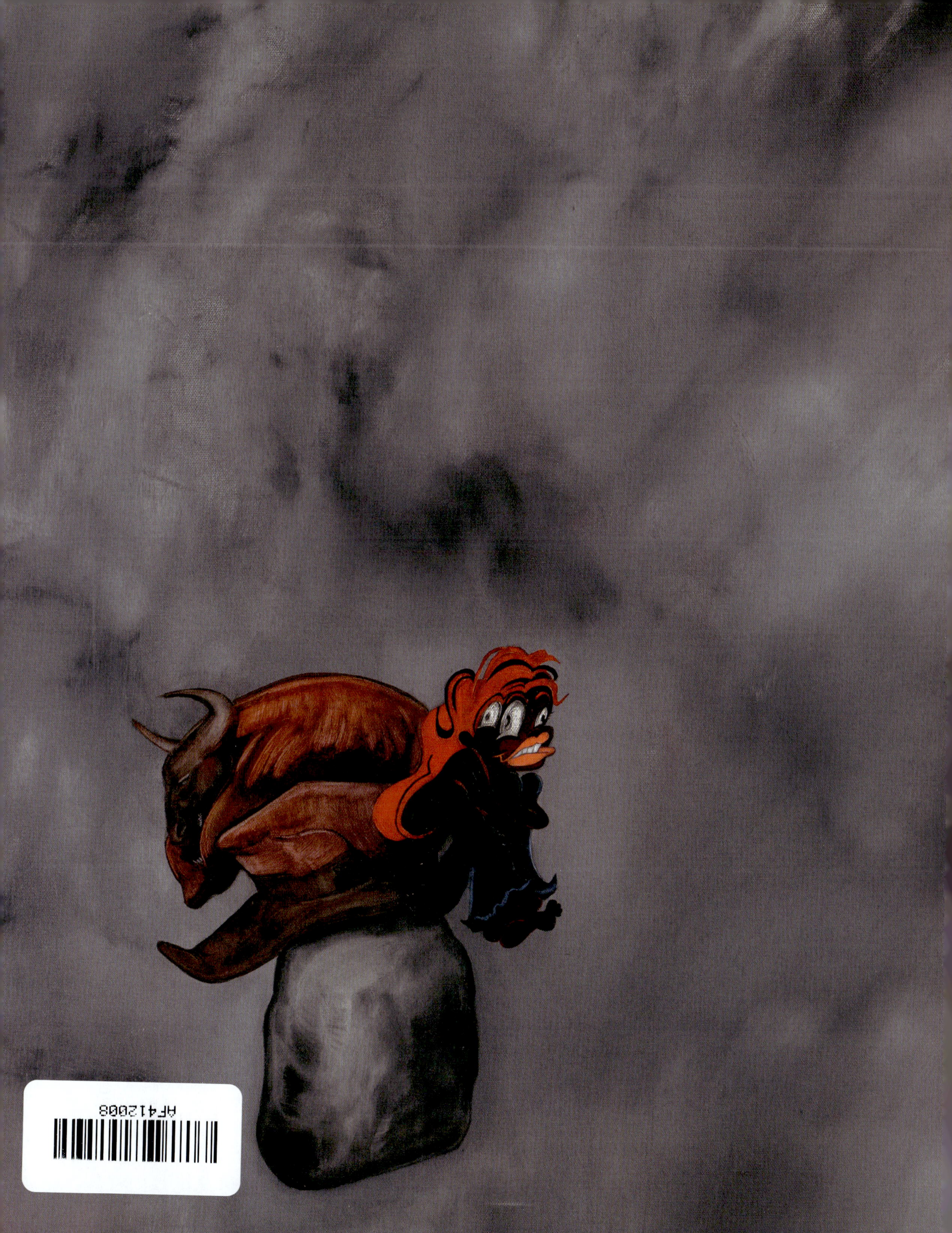